The Pursuit of the

ATLANTA

CHILD KILLER

D1104698

The Pursuit of the

ATLANTA
CHILD KILLER

FACTS, FIBERS, AND FORENSICS

JOSEPH DROLET

BOOKLOGIX

Alpharetta, GA

ISBN: 978-1-6653-0373-6 - Paperback
eISBN: 978-1-6653-0374-3 - ePub

Library of Congress Control Number: 2022912347

Printed in the United States of America   0 8 0 4 2 2

♾This paper meets the requirements of ANSI/NISO Z39.48-1992
(Permanence of Paper)

Larry Peterson provided his photo; the courtroom drawing by Eleanor Dixon Stecker was a gracious gift to the author; the cover art was provided by Mary Sage, who also produced for the author four charts used in the book.

FOR THE VICTIMS
AND THEIR FAMILIES

CONTENTS

AUTHOR'S NOTE

During a two-year period, Atlanta was engulfed by what became known as the case of the Missing and Murdered Children. The Pursuit of the Atlanta Child Killer: Facts, Fibers, and Forensics is the story of my involvement in that case and in the prosecution of a person believed to be responsible for the nightmare it produced. This work depicts actual events and is based on trial transcripts, newspaper accounts, court records, police reports, and other documents, as well as my own recollection of events and conversations set forth as truthfully as memory permits. When quoting directly from such sources, or from conversations, quotation marks are used. As the case unfolds, pieces of a puzzle fall into place, clearly revealing a picture of a serial killer.

PROLOGUE

Late in the evening of May 21, 1981, four law enforcement officers gathered near the James Jackson Parkway Bridge, which stretched across the Chattahoochee River on the northwest side of Atlanta and formed the dividing line between Fulton County and Cobb County. Traffic there was generally light, especially at night.

After a month of nighttime stakeouts on bridges throughout the area, this one would be the last. Atlanta police officer Carl Holden stationed his unmarked car near an abandoned liquor store at the south end of the bridge, where he could observe the gravel parking lot in front of the store. On the north side of the river—the Cobb County side—FBI Agent Greg Gilliland concealed his car on a quiet side road with a clear view of traffic leading to the bridge. Two Atlanta police recruits completed the team. Recruit Freddie Jacobs crouched in the bushes at the south end of the bridge, on the Fulton County side of the river. He could peer out and see any cars that might pass on the bridge. Across the river, recruit Robert Campbell was assigned a position on the muddy riverbank, below the bridge on the Cobb County side. He could see the bridge from below and was close to the water.

The four officers waited. The night was long, and for the two recruits exposed to the elements, the conditions were not pleasant. The weather was muggy; insects couldn't help but notice their presence. The hours dragged on. Traffic on the bridge had dwindled to an occasional vehicle.

It was nearly 3:00 a.m. on the morning of May 22, 1981, and no one noticed a car approaching the bridge, heading south toward Fulton County. The bridge had a steel-plate expansion joint that normally made a loud noise when a car ran over it. At slow speeds, though, the joint made almost no noise. While no one heard the car, Campbell, sitting quietly on the river bank, heard a loud splash in the river directly in front of him. Grabbing his flashlight from the muddy bank, he shined it on the river. The concentric circle of waves showed where something large had hit the water. Campbell was looking directly above the splash, when suddenly a light came on, visible through the bridge railing. The light began to creep across the bridge, moving slowly toward the Fulton County side. Campbell radioed to Jacobs, who peered out from his spot at the end of the bridge. "Is there a car on the bridge?" Campbell asked.

"Yes," Jacobs exclaimed, "it's coming toward me."

Jacobs watched as the car passed him and turned into the gravel parking lot of the abandoned liquor store. The car hastily made an immediate U-turn and crossed back over the bridge. Carl Holden watched the U-turn from his position near the liquor store. As the car started back across the bridge toward Cobb County, Holden pulled onto the bridge and followed. As the cars passed Gilliland's position, he, too, joined the procession. The car led them the short distance to Interstate 285, the highway that encircles Atlanta. With blue lights flashing and siren blaring, Gilliland and Holden pulled the car over as it turned onto the interstate. The car stopped, and Gilliland approached.

The driver, alone in the vehicle, was noticeably nervous. Among the first words uttered by the man in the white Chevrolet station wagon were these: "This is about those boys, isn't it?"

Despite the summerlike weather, there was a pair of suede gloves on the front seat of the car, and a flashlight lay on the seat near the man. A two-foot-long piece of nylon ski rope was on the floor in the back seat area. The car was messy, and the officers could see clumps of dog hair clinging to the upholstery. The twenty-three-year-old driver claimed he was checking out an address for a woman he was scheduled to interview later in the morning. He denied stopping on the bridge and denied making a U-turn at the end of the bridge; he claimed that he simply had driven over the bridge and continued another half mile to a convenience store.

To a second investigator at the scene, the driver claimed he was trying to locate two sisters about an interview. Having nothing but a splash as "evidence," the FBI agents decided to let him go.

Two days later, on May 24, 1981, the naked body of Nathaniel Cater was pulled from the Chattahoochee River, 1.2 miles downriver from the James Jackson Parkway Bridge. The medical examiner would later determine that the cause of death was asphyxia resulting from strangulation.

Chapter 1

CHILDREN DISAPPEAR

I began my law career in the small midwestern town where I was born, Kankakee, Illinois, which was a mix of farms and gritty industries. My family had deep roots there, descended from the influx of French Canadians who migrated from Quebec in the middle of the nineteenth century, seeking opportunity in the rich farmland of northern Illinois. My father, Edward Drolet, was the first of the family to go to college and the first to become a lawyer. He had served as an assistant prosecutor for sixteen years before being elected as the state's attorney of Kankakee County in 1960.

Like our father, my older brother and sister and I had attended the schools associated with the French parish of St. Rose. I was baptized there, in St. Rose Church, a beautiful 1870 limestone structure. Among its colorful stained-glass windows depicting saints and religious scenes, is a window inscribed with the name of the donor, my great-grandfather Joseph Lecours, an immigrant from a town near Montreal.

I was a paperboy for the *Kankakee Daily Journal* and developed an interest in coin collecting after finding a 1922 penny among the piles of change collected from my customers. I was inspired by the lofty principles of the Boy Scouts, eventually becoming an

Eagle Scout. I greatly admired the tenets of duty to God and country and the idea of helping other people.

I enrolled at the University of Illinois at Champaign-Urbana, a huge impersonal institution with a perennially losing, Big Ten football team. From there, I received a degree in economics followed by a degree in law. My father had always wanted one of his children to follow in his footsteps. The job fell to me, despite, at that time, my general lack of interest in being a lawyer.

Summer work as a locomotive fireman and then brakeman on the New York Central Railroad helped supplement the cost of the schooling. To repay my father for his assistance, I worked as an assistant state's attorney in his office for two years. I've since come to appreciate my father's encouragement to pursue the practice of law. With it, I would find opportunities for community involvement that I had never before envisioned.

Over the years, however, I grew tired of being known as "Eddie's son." I wondered what I would be were it not for my father's influence. So, in September of 1971, I moved to Atlanta, Georgia, and accepted an opportunity with the Fulton County District Attorney's office.

And now, here I was, ten years later, in a city becoming infamous for a series of unsolved murders. I had watched the case unfold in a morbid drama that engulfed the entire Atlanta community in heart-wrenching pain and widespread fear.

The murders had blossomed into national news during the summer of 1980. While Jimmy Carter was in the final year of his presidency and Ted Turner was starting a new company called Cable News Network (CNN), a group of mothers on the southwest side of Atlanta were distraught that the Atlanta Police Department wasn't doing enough to investigate the disappearance of their children. Some of the victims had been left in remote locations around southwest Atlanta. All the children were Black, ranging in age from seven to fourteen years old. The mothers began holding press conferences, which both publicized their distress and embarrassed the police.

The mayor of Atlanta, Maynard Jackson, had been elected in

1973. As chairman of a coalition of fifty-three neighborhoods throughout the city, I had supported his election. He was a champion for neighborhood issues, willing to protect communities from encroaching superhighways and bad zoning policies. In his first year in office, he gave neighborhoods a direct voice in planning decisions for the city.

Soon after being elected, Mayor Jackson attempted to appoint a new police chief. The incumbent chief refused to relinquish the office and a standoff ensued. As an alternative, Mayor Jackson created a new position to oversee all public safety agencies, including the police. The White police chief now had a Black commissioner supervising him. Legal challenges followed, and the matter was tied up in the courts for years. Meanwhile, the murder rate rose, and some national surveys labeled Atlanta as the "murder capital" of the country.

Maynard Jackson ultimately prevailed and, by the late 1970s, Lee Brown, an experienced, well-respected law enforcement official who would later serve as police commissioner in New York City, emerged as the new commissioner of public safety. The ever-present problem of missing and murdered children fell to him. Despite Brown's appointment, confidence in the police department, particularly in minority and poor communities, remained low.

Meanwhile, in the summer of 1980, the disenchanted mothers pressured the police department for answers. Camille Bell, a thirty-three-year-old divorced mother of four, emerged as their main organizer. Mrs. Bell's nine-year-old son, Yusef, had disappeared on October 21, 1979, when he went to the store for an elderly neighbor, an errand that would have earned him seventeen cents. Eighteen days later, his partially clothed body was discovered in an abandoned school building. The cause of death was asphyxia due to strangulation. Yusef's father, who did not live with the family, was initially considered a suspect, but there was no evidence tying him to the crime and no other obvious suspects. The case remained open but public interest gradually faded over the months that followed.

Across the country, bigger stories crowded out the murders of poor, Black children in Atlanta. Mount St. Helens erupted, causing massive destruction and killing fifty-seven people. There was a national election, and Jimmy Carter was being challenged from within his own party by Ted Kennedy.

On July 7, 1980, at least partly due to pressure from the community and the grieving mothers, the Atlanta Police Department unofficially created a task force to look into the murders and disappearances, assigning a sergeant and four investigators. That very day, another young man was found murdered.

First, the new Task Force had to decide which cases it would investigate. The answer would be dictated at least in part by the concerns raised by the children's mothers, who had been pressuring the police for action. By this time, the women had organized as the Committee to Stop Children's Murders, and their children were now included on the list of cases upon which the new Task Force would focus. I read about the cases in the *Atlanta Constitution*. Like others in Atlanta, I didn't know if any of the murders and disappearances were related.

Then another young man disappeared. Earl Lee Terrell was ten years old. His name was added to the list, now totaling twelve. The fact that there were twelve children missing or murdered in less than a year began to creep into national news reports. More law enforcement agencies began looking at the cases. Fulton County, encompassing most of the city of Atlanta, began working with the city. Nearby, DeKalb County, to the east of Atlanta, also began coordinating information. City officials requested the assistance of the FBI Behavioral Science Unit, with the hope that a profile of a kidnapper and killer could be developed. However, concerned about whether they had jurisdiction, the FBI remained on the sidelines.

On August 21, 1980, what was now referred to as "the Missing and Murdered Children's Task Force" was expanded. A captain was placed in charge, along with four supervisors and thirteen investigators. This brought the total to eighteen Atlanta police officers working full-time, investigating the cases. The Task Force was given larger space in the basement of the Atlanta Police headquarters. Atlanta was now pouring resources into solving the perplexing cases.

The same day, August 21, 1980, the body of thirteen-year-old Clifford Jones was discovered. He had been strangled, his body laid out on his back with one arm out to his right side. He had been placed next to a dumpster, behind a coin laundry on Hollywood Road in northwest Atlanta, not far from James Jackson Parkway and the Chattahoochee River. Some of his clothing was missing. Clifford Jones became victim number thirteen. The story was too big to be contained; it was now national news.

A young forensic scientist with the Georgia Bureau of Investigation, twenty-seven-year-old fiber expert Larry Peterson, studied the crime scene and meticulously recovered evidence from the hair, clothing, and skin of the young victim. Peterson, from the time he was a teenager, had developed a passion for microscopic evidence. That passion had led him to his position as chief analyst of trace evidence at the GBI. I did not know it at the time, but our paths would soon cross.

On a Sunday morning soon after the body of Clifford Jones had been discovered, Homicide Detective Sidney Dorsey called my boss, District Attorney Lewis Slaton. Dorsey said he had a suspect in the murder of Clifford Jones. As I was a frequent advisor to Slaton and head of the office's Appellate Section, Slaton asked me to meet him at our office. At Atlanta Police headquarters, Dorsey was anxiously waiting. He was a flamboyant detective, a flashy dresser, and a man who never concealed his opinions. He told us about a man who operated a coin laundry on Hollywood Road; his name was Jamie Brooks and he was a convicted sex offender. Clifford Jones' body had been discovered behind the business. A young man claimed to have seen Jamie Brooks murder Clifford Jones, and Dorsey wanted to obtain a search warrant for Jamie Brooks' coin laundry and residence on Hollywood Road. Brooks looked like the perfect suspect.

I helped Dorsey but after a few days, I learned that nothing found in the search matched any evidence found on Clifford

Jones. And the "eyewitness" was not much of a witness; he claimed to have seen things that simply didn't happen. He described events and evidence that conflicted with reality. Even the witness' mother cast doubt on his credibility. Shortly after the death of Clifford Jones, Jamie Brooks was returned to prison on an unrelated case. But the killings continued. A likely suspect turned out to be a dead end.

Another young man disappeared—he was ten years old, victim number fourteen. Darron Glass would never be seen again. A few days later, Major W. J. Taylor was placed in charge of the Task Force, now numbering thirty-four people. For the first time, my office assigned an assistant district attorney to assist with the investigation. Our own Gordon Miller became our link to the investigation.

My own job had continued without any direct contact with the Task Force. My Appellate Section always had plenty of business, given the numerous convictions being generated by a dozen trial divisions. And I had other duties that kept me busy: office administration, reviewing job applicants, and acting as the district attorney's representative on a committee rewriting the Judicial Article of the Georgia Constitution. But like everyone else in Atlanta, I watched and wondered as the unexplained killings unfolded. The list of missing and murdered children served as a heartbreaking reminder for everyone in law enforcement in the Atlanta area. We all felt helpless as names were added and the disappearances continued.

Psychics began bombarding the city with tips from dreams and premonitions. With great fanfare, a group of five "super-cops" came from Detroit, New York, Los Angeles, and other major cities. After two weeks in Atlanta, they all returned home, unable to solve the mystery. Frustration grew even greater. What would it take to catch the killer or killers?

On October 10, 1980, the body of twelve-year-old Charles Stephens was discovered along a roadside in East Point, Georgia, just south of Atlanta. Stephens was laid out much like Clifford Jones, on his back with his right arm out to the side. The cause of death was asphyxia. Fiber expert Larry Peterson from the crime lab was again at the scene, retrieving evidence. Charles Stephens became victim number fifteen on the list.

The East Point police now joined the thirty-four Atlanta police officers on the Task Force. The Task Force itself was becoming the size of a police department—its sole mission: to solve the mystery of the fifteen missing and murdered children.

The community was growing impatient; everyone wanted action. Reverend Arthur Langford, a local religious leader, called for volunteers to search wooded and overgrown areas of southwest Atlanta. On the first weekend of searches, the remains of Latonya Wilson were discovered. She had been abducted from her home 118 days earlier. Sadly, her skeletal remains yielded little in the way of evidence.

On October 23, 1980, Atlanta imposed a citywide curfew for youths fifteen years of age and younger. Maybe the abductions could be stopped by keeping young people off the streets at night. Meanwhile, a reward fund was announced by Mayor Maynard Jackson. The mayor held a press conference surrounded by a huge mound of cash—bundles of twenties, tens, and fives. The mayor implored anyone with information to come forward. "Someone," he said, "must have seen something. Come forward and get $100,000! Do it for the children!"

One week later, on November 2, 1980, another Black child was added to the list, dead of asphyxia. He was victim number sixteen. GBI fiber expert Larry Peterson was there again gathering evidence at the scene. The next day, Atlanta added ten more investigators to the Task Force. There were now over fifty officers working on the cases, and the Task Force was moved to a space previously occupied by a car dealership just north of downtown Atlanta. A few days later, the FBI officially entered the investigation. As the list grew, it became like a scorecard that drew the national media to the unfolding drama in Atlanta.

Meanwhile, Ronald Reagan and Jimmy Carter were in the final stages of the 1980 presidential election. On November 4, 1980, Reagan was elected president. Just six days later, another fifteen-year-old was reported missing.

The Atlanta Police continued trying everything, including roadblocks in isolated areas. My boss, District Attorney Slaton, assigned one of his investigators to the growing Task Force. More and more people were involved in the effort, but nothing seemed to stop the disappearances. As the year ended and the nation prepared to inaugurate a new president, Atlanta was a city under intense pressure. Since the Task Force had been created, seven more victims had been added to the list of missing and murdered children.

The large force of officers, even with FBI and regional support, had come up empty. Somehow, someone was luring young people off the street and leaving bodies scattered in southwest Atlanta. After many months, four young Black males were still missing. Family members from Atlanta's most economically disadvantaged communities could only grieve the deaths and disappearances of their children.

Chapter 2

THE NIGHTMARE ACCELERATES

For me, the new year had much in store. I was getting married on January 3, 1981, and soon after that the Georgia General Assembly would be returning for a new forty-day session. During the legislative session, I would be spending time at the State Capitol, attending judiciary and public safety committee meetings. This was in addition to my normal duties writing briefs, assisting lawyers on trial, and supervising some of the office staff. My wife and I had decided to wait until after the General Assembly to take a planned trip to Europe.

On my wedding day, other events were playing out elsewhere in Atlanta. A young man named Lubie Geter was reported missing. Geter was fourteen years old and had last been seen trying to sell car deodorizers to motorists at a rundown strip mall on Atlanta's south side. Lubie would become victim number eighteen.

On January 5, 1981, police officers and police recruits formed search parties and began searching wooded and overgrown areas on Atlanta's south side, looking for bodies. On January 9, 1981, the skeletal remains of two of the missing children were discovered. Christopher Richardson and Earl Lee Terrell had been missing for nearly six months.

On January 23, 1981, the body of yet another child was discovered discarded along a roadside in Rockdale County, east of Atlanta. He was fifteen years old and became victim number nineteen. In the weeks before his body was found, the very same area had been searched, without success, in response to an anonymous caller who had told the sheriff's office that a body would be found there.

In early February, the chief of police in DeKalb County made an offhanded comment that appeared in print. He suggested that if any of the bodies had been found in unincorporated DeKalb County, the cases would probably have been solved by now. Shortly thereafter, the body of Patrick Baltazar was dumped down an embankment near an office park in DeKalb County. He had been strangled. The killer seemed to be responding directly to the remarks.

On February 17, 1981, the *Atlanta Constitution* reported that analysis of fibers and hairs recovered from the bodies of victims could help identify the killer or killers. Some of the fibers were quite unusual, the paper reported. Shortly after this information was reported, the pattern of the killings changed. Some victims began appearing in rivers, stripped of clothes, in conditions that could cleanse the bodies of identifying evidence.

On February 19, 1981, a thirteen-year-old was reported missing; he became number twenty-one on the list. On March 6, his body was pulled from the South River in DeKalb County, stripped to his underwear, and dead of asphyxia.

In early March, fifteen-year-old Jo-Jo Bell was the next child reported missing and added to the list of missing and murdered children. Weeks later, Bell's body was retrieved from the South River, snagged on fallen tree branches. He, too, was stripped to his underwear. The cause of death was asphyxia. On May 3, 1981, the *New York Times Magazine* published an article about the murders in Atlanta, reporting that Jo-Jo had boasted that "no kid snatcher was going to get me."

There was a killer out there somewhere, reading and watching news reports and then responding. Concerned citizens began wearing green ribbons on their lapels. I wore one myself. Earlier in the year, people had worn yellow ribbons in solidarity with the Americans held hostage in Iran. Now, everyone seemed to be wearing green in solidarity with the missing and murdered children. It was a small thing, but it was a reminder to everyone that this ongoing nightmare hung over Atlanta.

Sammy Davis Jr. held a concert, and Frank Sinatra soon followed with one of his own—both hoping to raise money for the families of the victims. The new vice president of the United States, George H. W. Bush, came to Atlanta to lend support and to announce a half-million-dollar grant to assist in the investigation. From New York, a dozen red-beret-clad "Guardian Angels" came to Atlanta to help patrol the streets. A man with a tracking dog came to Atlanta, certain that he could help find the killer. Known as "the Dog Man," Don Laken and his dog were unsuccessful.

Meanwhile, another teenager was reported missing. He became victim number twenty-three on the list. As the numbers grew, and word spread that another victim had been added to the list, the case drew even greater attention. Frustrated citizens took matters into their own hands. Residents of Techwood Homes, an Atlanta housing project near the Georgia Tech campus and nearby Coca-Cola's headquarters, formed what they called the "Bat Patrol." The patrol held a press conference on March 20, 1981, and displayed rows of baseball bats and handguns; they were going to defend themselves and find the killer, they boasted. One day after their press conference, on March 21, 1981, yet another young man, a twenty-one-year-old, was reported missing. He was number twenty-four. He was a resident of Techwood Homes, the area that had organized the patrol. The killer appeared to be mocking the "Bat Patrol."

Then two more young men were reported missing.

As April approached, I was preparing for my first trip to Europe—London and then on to Paris and a tour of the Loire Valley. Meanwhile, in Washington, on March 30, 1981, the new president, Ronald Reagan, was seriously wounded by gunman

John Hinckley. The same day in Atlanta, the body of Timothy Hill, clad only in his underwear, was discovered in the Chattahoochee River. Like so many before him, he had died of asphyxia. The next day, on March 31, the body of the young man reported missing ten days earlier was also found floating in the Chattahoochee River, not far from where Hill's body had been discovered.

The Task Force continued to grow. The Georgia Bureau of Investigation was now actively involved, as were police agencies from the surrounding counties of Cobb, Douglas, DeKalb, Rockdale, and Clayton. There were now ninety-two investigators working together to stop the killings. In addition, the FBI had another two dozen agents working independently from the Task Force.

Chapter 3

THE NIGHTMARE CONTINUES

As April dawned, I was enjoying life on another continent. My wife and I were exploring London, enjoying the convenience of the London subway and exploring landmarks, from Westminster Cathedral to Hyde Park. I had put the events in Atlanta out of my mind. Then on April 5, 1981, as I stood at a newsstand, I noticed a headline in bold letters in the *London Observer*: "The Killings in Atlanta." There was a full-page story with a large picture of Coretta Scott King and a host of people I recognized marching in memory of the victims. The article set out theories gleaned from a variety of sources. Perhaps it was a cult of some kind, performing rituals on the children. Perhaps an "invisible man" case, like one from the Father Brown crime series by author G. K. Chesterton—someone so obvious that he would be overlooked—a deliveryman, a postman, or someone else in a uniform. The story in Atlanta was now a big story in London.

In Paris, again I was unable to escape the news from Atlanta. A headline in *Le Figaro* on April 11, 1981, announced: *"Atlanta: le Cauchemar Continue"* (Atlanta: the Nightmare Continues). A photo showed police officers I knew loading a body into a hearse, with a caption: *"un 23e jeune Noir assassiné"* (A 23rd young Black murdered). Another article appeared in *Le Figaro* on April 16, 1981, about different theories being put forth to explain the killings in Atlanta. On April 21, 1981, *Le Figaro* blared another headline about the murders in Atlanta: *"Atlanta: Toujours le Cauchemar"* (Atlanta: Still the Nightmare). I returned to Atlanta the next day.

While I had been in Europe, the nightmare had indeed continued in Atlanta. And the pace of killings had quickened. And still, there were no solid suspects.

I had barely returned to work when Jimmy Ray Payne was reported missing on April 22, 1981. He was victim number twenty-seven. Like many of the recent victims, Payne was in his early twenties, and his body was pulled from the Chattahoochee River five days after he disappeared. He was clad only in underwear shorts, and the cause of death was asphyxia.

During the first week of May 1981, Heavyweight Boxing Champion Muhammad Ali came to Atlanta and met with Mayor Jackson. Ali donated $400,000 to the reward fund, which had yet to yield any useful information. Meanwhile, the Task Force now numbered 102 full-time investigators, and every river bridge in the Atlanta area was being staked out, in hopes of catching the killer in the act. The stakeouts were costly and labor-intensive; surveillance of each bridge required four officers. Because of the drain on resources, they were scheduled to end on Friday, May 22, 1981—the very morning when a man in a white Chevrolet station wagon had been stopped near the James Jackson Parkway Bridge.

Chapter 4

WHO IS THIS SUSPECT?

Over the following two weeks, more information came to light. There was reason to believe that the body found in the river, later identified as Nathaniel Cater, was connected to the splash heard at the bridge. On June 3, 1981, a home on Penelope Road, west of downtown Atlanta, was searched. A white Chevrolet station wagon had been towed to the local FBI office. The young man who had been stopped near the bridge was escorted to that office to get hair samples. His name was Wayne Williams.

After leaving the FBI offices, Williams held a press conference at the house on Penelope Road. A *New York Post* headline blared: "Atlanta Monster Seized!" The name Wayne Williams was now known to the world.

Later that same day, I heard the voice of District Attorney Lewis Slaton erupting from one of the speakers located in the ceiling panels of our offices on the seventh floor. I had worked for Slaton for ten of his sixteen years in office. Sporting slicked-back dark hair and a receding hairline, Slaton liked to know about everything going on in the courts and in the community. He depended on his staff to let him know if any case or event was likely to generate media attention. The raspy voice announced: "Drolet, come to the front office."

"Drop everything," he said. "Start working on this case with Jack Mallard and Gordon Miller," (our lawyer working with the Task Force). Like me, Jack was new to the case; he was among our best witness examiners and a twenty-year veteran of the office. Born in Claxton, in rural south Georgia, the balding Mallard had an easygoing manner that was disarming to most witnesses. His country accent and deliberate style led many a lawyer to underestimate his ability.

In the event we proceeded with a case, I would be expected to know the law and be able to defend every move we made. Over the next few days, I would begin to appreciate the host of legal issues that could be confronting me, from searches to the admissibility of statements to the viability of scientific evidence. This would not be a simple case.

I now had access to much more information about the evidence that was being gathered. Wayne Williams was a twenty-three-year-old music promoter, living in the family home with his mother, Faye, and his father, Homer. He was their only child. Both parents were retired schoolteachers living in the middle-class Dixie Hills neighborhood, west of downtown. Williams was known to many in the Black community as a bright young man, full of promise.

I soon learned that Wayne Williams had thus far given six statements explaining his presence on the James Jackson Parkway Bridge. The explanations varied, sometimes contradicting each other, and other times claiming things that were clearly untrue. Williams had taken a lie detector test, and the results indicated deception.

Larry Peterson, the fiber expert from the state crime lab, had matched some man-made fibers and hairs found on the naked body of Nathaniel Cater, whose body had surfaced downriver from the James Jackson Parkway Bridge. The fiber analysis suggested a link between Williams, the incident at the bridge, and the victim. This was promising. There had been previous suspects, but there had never been reliable evidence connecting them to victims. And Williams had, not long before, decked out a Plymouth sedan as a police detective car, complete with a police radio, scanner, blue light, and siren. Although he looked like a nerdy kid— not what most people imagine as a killer—he was becoming a most interesting suspect.

In preparing for the possibility of charges against Wayne Williams, I reviewed the files of the twenty-nine missing and murdered children and gathered every bit of information I could from Gordon Miller, who had been keeping Lewis Slaton advised of everything happening at the Task Force.

Hundreds of reporters from around the world descended on Atlanta. Dozens of cameras were set up in the street across from the Williamses' home. Reporters scampered to any location that might be related to the murders or to Wayne Williams.

Williams went on the offensive. On June 12, 1981, his lawyers sued seventeen local and national media organizations as well as various law enforcement officials. Despite the fact that Williams had held his own press conference, referred to himself as the "prime suspect," and distributed his three-page résumé, the federal lawsuit sought to bar the use of his name in relation to the case and to seal court records that might disclose his personal information. A hearing was held on this request on June 16, 1981. Not surprisingly, a federal judge declined to bar the media from identifying Wayne Williams as a suspect.

A MEETING OF FIBER EXPERTS

Unknown to the media, a meeting was held at the Georgia Police Academy building on Saturday, June 13, 1981. The 1950s-era building was tucked away on a back lot of the southeast Atlanta grounds occupied by the Georgia State Patrol, the Georgia Bureau of Investigation, and the Georgia National Guard. The meeting had been scheduled weeks earlier, long before Wayne Williams was stopped near the Jackson Parkway Bridge. The director of the State Crime Laboratory had called the meeting to invite fiber experts from around the country and Canada to assess the significance of the fiber evidence that appeared on many victims. Of particular importance was a green trilobal carpet fiber with an unusual cross-section. While trilobal fibers were made with three equal-length lobes, like the blades on an airplane propeller, this trilobal fiber had two long lobes and one short lobe. The manufacturer of this distinctive fiber was unknown. A classroom had been turned into a makeshift laboratory for the experts. Given that we now had a suspect, the meeting could not have been more timely.

Walter McCrone, founder of the highly respected McCrone Institute, and two experts from DuPont's Textile Fibers Department exclaimed at the unusual nature of the mystery fiber. Experts from the FBI and the Royal Canadian Mounted Police contributed their opinions, joined by experts from half a dozen state crime laboratories. They all agreed that the carpet fibers found on the victims were extremely rare and appeared to match fibers from the carpet in the Williamses' home. I was impressed, and so was Lewis Slaton, my boss. Although many in attendance at the meeting urged him to make an arrest, Slaton, ever cautious, chose to assess evidence still flowing into our office, to be sure our evidence was strong and on sound legal ground. The evidence looked good to me, but Slaton knew that in a high-profile case, you had to be armed with rock-solid evidence. I was excited; he was calm and noncommittal.

Days later Lewis Slaton and FBI officials met with Governor George Busbee at the governor's mansion. Although urged by some to proceed with a prosecution, Slaton bristled at the idea that anyone would tell him how to do his job. The decision to prosecute rested solely with the district attorney, and for Slaton, no one was going to dictate when or how a case was prosecuted. If the matter was mentioned, his irritation became obvious, and he had no interest in discussing it.

The next day, June 20, 1981, Wayne Williams startled the crowd of reporters and police watching his house as he hurried from his house, jumped in a car, and led a trail of police and media in a parade around Atlanta. He was mocking the police, knowing they would follow wherever he went. He even went by Mayor

Maynard Jackson's home, stopping briefly to harass the mayor by holding down his car horn and yelling for the mayor to come out.

Jack Mallard, Gordon Miller, and I met Slaton at the office on Sunday, June 21, 1981. We discussed the evidence and any potential legal obstacles to prosecution. We went around the room, offering opinions. We all agreed that we had sufficient evidence to charge Williams with killing Nathaniel Cater, whose body had been discovered just two days after Williams was stopped near the bridge. The crime lab confirmed they could show a connection between fibers found on Cater's body and Williams' environment. The evidence was far from overwhelming, but Slaton had decided. An arrest warrant was prepared, signed by a judge, and investigators from the office headed to Penelope Road. There, at the Williamses' family home, they arrested Wayne Bertram Williams for the murder of Nathaniel Cater. I felt like I had just jumped out of an airplane, committed to a journey with no turning back.

Chapter 5

MORE THAN A SUSPECT

t the Fulton County Jail, Williams was met by his attorney, Mary Welcome, a former solicitor for the Municipal Court of Atlanta. As city solicitor, she was well known in Atlanta and had been responsible for prosecuting city ordinance violations and presenting evidence at probable cause hearings on more serious cases.

The next day, June 22, 1981, a second search warrant was executed at the Williamses' home. Some items that had been noted during the first search were no longer in the home. During the first search, a crime lab expert had taken a small cutting from a yellow blanket under Wayne Williams' bed. The blanket was now gone. It was later determined that fibers from that blanket matched those found on numerous victims. Also missing was a book called *The Egyptian Book of the Dead*. It featured descriptions for positioning bodies after death, descriptions that bore a strong resemblance to the position of many victims, who had been discovered along roadsides on their backs with one arm out to the side.

On June 23, a hearing was held before a State Court magistrate to determine whether there was adequate evidence to hold Wayne Williams in custody. GBI fiber expert Larry Peterson, Chief Medical Examiner Bob Stivers, and two witnesses from the bridge encounter testified. The judge found that there was sufficient probable cause to believe Williams had murdered Nathaniel Cater.

After the two-year nightmare in Atlanta, we now had a man in custody. The pressure on our office was intense. Media representatives from around the world hounded us, wanting to know what would happen next, what evidence we had on Wayne Williams, and when there would be a trial. This case was bigger than anything I had ever experienced. I was pleased to be chosen, but the enormity of the task was daunting. We had a man in custody and now we had to figure out what to do with him.

Then, suddenly, our efforts were dealt a blow. My fellow prosecutor Jack Mallard, who, like me, was still digesting a year's worth of investigative material, suffered a personal tragedy, learning that his wife Jo had late-stage cancer. Jack could be called away at any moment. A new member had to be added to our team; Wally Speed would be a backup for Jack. Bulldog-like in the courtroom, Wally had been with the office almost as long as Gordon and I had.

It was late June 1981, and our suspect had been arrested but not yet officially charged. An official charge would be triggered by the return of an indictment by the Fulton County Grand Jury. An indictment is simply a document reciting the criminal offense or offenses alleged against a person; it officially launches the process of prosecution in the criminal justice system. While we could seek an indictment for the murder of Nathaniel Cater, the question was whether to add any other murders to the indictment. One of the other murders was clearly similar.

Just a month earlier, the body of Jimmy Ray Payne had been pulled from the river a short distance from where Cater's body was found. Both had been stripped of clothing, and both died of asphyxia. Cater's asphyxia had apparently been caused by strangulation; the exact method of Payne's asphyxia was undetermined. Both lived on the margins of society and frequented the streets of Atlanta; neither had an automobile. Both had fibers that matched fibers in Wayne Williams' environment. Additionally, there was a possibility that witnesses may have seen Williams with one or both young men. We concluded that the indictment should consist of two counts of murder: the murders of Nathaniel Cater and Jimmy Ray Payne. We would need to be able to prove our cases beyond a reasonable doubt, and at the time, these were the two strongest cases we had, linked by connections to the bridge incident and by strong fiber evidence.

There were other related cases on what had become known simply as "the list." We didn't know which of them might be connected; evidence was still being gathered. If they turned out to be connected, there was an effective way to use this evidence, even if we didn't include the cases in the indictment. In the state of Georgia, as in most other states, related cases that were part of an obvious pattern could be offered as "similar transactions," serving as evidence that Williams murdered both Cater and Payne. As the United States Supreme Court once noted, there is a "widely recognized principle that similar but disconnected acts may be shown to establish intent, design, and system." The law clearly authorized such evidence to be considered if we could show that the evidence was logically connected, or bore similarities, to the murders of Cater and Payne.

Another obstacle to indicting other cases was a lack of jurisdiction over some of the murders—bodies had been found, not just in Fulton County, but also in surrounding counties. We couldn't prosecute cases from other jurisdictions, but as similar transactions, we could use those cases to support ours. I just needed to figure out whether we could demonstrate that Wayne Williams was the perpetrator in any of those cases.

THE GRAND JURY

The Fulton County Grand Jury consists of twenty-three citizens selected, like regular jurors, from voter lists and other sources. Grand jurors are supposed to be "upright" citizens, but just about anybody can actually serve on a grand jury. In Fulton County, grand jurors serve for a two-month term and meet twice per week, on Tuesdays and Fridays. On routine days, a grand jury will hear scores of brief presentations, in almost summary form, from law enforcement officers who have arrested people in Fulton County for felony offenses. By "returning an indictment," the Grand Jury simply accuses the person of a crime; it does not make a final determination of guilt or innocence. It is simply the mechanism that allows the prosecution to move forward.

We began preparing for the Grand Jury presentation scheduled for Friday, July 17, 1981. We would call witnesses from the bridge incident and provide testimony on the changing stories told by Wayne Williams. Larry Peterson would discuss the fibers found on Payne and Cater.

Wayne Williams began to expand his legal team. He already had Mary Welcome as a lawyer, and now added Tony Axam. The two lawyers could not have been more different. Mary was comfortable in front of television cameras. She was attractive and quotable and could distill legal matters into catchy sound bites. Tony rarely did interviews, and he was always well prepared. He thought strategically and could make an impressive presentation in court, even with almost nothing to work with.

Williams' new legal team quickly went on the offensive, trying to keep us from even presenting our case to the Grand Jury. They attacked the Grand Jury process itself and demanded to question grand jurors about whether they had been tainted by pretrial publicity. They petitioned the court to allow Williams' lawyers to be present when the Grand Jury met and to give Williams an opportunity to address the grand jurors. They wanted a delay in the process and petitioned for Williams' release on bond, claiming he was not a flight risk and was unlikely to commit another crime.

Gordon Miller and I, along with District Attorney Lewis Slaton, attended a hearing on the defense motions. I had provided Slaton with the latest cases from the Georgia Supreme Court and the Court of Appeals regarding Grand Jury procedures, the right to appear before a grand jury, and the granting of bail. Williams claimed to have grand-sounding recording deals negotiated with major record labels. Axam described our case as marginal, describing Williams as a successful businessman who was harmless and had been wrongly accused. Slaton took full advantage of the materials we provided as Gordon and I sat at the counsel table and passed notes to him as needed.

For two days we waited, wondering whether we had failed in our mission and whether a potential serial killer would be put back on the street. Finally, on July 16, 1981, the judge filed a written order denying the motions. We were now clear to proceed with our final presentation to the Grand Jury.

Although I normally did not assist in presenting cases to the Grand Jury, the week of July 13, 1981, was an exception. The Grand Jury had been warned that a complicated, high-profile case was coming and that it would take longer than usual to present.

Unlike jurors in a trial, grand jurors may ask questions of witnesses and the prosecutors. While Officer Carl Holden was answering our questions, one grand juror asked how a person could lift a body and throw it over the rail of the James Jackson Parkway Bridge. Holden, who regularly worked out with weights, jumped at the chance to show the Grand Jury. As I stood, unsure exactly what Holden had in mind, he asked me to hold my body straight, then suddenly lifted me off my feet and held my now-horizontal body over his head. It felt a bit awkward being held in the air, and I was much relieved when he was able to return me to the floor without dropping me. However, being lifted off my feet was unnecessary as we had other evidence to show how a body could easily be moved the short distance from the tailgate of Williams' Chevrolet station wagon to the unusually low concrete railing on that particular bridge.

We called Williams' mother, Faye Williams, to testify. She described her role in providing the address Williams claimed to be searching for in the middle of the night. He had told us that his "answering service" had taken the call and that "one of my workers" took the call. His mother was that worker. In other interviews, he had stated that he, himself, had spoken to the woman he was searching for. Faye Williams was now under oath before the Grand Jury. I asked Mrs. Williams if she or her son, Wayne, had communicated with the woman he claimed to be looking for. Mrs. Williams insisted that she, and she alone, had spoken to the young lady, and the only information she had been given was the name, an address, and a phone number. She was certain of all of this, she told the grand jurors.

Late in the day on July 17, 1981, the Fulton County Grand Jury returned an indictment, charging Wayne Bertram Williams with the murders of Nathaniel Cater and Jimmy Ray Payne.

Chapter 6

BATTLES BEFORE A TRIAL

𝕿he first step after indictment was the appointment of a judge. Each indictment number went on what was referred to as "the wheel," a random selection process by which one of the twelve Fulton County Superior Court judges would be chosen. On Tuesday, July 21, 1981, Judge Clarence Cooper became the recipient of Indictment Number A-56186, *The State of Georgia v. Wayne Bertram Williams.*

I had known Clarence Cooper for more than ten years; he had worked in the district attorney's office as head of the Child Support Recovery Unit. Our paths only occasionally crossed as I had worked in other divisions of the office. Cooper had run for a position on the Fulton County Commission and lost, but later was appointed to a judgeship in the Atlanta Municipal Court. Some years earlier, he had presided over a case in which I was the complaining witness, and Mary Welcome—now serving as Wayne Williams' defense attorney—was the prosecuting attorney. The defendant in that case also happened to be named Williams (but no relation to Wayne Bertram Williams). That Williams had been arrested for disrupting a congressional forum I was chairing in the basement of historic Friendship Baptist Church, one of the oldest Black churches in Atlanta. Now, Cooper would be dealing with another case in which Mary and I were involved. After Municipal

Court, Cooper had run for a vacant position on the Fulton Superior Court and won, becoming the first African American elected to such a post in Fulton County history.

When assigned the Wayne Williams case, Cooper had only recently been elected to the Superior Court bench, and there was some concern about his inexperience. I felt comfortable with Judge Cooper and confident in his ability as a judge. He had always been fair with anyone who appeared before him. He was friends with Mary Welcome and Tony Axam, but also friends with many in my office, and he occasionally still referred to Lewis Slaton as "boss."

Now that we had an indictment, the law required that we address whether we would seek the death penalty. If certain aggravating circumstances are present, a murder case may be eligible for the sentence of death; otherwise, life imprisonment is the penalty for murder. I didn't think we should seek the death penalty. It wasn't that I thought the crimes didn't warrant it. My thinking was that if Wayne Williams was convicted of killing Nathaniel Cater and Jimmy Ray Payne, and if we could bring enough other cases to convince a jury that he was the serial killer who had long tormented Atlanta, there was no way he would ever get out of prison. Death penalty trials can take on a life of their own, not based on the circumstances of the crime committed, but based on the long-running debate over capital punishment. Juries can be influenced in the finding of guilt or innocence when they know a defendant may be executed. I wanted the jury in this case to have only one question before them: Did he do it?

Our team, now consisting of Lewis Slaton, Jack Mallard, Gordon Miller, Wally Speed, and me, met frequently to discuss our options. In addition to my concerns over seeking the death penalty, there was another obstacle to seeking it. According to Georgia's death penalty statute, we would have to prove the existence of an "aggravating circumstance" listed in the statute. We didn't have one. Wayne Williams did not have a history of violence, he had not murdered a police officer, he was not a hired killer, and he had not killed someone during an escape from prison. The killings did not qualify as "outrageously or wantonly vile, horrible, or inhuman in that it involved torture, depravity of mind, or an aggravated battery to the victim." The victims may have gone quietly with the killer and, at some point, they were asphyxiated; there was no evidence of torture. On August 4, 1981, Slaton issued a public statement indicating that the office would not seek the death penalty, as the facts of the case did not meet the standard under the death penalty statute.

Judge Cooper was now faced with presiding over an enormous undertaking. Hundreds of reporters, film crews, photographers, and the generally curious began descending on the courthouse and visiting the locations where bodies had been found. Every day I had to gently decline comments to reporters who would drop by my office to visit. One day, a *Washington Post* reporter and a reporter from the *Chicago Tribune* came by together. They had just one question: Why did he do it? I told them I couldn't discuss the case, adding that maybe Wayne Williams just wanted to make a big splash. They assumed I was making a pun about the splash heard when a body hit the waters of the Chattahoochee River. I was actually suggesting that Wayne Williams desperately seemed to seek attention and control. They left my office disappointed.

Judge Cooper became concerned about security. He feared someone might try to kill Wayne Williams, in addition to concerns about publicity and the effect it could have on the trial. After August 12, 1981, everyone entering the courtroom had to be searched. And Cooper formed an advisory committee to create guidelines regarding publicity.

As required by law, an arraignment date was set for Wayne Williams: August 17, 1981. An arraignment is the court proceeding at which a person charged with a crime will appear to answer the charges. There, the defendant is entitled to a copy of the charges and a list of witnesses against him. He may ask for a lawyer and can plead guilty or not guilty. Williams was present with his lawyers, Mary Welcome and Tony Axam, and loudly proclaimed that he was "not guilty." Judge Cooper gave the defense ten days to file any motions they deemed appropriate, and he set a trial date for October 5, 1981. He warned everyone to stop talking to reporters and holding interviews. *There was no way,* I thought, *that we would be ready by early October; and there was no way Williams' team could be ready either.*

Elsewhere in the world, technology was evolving quickly as the first personal computer was sold for $1,565, a sizeable sum in 1981. It would be years before such computers would become common in offices. For now, our secretaries continued to prepare documents on paper using typewriters.

Meanwhile, we hurried the pace of our preparation; weekends were no longer our own. Jack Mallard and I had already begun going to the Task Force office each day to go over the multitude of reports, statements, letters, and other material gathered over the prior year. The main showroom of the old car dealership had been divided into small cubicles and workrooms. Some rooms had wall charts noting details relating to each case, such as the time of day a victim disappeared, some showed maps of key locations where victims had last been seen, and others showed major highways and roads connecting locations.

Everything had been studied by the host of officers who had tried, for over a year, to make sense of the unfolding killings. Rows of four- and five-drawer file cabinets were filled not only with police reports but also with letters from psychics and tips from around the world. Our guide in reviewing the material was Major W. J. Taylor, who had for a time headed the Task Force. Major Taylor, a slightly graying veteran of the police department, was calm and reassuring. Whatever we needed, he was going to help us find it, and Taylor proved a lifesaver. Without him, we would have spent hours wading through files to find what we needed.

Jack and I would report to the Task Force office on West Peachtree Street at about 9:00 a.m. and often stay until well after 5:00 p.m. We reviewed files on the many suspects that came and went over the course of the investigation—people like Jamie Brooks, the sex offender Sidney Dorsey had suspected of being the killer. There had been many who looked, for a time, as perfect suspects; they were unsavory characters, involved in a variety of depraved criminal activities, and they were, in some way, in close proximity to one victim or another. But—like Jamie Brooks—as each was examined, the lack of evidence became obvious. Each looked like a person capable of a horrific crime, but each faded as no evidence tied them to the murders.

Meanwhile, the Atlanta Press Club filed a motion requesting to televise the trial. A host of television stations and networks weighed in, supporting the idea. Williams' parents, Homer and Faye Williams, objected, as did Williams and his lawyers. We feared that televised witnesses might clam up on the witness stand or showboat, knowing they had a national audience. We wanted the trial to be contained to the courtroom—the jury was the only audience we cared about. Judge Cooper set a hearing on the request for August 21, 1981, where we let the defense and the media fight it out. We took a neutral position, not objecting to cameras but not advocating for them. Judge Cooper released a seven-page order on August 25. Based in large part on concerns about preserving Williams' right to a fair trial, the judge denied the Press Club's request.

On August 27, Judge Cooper, frustrated by continuing leaks of information to the press, issued a gag order. Only ten days earlier, the judge had issued a judicial warning to lawyers involved in the case, imploring them not to discuss the case with reporters. Williams' lawyers had been making almost daily declarations suggesting that the real killers remained at large, and that Wayne Williams was being railroaded. Now Judge Cooper filed an "order restricting extrajudicial statements by the prosecution, counsel for the defense, potential witnesses, court personnel, and members of the Special Task Force."

During the last week of August 1981, as we struggled to prepare for trial, Tony Axam and Mary Welcome showered us with written motions. Some were routine: boilerplate language used in every criminal case, invoking disclosure of scientific reports or a listing of witnesses. Some motions were inventive creations. Williams' lawyers asked the court to have every potential witness fingerprinted by the FBI and asked that the court order us to state in detail at what time Wayne Williams murdered each of his victims and who exactly was present at the time. There were nearly forty such motions to research and respond to at the motions hearing scheduled for September 4. On August 28, 1981, Gordon Miller and I met with Tony Axam and Mary Welcome and turned over copies of the eighteen-page affidavits that supported issuance of the search warrants for Williams' home and automobile. After that, Axam and Welcome filed even more motions, these attacking the validity of the search warrants that had been executed the previous June.

PRETRIAL HEARINGS

For weeks I had been preparing for the hearing set for September 4, 1981, totally immersed in preparing legal arguments for every request in the tall pile of written motions. Whether at work or at home, I was consumed by the task. Renovation work on my 1892 house would have to wait, as would work on neighborhood committees. The hearing was scheduled for 9:00 a.m. in a fourth-floor courtroom, the largest in the Fulton County Courthouse. Tony Axam was present, while Mary Welcome had not yet arrived. Tony said he would move ahead without her.

First he said, "I have some housekeeping matters." He then cited Rule 23 of the local rules of court, claiming that all of his motions should be granted without argument because I had filed no written responses to his motions. I was caught completely off guard. In criminal cases, we never filed written responses to defense motions. Tony suggested that Rule 23 of the local rules required otherwise. I awkwardly noted that we would be responding to anything considered to be contested matters in the case. I also noted that Rule 23 would not apply to this case and that neither state statutes nor court decisions supported his argument that written responses were required.

I was basically winging it, until suddenly, I felt an uncomfortable tug on my coattail. It was Lewis Slaton, who was seated at the end of the counsel table a few feet behind me. Slaton loudly whispered, "Tell him that that rule applies only in civil cases, not in criminal cases." I was mortified; it was bad enough to have someone pulling at your coattail while arguing, but it was even more embarrassing to have your boss doing it. Judge Cooper, sensing that I might have more to say, said, "Anything further, Mr. Drolet?" I responded, "I just want to add that this is a criminal case, and I believe those rules that Mr. Axam cited are normally applicable to civil cases." I again offered to provide written responses to anything the court requested.

The judge reserved ruling, and we moved on. I had survived. Fortunately, the focus of the hearing shifted, and we were now on the playing field of constitutional law and the rules of criminal procedure. Tony Axam was adept and could be very persuasive, but I knew the law, and for most of the positions we were taking, the law was clearly on our side. I conceded many points, agreeing with Tony when I knew he was right, but I had at least one case precedent for every point. Whatever he would argue, I would respond with applicable case law from the Georgia Supreme Court and the Georgia Court of Appeals. The hearing went on all morning as we proceeded from one written motion to the next. After a short lunch recess, we continued. For me, the hearing had become energizing. I was prepared for everything that was coming at me; it was one of the moments when I really enjoyed being a lawyer. I was doing what I did best, and it was working.

At the end of the hearing, Judge Cooper acknowledged that there was no way we were going to trial in early October. He announced that no trial would be held until all motions had been completed and the court had reviewed all the files.

Six days later, on September 10, the court held a hearing on the defense motion to suppress evidence from what they characterized as an "illegal detention" of Wayne Williams near the James Jackson Parkway Bridge on the early morning of May 22, 1981. I opened the hearing by pointing out the legal deficiencies in the defense motion: no evidence had been seized and Wayne Williams had made no confession. There was no evidence to suppress, legal or illegal. Gordon Miller then presented three of the witnesses from the bridge incident: Carl Holden, who had been in an unmarked car on the Fulton County side of the river, Greg Gilliland, the FBI agent who had been in a car on the Cobb County side of the river, and FBI Agent Mike McComas, who had interviewed Williams along the roadside.

Mary Welcome, who was handling the hearing for the defense, was quite aggressive and Slaton, who had planned to sit quietly as Miller handled the examination of witnesses, became exasperated and jumped into the fray. He and Mary Welcome exchanged sarcastic comments for the remainder of the hearing. Welcome then called five witnesses related to the bridge incident and used the opportunity to squeeze whatever information she could from them. Slaton fumed. I quietly watched and took notes. I was relieved when the hearing ended. That afternoon, Judge Cooper issued a written order in regard to the various motions we had heard a week earlier. He granted some of the requests but generally ruled according to established law.

On September 21, Judge Cooper ruled on another matter. Williams' motion for severance of the two murders was denied. The two murders in the indictment would be tried together. In the same order, the judge also considered the evidence he had heard at the contentious hearing regarding the initial questioning of Williams when he was stopped on I-285. Judge Cooper found that Williams had consented to talking to the police and allowed them to look in his car. In addition, nothing was seized from Williams, so his motion to suppress evidence was denied.

That same day, in Washington, DC, Sandra Day O'Connor was confirmed, in a 99–0 vote in the US Senate, as the first female member of the United States Supreme Court.

Chapter 7

CARPET FIBER

Τhis was my first case involving fiber evidence, and I had a lot to learn. I met with Larry Peterson at the Georgia Bureau of Investigation's Crime Laboratory, crammed into a small space in the back of the Public Safety Complex on what was then called Confederate Avenue in southeast Atlanta. The complex was a one-story building built in the 1950s for the Georgia State Patrol. In the basement, office space overflowed into a warren of hallways. The agencies stuffed into the building had long since outgrown the space.

Larry Peterson, an earnest public servant who loved his work, was dressed casually under his white lab coat. He loved nothing better than microscopes and minuscule fragments of matter. I asked Larry to tell me about the fiber evidence. He started by showing me two eight-by-ten-inch glossy photos. The one on the left looked like a picture of an elongated thick green stripe; the companion photo was a similar elongated stripe. The two photos were very similar, both the same sickly color of green, except for what appeared to be tiny air bubbles each displayed. Larry looked at me as he proudly held up the pictures. "What do you think?" he asked.

I didn't know what to think. I had no point of reference. I said, "Are they the same or are they different? What am I looking at?"

Larry looked at me in disbelief and said, "They're a match." I realized then that explaining fiber evidence to a jury would be challenging.

Larry showed me how the color of the two fibers shown in the photos could be measured on an instrument called a microspectrophotometer. The instrument produced a graph, and different specimens could be compared to see if the color was exactly the same. Larry now showed me examples of other fibers and hairs. They looked completely different from the photos of the green carpet fibers. I was learning that man-made fibers varied in size, shape, color, cross-section, and chemical composition. As Larry explained the fiber comparisons, I realized that we would have to educate the jury, just as Larry was educating me. I had never seen a fiber blown up four hundred times actual size. If I didn't know what I was seeing, it was likely that any group of twelve jurors would have the same difficulty. Figuring out how to explain this microscopic world was now a priority.

Meanwhile, Gordon Miller had been speaking to experts at the FBI. They mentioned that prosecutors in a case in Federal Court in North Carolina had done a fine job of explaining complicated scientific evidence, and suggested we contact Brian Murtagh, one of the assistant US attorneys who had presented the case. In late September 1981, Gordon and I met with Brian Murtagh at the old Federal Courthouse in Columbia, South Carolina. The case involved an Army Green Beret doctor named Jeffrey MacDonald. On February 17, 1970, Captain MacDonald's pregnant wife and two young daughters were brutally stabbed and clubbed to death in the MacDonalds' quarters at Fort Bragg, North Carolina. MacDonald claimed drug-crazed hippies, saying things like "acid is groovy" and "kill the pigs," had invaded his home and beaten him unconscious. He had awakened to find his family dead and the word "pig" written in blood on the headboard of a bed.

Dr. MacDonald's wounds were minor compared to those inflicted on his family. He had a neat incision between two ribs, a lump on his forehead, a cut on his left arm, and other superficial cuts. For years, doubts about his story had lingered; his version of events did not fit with the physical evidence at the scene (blood-stains and blood spatters). And then there was his pajama top, which he claimed was pulled over his head by the attackers as they stabbed at him with an ice pick, and he fought them off with the pajama top wrapped around his arms. The top was found draped over his dead wife, Colette. It had forty-eight round, smooth holes in it.

Brian Murtagh began showing us the visual aids and charts that he had used in the 1979 trial of Captain MacDonald. The clarity and power of his presentation became evident. Gordon and I began to understand the significance of bloodstains and the fact that the pajama top could not have been on Captain MacDonald's arms as he fought off crazed hippies. If folded, the forty-eight holes in the pajama top lined up neatly as holes through multiple layers of the garment. Those holes showed no sign of having been ragged or torn as would have been the case had MacDonald been using the pajama top to protect himself during a struggle. They were neat, clean, and, more important, the holes matched up per-fectly with twenty-one identical holes in the chest of Colette MacDonald. Jeffrey MacDonald had no wounds on his arms or body that were consistent with the holes in the pajamas and with his version of the attack. The evidence suggested that the folded pajama top had been placed on Colette's chest and she had been repeatedly stabbed with the ice pick. Other bits of blood evidence reinforced that conclusion, and the visual exhibits made the evi-dence clear. A verbal explanation of the evidence, without the cor-roborating visuals, would have fallen short.

We began constructing a framework to explain the significance of fiber evidence. We would need to show how fibers differ, with varying cross-sections, thickness, chemical composition, color, and rarity. We would have to educate both the court and the jury on how fibers are made and how groupings of fibers can function almost like a fingerprint in connecting a killer to his victim.

While we reviewed files at the Task Force and developed a strategy for presenting the fiber evidence, Wayne Williams had not been idle. Despite the judge's gag order, Williams was communicating with reporters, using his father as a courier to radio stations, making calls from the jail, and even doing interviews with national magazines, complete with photos of his childhood triumphs from the family scrapbook. He attacked the police, ridiculed evidence, and proclaimed his innocence.

On September 24, 1981, Judge Cooper issued another order, granting two requests made by Williams' lawyers. The first was a request for the court to review all the files at the Task Force, not just the files related to victims Nathaniel Cater and Jimmy Ray Payne. The court would be searching for any material evidence that would support the proposition that Wayne Williams did *not* kill the victims as alleged. Judge Cooper appealed to his fellow judges to loan him their law clerks.

Beginning in early October of 1981, Judge Cooper and a dozen law clerks virtually took up residence at Task Force headquarters, the old car dealership on West Peachtree Street. As Jack Mallard and I were in one part of the building reviewing files, the judge and his team of clerks would be out of sight in a conference room, poring over thousands of pages of documents. During the years of the investigation, the Task Force had amassed a trove of over fifty thousand separate documents, statements from some fifteen thousand witnesses, files on hundreds of suspects, and a host of letters from psychics.

Judge Cooper's order on September 24 also granted a request by the defense that jurors be questioned individually, not in groups. The judge allowed general questions to be asked of jurors in groups, but each prospective juror would then have to be questioned individually.

On September 25, Tony Axam and Mary Welcome filed another motion to suppress evidence. This time, they attacked the June 3, 1981, search warrant and its eighteen-page affidavit, which explained what evidence police had expected to find at the Williamses' home and in the Williamses' white station wagon. They didn't want us to be able to use any of the evidence recovered from the Williamses' home or automobile. The defense team also filed additional motions the same day: a motion to "cause witnesses to confer with defense," a notice "to produce witness statements, criminal records of state witnesses, and all forensic reports," a motion to "compel the state to identify whether any expert witness will testify as to voice spectrogram comparisons," a motion for a hearing to determine "the reliability of methods used to refresh witness recall through hypnosis," and a motion to "suppress the testimony of any witness who has been hypnotized." The defense had now filed a total of forty-two motions.

On October 1, 1981, we filed a written response requesting that no more motions be permitted, as the deadline for filing defense motions had long since passed. The judge had set a deadline for more than a month earlier; the defense ignored it and instead buried us in legal reading material. Our response had no immediate effect. Now Tony Axam, Mary Welcome, and a newly added lawyer, Harold Spence, filed yet another motion, this one to dismiss the case based on pretrial publicity. Judge Cooper apparently sensed our frustration. On October 9, he entered an order requiring that any future motions, by prosecution or defense, could be filed only with the consent of the court.

The defense's motion to dismiss the indictment because of "pretrial publicity" was now on my desk for response. On this issue, the law was clearly on my side. Cases were not dismissed because of pretrial publicity. Were it otherwise, a person could shoot the president in front of hundreds of witnesses on live TV and claim that no charges should be filed because there was too much publicity. The usual remedy in such cases was to move the trial to a place where few people were familiar with it, or to question potential jurors until attorneys on both sides agreed upon a group of people who were willing to decide the case based solely on the evidence presented in court.

But the part of my response I enjoyed writing the most had to do with Wayne Williams himself. The motion his lawyers filed claimed that the defense had "in no way instigated or solicited any type of publicity." I attached twenty-five exhibits to my response. Among these was a letter Williams had sent to a radio station declaring his innocence, phone calls he had made to reporters, and his "exclusive story" told to *Us* magazine, in which he swore he was innocent and a scapegoat. According to articles in the *Atlanta Constitution* and the *Atlanta Journal*, his lawyers had helped arrange the magazine interview, and one of Mary Welcome's associates even distributed flyers to reporters on behalf of the defense team, attacking both Lewis Slaton and Judge Clarence Cooper, claiming Williams was being ambushed and railroaded. Many of these publicity stunts took place long after the court's gag order went into effect.

Chapter 8

CHANGE OF LAWYERS

On October 16, 1981, Wayne Williams fired Tony Axam. The terms of Williams' release of Axam "expressly" prohibited him "from participating in any manner as an attorney . . . in the investigation, trial, and activities" of his case. We had heard rumors of friction between Mary Welcome and Tony Axam. Wayne apparently preferred Mary Welcome. Tony Axam was quiet, businesslike, and competent, and, for some reason, banished by Williams. We were not sorry to see Tony go, but we wondered what precipitated his abrupt departure and who would fill the void on the defense team.

On October 20, a hearing was scheduled on Williams' second motion to suppress evidence, which sought to bar evidence from the June 3, 1981, searches of his home and automobile. Mary Welcome was there, joined by one of her associates, Cliff Bailey. Mary argued for a continuance of the hearing. I argued against delaying the hearing. It had been delayed at least once already and the focus of the hearing was Ms. Welcome's own motion. We proceeded with the hearing.

Gordon Miller, my fellow prosecutor, presented testimony from Judge John Langford, who had reviewed the request for a search warrant and found probable cause to issue the warrant.

Mary Welcome then called Miller as her own witness, which surprised us, considering that Gordon had just presented the evidence on our behalf and had helped draft the search warrant. With Gordon on the witness stand, Mary Welcome attempted to elicit information about the case, but there was nothing Gordon could contribute that would help her defense of Wayne Williams.

Welcome then called Morris Redding to the stand. Redding was head of the Task Force investigating the murders. He had signed and sworn to the affidavit supporting the search warrant. Ms. Welcome tried to show that he could not have been privy to all the information in the eighteen pages of the affidavit. We conceded that point and showed that, by law, Redding could rely on information provided by officers under his command. This was the law in Georgia, and the concept had been upheld by the United States Supreme Court. Judge Cooper did not rule at the end of the hearing, but took the matter "under advisement," meaning he would rule at a later time.

By the end of October, Williams had added another lawyer to his team. Alvin Binder came with an excellent reputation. Binder was a high-powered lawyer from Mississippi with a slow, mellow southern drawl. At fifty-one years old, he was ever the gentleman, polite and respectful. And he was reputed to be excellent at cross-examining witnesses. Binder would undoubtedly be a formidable opponent.

More lawyers continued to join the defense team. Cliff Bailey had been present for the hearing on October 20, and was now part of the team with Mary Welcome, Al Binder, and Harold Spence.

During this time, Jack Mallard and I were still making our almost daily trips to the Task Force offices to review files. Now began the marathon task of interviewing hundreds of witnesses. Major W. J. Taylor continued to be our guide at the Task Force. He would help find witnesses, get them to the Task Force offices, and have them ready to be interviewed. We scheduled witnesses at fifteen-minute intervals and interviewed them in a small cubicle. Many witnesses provided nothing helpful, while with others, we felt like we were striking gold.

Sharon Blakely was one of those witnesses. She was a friend of Wayne Williams, and we expected little when she entered the room. She was a small, pleasant young woman who ran a jewelry store with her husband, Eustis, in Decatur, Georgia. She knew Williams well and seemed somewhat protective of him. Even so, she offered certain details that grabbed our attention. Williams had shown her and her husband how to squeeze a person's neck until he would lose consciousness. He had made disparaging comments about the missing and murdered children, saying that they had "no business on the streets," and he referred to them in degrading terms. After the incident on the James Jackson Parkway Bridge, Williams had visited the Blakelys' store and acknowledged that he dropped "garbage" from the bridge. This was the same Wayne Williams who had denied even slowing down on the bridge.

Every few days we would encounter other helpful witnesses, each with a tidbit of information that provided us with a fuller picture of Wayne Williams. Some witnesses had seen Williams with one or more of the victims, while others had seen his father, Homer, with victims. Some reported seeing Williams at the funerals of some of the victims. After days of talking to these witnesses, we were left with piles of notes to be organized. The case became my full-time companion.

A VISIT TO THE FBI

On November 5, 1981, Gordon Miller and I took an early flight to Washington, DC, and the downtown headquarters of the Federal Bureau of Investigation. Although the FBI had not been part of the 102-member Task Force, two dozen agents had been working on the case for months. We were escorted through the labyrinth of hallways to the office of the assistant director who oversaw the FBI laboratory. After a brief introduction, he guided us to the lab, where we met with Dr. Harold Deadman, the FBI fiber expert. Hal was a scholarly, slender, middle-aged man with slightly graying hair and dark-rimmed glasses. Like Larry

Peterson, Deadman was focused and businesslike; the examination of trace evidence, like hairs and fibers found at crime scenes, was his passion. He had years of experience and was well respected in the scientific community. Along with Larry Peterson, our Georgia fiber expert, he had been reviewing the potentially significant hair and fiber evidence in the case.

Gordon and I discussed with Deadman how the fiber evidence would be presented. Deadman and the FBI lab would help produce thirty-by-forty-inch foam-core display boards as visual aids in the presentation. The exhibits would show how man-made fibers were created, and how natural fibers varied in color, size, and texture. They would illustrate different cross-sections of fibers, and they would provide photos comparing fibers found on various victims with the identical fibers found in the Williamses' home and automobiles. Charts would outline the process for creating carpeting composed of man-made fibers. All visual aids would be supported by the testimony of experts.

While at the lab, we also met with agents who were preparing a scale model of the James Jackson Parkway Bridge as well as mounted aerial photographs of the Chattahoochee River. We returned to Atlanta that evening pleased with the assistance and cooperation from the FBI.

By this time, I was also learning a lot about serial killers. People kill for a variety of reasons, and circumstances often point to an obvious suspect. Serial killers are different. A victim picked at random can be baffling to law enforcement. Until there is a pattern, the serial killer is undetectable. He leaves a trail of death hard to follow, and he becomes visible only when he makes a mistake.

Wayne Williams made a mistake when he dropped Nathaniel Cater's body from the James Jackson Parkway Bridge.

Before Wayne Williams became a suspect, the FBI's recently formed Behavioral Science Unit, headquartered in Quantico, Virginia, had developed a psychological profile of the killer. Profiling was a new science, and many police officials were skeptical. Psychologists John Douglas and Roy Hazelwood had been studying the murders since January of 1981, and based on their analysis, they expected the killer to be an articulate, Black male of average to above-average intelligence, who closely followed media coverage of the cases, changed homicidal methods to suit his needs, and was likely the only son in his family. He might be a police buff, could be driving a police-type vehicle, and might even insinuate himself into the investigation. They expected the killer to have frequent changes in employment or be self-employed. Killers of children, they had found, were often pampered and overprotected in their youth and might fixate on either boys or girls. They believed the killer would be in his mid-to-late twenties, and they did not expect him to have a girlfriend. This profile described Wayne Williams perfectly, but it was unclear whether it would be allowed as evidence in a courtroom.

The day after I returned from our trip to Washington, I attended a training class provided by a new company claiming to have the ability to perform legal research in a revolutionary way, by connecting to a computer in Dayton, Ohio. Salespeople from the firm were pushing their rather pricey services, claiming that they offered lawyers an alternative to the tedious and time-consuming process of going through numerous books and digests to find cases on a particular point. In 1981, few people were using computer-assisted research, and the emerging technology was beyond the budget of most lawyers and governments, including Fulton County, Georgia. I attended the training session at temporary offices the company had opened in Peachtree Center, an office complex on Peachtree Street in downtown Atlanta.

As part of the session, we were permitted two hours of unlimited legal research on the system. These two hours would have cost thousands of dollars, as it charged by the minute, and fees were based on which "library" you searched. A brief search of an issue from just one state would be relatively affordable, but a search of state and federal libraries from across the country was financially prohibitive for an office like ours. With my allotted two hours, I could search in any of the libraries. I had prepared a list of subjects I had been researching, with one, in particular, proving frustrating: If a person fabricated evidence in regard to an event, was that in itself evidence of his guilt? Using traditional methods, I had found nothing. I used my free time and entered words such as "fabricate" and "evidence" and "guilt." To my surprise, there was an 1896 case from not just any court, but the United States Supreme Court, supporting the proposition that fabricating or concealing evidence showed a consciousness of guilt. That case led to other cases, including Georgia cases supporting the principle. I was impressed with the new system, and soon our office, with an addition to the office budget, became a subscriber to the service. What would today be considered an absurdly large and awkward desk-sized terminal was installed in the library outside my office with special permission required for anyone wishing to use the expensive new device. This wondrous machine was a crude early version of a personal computer. At the time, it seemed like magic.

On November 10, 1981, Judge Cooper and his team of clerks had completed their review of every file at the Task Force. Cooper turned over a box of materials that could be considered "exculpatory," consisting of reports that called into question or contradicted the allegations of the state's case.

Two days later, the defense announced that they had brought in Charles Morton as their fiber expert. A well-respected fiber analyst familiar to both Harold Deadman and Larry Peterson, Morton was director of the Institute of Forensic Science Criminalistics Laboratory in Oakland, California. Fiber evidence formed the basis for much of our case. What could Morton possibly say that would challenge its relevance? The answer to that question would come three months later, after the trial began.

The defense team requested permission to file a third motion to suppress evidence, involving items seized in the second search of the Williamses' home on June 22, 1981. Judge Cooper permitted the filing and set a hearing for November 20. He also set a date for the trial: December 28, 1981. Time was getting short, and my anxiety was growing. I wondered whether we could possibly be ready in one month. Meanwhile, the defense added another lawyer, Ken McLeod Jr.

At the November 20 hearing, Williams' lawyers claimed the affidavit for the second search of the Williamses' home contained falsehoods, rendering it invalid. Gordon Miller questioned Albert L. Thompson, the judge who had issued the June 22 search warrant. Before signing the search warrant, Thompson had read the lengthy affidavit and heard from Morris Redding, head of the Task Force, who swore to the truthfulness of what was contained in the affidavit. Williams' new lawyer, Al Binder, made his first courtroom appearance. He was calm and respectful and had a deep soothing voice that could lull you into a state of relative comfort. He went through the lengthy affidavit meticulously, gently bringing out the fact that Redding was swearing to information told to him by other people. Binder objected to the admission of the search warrant and gave an impassioned argument about its inadequacy. I responded, explaining that Binder was arguing matters that had nothing to do with the admissibility of the warrant. The only question was whether the affidavit established probable cause to believe the items listed could be found at the Williamses' home.

After hearing the testimony of the judge who issued the warrant, Judge Cooper admitted the affidavit and warrant as evidence. Binder then called Morris Redding as a witness. Jack Mallard and I both objected to the wide range of subjects Binder tried to explore. Binder, claiming the affidavit was infected with falsehoods, wanted the results of the search thrown out. I argued that Binder had shown no intentional falsehoods and no evidence of any intent by Morris Redding to deceive Judge Thompson. In addition, the United States Supreme Court case Binder was relying upon, *Franks v. Delaware*, said a search warrant was still good, even if it had errors, as long as the warrant as a whole still established probable cause, even after disregarding the objectionable parts. In other words, Binder's argument fell flat on two different grounds: he had established no lying, and even if he had, it did not infect the warrant. The judge took a recess for lunch and to read the law I had presented. When he returned at 1:15 p.m., he disappointed the waiting Al Binder, who wanted to grill more of our witnesses. Judge Cooper ruled that "the requirements clearly enunciated in the case of *Franks v. Delaware* have not been met. Therefore, the motion to suppress is hereby denied." Binder's attempt to get at our witnesses was repelled.

From the hearing, we learned a lot about Al Binder. He was a good lawyer, thorough and capable of stretching the law to his advantage. On November 23, just three days after the hearing, Binder filed a written motion asking the judge to reconsider his ruling and to allow him to examine police officers and Larry Peterson in an attempt to show falsehoods. I spent my Thanksgiving weekend preparing a response, which I filed on Tuesday, December 1. The next day the judge entered a written order, denying the request to reconsider.

The trial was now just four weeks away. Our team was in high gear and weekends turned into workdays. I prepared a separate manila folder on each issue I could imagine being raised by the defense.

On the morning of December 3, Judge Cooper invited me and representatives of the defense team to discuss media and public access for the upcoming trial. There were more press people than there were seats in the courtroom; if the press got all the seats, no members of the public would get to see the trial.

Later that day, Cooper issued an order setting guidelines labeled "Fair Trial—Free Press." Passes would be issued for representatives of television, radio, and print media; the sheriff would issue press credentials. Those with passes would get numbered badges each morning, and the badges would be collected at the end of each day. A list of those already approved for passes was attached. CNN, ABC, NBC, CBS, the Associated Press, and United Press International were each allowed two representatives, as were the *New York Times*, the *Atlanta Journal*, and the *Atlanta Constitution*. *Newsweek*, *US News and World Report*, the *Los Angeles Times*, *Time* magazine, the *Miami Herald*, and the *Chicago Tribune* were allowed one representative each. A host of other regional and local radio, TV, and print media were given passes as well. Sketch artists were permitted in the front row, where they could get a good view of their subjects.

After passing through security, members of the public would enter from the rear of the courtroom. Press access would be from the side entrance. The spectator area of the courtroom was divided—the left side of the courtroom for the press, the right side for the public. The jurors' assembly room, a large open hall on the same floor as the courtroom, would be a secondary area for the overflow of media to view proceedings, which would be piped in live to large TV monitors positioned throughout the room. Hundreds of reporters were expected.

On December 7, Judge Cooper issued a petition for contempt against Mary Welcome and Al Binder for repeatedly violating the court's gag order. The defense lawyers had continued to criticize the court and attack the credibility of our witnesses; two defense witnesses had publicly shared their belief that Wayne Williams was innocent. One article, quoting a Utica, New York, pathologist hired by the defense, had questioned whether the victims had actually been murdered. The article had appeared in local newspapers just days before, on December 4, 1981. Although the judge did not schedule a hearing on the matter, the judge was clearly trying to rein in the talkative defense team and their minions.

Meanwhile, Jack Mallard and I toured the crime scenes. Guided by Major Taylor and a detective, we visited the places where bodies had been found. For victims found in rivers, we inspected nearby bridges, noting the height of the railings, the width of the sidewalks, and the ways in which a body could've been dropped into the river. We toured downtown spots where many of the victims hung out, and we met with lead detectives involved in each of the cases.

In December, I developed a chart of related murder cases we could offer to support our case. Evidence of other crimes was admissible if the cases were logically connected or similar to the cases on trial. The principle of using such "similar transactions" was universally permitted in American and English courts. As early as 1842, the United States Supreme Court had ruled that it had "always been deemed allowable" to introduce evidence of other acts of a kindred character to establish a pattern, intent, motive, or scheme.

As I studied the murders, it became clear that none of the young, Black males had been snatched from their homes. They had all been picked up from places where they hung out. They were all poor, streetwise, and vulnerable, and they hung out at places like the Omni Complex in downtown Atlanta or at other local game rooms. None of them, not even those in their twenties, had access to an automobile. The bodies were all found in places easily accessible by major highway arteries. Even the bridges over the South River and the Chattahoochee River were close to interstates or major highways. I considered personal characteristics, cause of death, wounds and other marks on the bodies, and clothing missing from the bodies. My first charts listed twenty connected cases. But we didn't really need twenty. That number of cases would be unwieldy and half that number would serve the same purpose: to show that there was a two-year pattern of murders by a serial killer and that we had reason to believe that Wayne Williams was that killer.

I eliminated the weaker cases from the list. Some cases had strong fiber evidence and eyewitnesses who had seen Wayne Williams with the victim. Others fit the pattern perfectly but lacked the strong fiber evidence. Close scrutiny of victims Mickey McIntosh and Bubba Duncan revealed many similarities to Nathaniel Cater and Jimmy Ray Payne. Duncan was mentally challenged, hung around the Omni, had no vehicle, and could be described as a classic street person. McIntosh had recently been released from jail, was a street hustler, often high on drugs or alcohol, and hung out near the Omni. Timothy Hill was like the others and was known to prostitute himself as he worked the nighttime streets. Duncan, Hill, and McIntosh had all been found floating in the Chattahoochee River in the same general area, each stripped of all but underwear. Hill and McIntosh were dead from asphyxia. But the bodies of these victims had been subjected to the river currents for extended periods of time; there was little fiber evidence still clinging to their hair or underwear. Because the fiber evidence had washed away, these cases would've been more difficult to prove beyond a reasonable doubt. In some cases, we had only skeletal remains. Some fiber evidence was found, but there was no way to determine what had killed these victims. Then there was the Clifford Jones case. The body of Clifford Jones was laid out like that of many of the victims. He had been strangled, and he had dog hair, green carpet fibers, and violet acetate fibers clinging to his body and clothing. But Jones' clothing also revealed more than two dozen beige carpet fibers. The problem was, we couldn't determine where they had come from. As far as we knew, Wayne Williams had no beige carpeting in his home and no car with beige carpet. We chose not to use the Clifford Jones case.

Finally, Jack, Gordon, Wally, and I agreed on ten cases we would use as similar transactions. We were aware that there were grieving families looking for justice for their loved ones. We hoped they would understand that the cases we chose were meant to represent *all* of Wayne Williams' victims. Our goal was to show that Wayne Williams was the serial killer who had tormented the community, and to see him sentenced to life in prison. That meant focusing on those cases that provided us with the most convincing evidence.

The ten chosen cases cut across the two years of murders, from the very first victim to the last. Among them was a murder so recent that it had not even made the list. John Porter resembled Nathaniel Cater, was about his age, and had a similar back-ground. He slept in an abandoned building, was unemployed, and hung out on the street, often drunk. He was found laid out on his back on a retaining wall in a vacant lot near downtown, and all the key fibers were found on his body and clothing. What appeared to be ritualistic horizontal stab wounds, like those on some other victims, punctured his abdomen and his clothing appeared rearranged. Some stab wounds pierced his shirt, while others, in the same area, had been inflicted directly into his body with no evidence he was wearing his shirt.

By mid-December, I feared we were losing Jack Mallard from our team. Jack's wife, Jo, had just survived cancer surgery on December 17, and Jack was at her bedside for most of the remainder of the month.

Meanwhile, those of us on the trial team were trying to figure out how involved Lewis Slaton would want to be in this high-profile case. Slaton had been the district attorney for over sixteen years. He was a master politician, cautious and at the same time conscious of the political impact of everything he said or did. He exuded self-confidence and liked to be on top of every aspect of the criminal justice system. But Slaton rarely tried cases. He managed; we prosecuted. For nine years I had been his mouthpiece at the General Assembly, and I knew what he was for and what he was against. He often attended political events and was seen everywhere. The last trial he prosecuted was that of Marcus Wayne Chenault, the man who shot up Ebenezer Baptist Church and killed Martin Luther King Jr.'s mother. Slaton took a lead role in that trial, which resulted in a death penalty verdict.

Media coverage was becoming more intense. Reporters were taking pictures of us and writing articles about the prosecution and defense teams, much like reporting for a sporting event. News articles summarized our specialties and our strengths. The attention was flattering but unnerving, and it reminded me that everything I said and did could erupt into a news item.

The defense team was busy serving subpoenas on federal, state, and local officials. City of Atlanta lawyers responded to defense subpoenas for all records of "any case involving negro children between the ages of 6 and 28 years of age, who have been reported missing or who have been found dead from January 1, 1981, to the present" and statistics as to "all homicides committed in the metropolitan area over a ten-year period, without regard to age, race or sex or whether the cases were resolved or unresolved." The defense was trying to get into the files of all police agencies in the metro area. They were trying to circumvent the procedural rules applicable to criminal cases. The judge had already reviewed all the relevant files and provided the defense with anything that would be helpful. On December 24, 1981, Judge Cooper quashed the subpoena for city records.

In late December, Judge John Langford assisted Judge Cooper, who was hearing from prospective jurors who claimed that for one reason or another, they couldn't serve on the jury. Seven hundred jurors had been sent notices to appear for the start of the trial on December 28, 1981, and hundreds of them wanted nothing to do with it. The case would be long, and the jury would be sequestered, meaning they would be isolated in a hotel, having little contact with the outside world, a level of confinement most people did not wish to endure.

Christmas Eve found me meeting with Al Binder to go over photos we would be presenting at trial and meeting with defense team member Cliff Bailey to develop stipulations of evidence, which would eliminate the need to bring certain witnesses to court. Gordon, Wally, and I met in our "war room," a large third-floor office, to discuss jury selection, surrounded by piles of exhibits, charts, maps, and case files. We took Christmas Day off, but I could think of little other than the case, set to start just three days later. Early on Saturday, December 26, Gordon, Wally, and I gathered in the war room and met with FBI Agent Bill McGrath, Major Taylor, and two detectives who were assisting us. Slaton would drop in now and then to check on our progress.

In the war room, we had many of the items we would be offering as exhibits and visual aids in the trial. Leaning against one wall was a tall cardboard box covered with white tape used to seal packages of evidence. The box was about eighteen inches wide and about ten inches deep, and it stood about five feet high. It was our understanding that the box contained the back seat from the white Chevrolet station wagon Wayne Williams had driven onto the James Jackson Parkway Bridge. Fresh blood, still containing active enzymes, had been found on the seat, matching the blood of two recent victims, William Barrett and John Porter. Gordon, Wally, and I had been eyeing the box for days and discussing different ways to dramatically slice open the evidence tape and pull out the bloody seat in front of the jury. This, we imagined, could be a huge moment in the trial.

We had not seen the exhibit before, so we wondered whether the blood would even be visible. We knew there were only tiny amounts on the seat, and most of it had been cut from the seat for analysis at the crime lab. We looked and looked at that box. Finally, our curiosity won out. We laid the long box on the large conference table and carefully sliced the tape on the end of the box. I reached in to pull out the seat. As I did, Wally and Gordon gasped, one of them exclaiming, "What the hell is this?" It was the steel cover from the front of a furnace with spatters of blood on it. It was *not* a car seat. After our shock subsided, we laughed about how embarrassing it would have been to dramatically open this box in front of a jury. After that, we looked in every box, making no assumptions unless we had checked it ourselves. The car seat, as it turned out, was safely in the possession of the Georgia State Crime Lab.

By Sunday, December 27, the entire block around the Fulton County Courthouse was surrounded by enormous trucks, all of them oozing cables and sprouting tall antennae. Hundreds of reporters, photographers, and film crews milled about, watching for anything associated with the trial. The jury assembly room was finally fully fitted out as a closed-circuit viewing area for the media overflow, as hundreds of reporters, unable to squeeze into the courtroom, would watch live on large monitors at each end of the room.

Amid this media frenzy, Gordon, Wally, and I nervously made final preparations for the drama that was about to begin.

Chapter 9

DOES ANYONE WANT TO BE A JUROR?

On Monday, December 28, 1981, people jammed into the courtroom. Members of the press began choosing seats on the left side of the courtroom, trying to figure out the best vantage point. Sketch artists jockeyed for the best seats in their reserved front row. Homer and Faye Williams were seated on the right side of the courtroom, in the front row of the public spectators' area, directly behind the counsel table where their son Wayne would sit. Five sheriff's deputies escorted Wayne Williams into the courtroom, as a murmur rose from the press and members of the public lucky enough to get a seat. Williams wore a bulletproof flak jacket as he sat at the counsel table directly to my right, about ten feet away. Additional press credentials had been issued, and the courtroom overflowed with the ballooning press corps.

As a deputy slammed his gavel and announced, "Everyone, please rise," Judge Cooper entered the courtroom from a passageway behind the bench. The judge quietly asked everyone to be seated. Forty-eight prospective jurors entered the courtroom, filling the jury box and chairs set up around the courtroom.

The 1913-era courtroom had been renovated, probably in the early 1960s. The ornate early-twentieth-century bench, jury box, counsel tables, and podium had been replaced with the latest in mid-twentieth-century institutional modern furnishings. From the judge's bench to the counsel tables, everything was blandly covered in faux-wood plastic laminate. The courtroom was functional but utterly lacking in charm or architectural detail.

Judge Cooper announced that this was the case of the State of Georgia versus Wayne B. Williams and that, by agreement with both counsel, jurors would be examined in panels of forty-eight. Additional panels of forty-eight would be brought in until a pool of sixty eligible jurors had been reached. The jury and alternates would be selected from those sixty people. Cooper asked Lewis Slaton if issue had been joined. The "joining of issue" had taken place when Wayne Williams and his attorneys signed the indictment, indicating that he was pleading not guilty. This meant there was now a legal dispute requiring a trial. We said he was guilty of murder, and he denied it. Cooper invited the forty-eight potential jurors to stand and swear an oath to give "true answers" to all questions concerning their qualifications and to swear they had truthfully filled out a written questionnaire.

Lewis Slaton now stood to read the indictment. He introduced himself and me, Gordon, Wally, and Major Taylor, who was seated behind us. Slaton also graciously introduced the defense team: Alvin Binder, Mary Welcome, Cliff Bailey, Harold Spence, Gail Anderson, and a psychologist named Bayless. By his actions, Slaton made sure the prospective jurors understood that regarding the lawyers in the courtroom, he was in charge.

Slaton read the indictment: "The Grand Jurors selected, chosen and sworn for the County of Fulton . . . charge and accuse Wayne Bertram Williams with the offense of murder for that said accused, in the County of Fulton and State of Georgia, on or about the 22nd day of April, 1981, did unlawfully and with malice aforethought cause the death of Jimmy Ray Payne, a human being, by asphyxiating him with objects and by means which are to the grand jurors unknown, contrary to the laws of the state, the good order, peace, and dignity thereof." Count Two of the indictment read the same and repeated the formal language of the charges, with the exception that it alleged murder "by strangulation and asphyxiating" of Nathaniel Cater "with objects and by means which are to the grand jurors unknown."

Judge Cooper read general questions to the forty-eight members of the jury panel. Could they be fair? Were they related to Wayne Williams or to any of the lawyers? Were they registered voters in Fulton County? Had they read about the case? (Nearly everyone raised his or her hand.) The general questions showed that almost everyone was familiar with the case of the missing and murdered children and the arrest of Wayne Williams. Williams' lawyers had earlier filed what they called a "reserve motion for change of venue," suggesting that they could not get a fair trial in Fulton County and asking that the case be moved elsewhere in the state of Georgia. I wondered if they really wanted to take the trial to some rural area of Georgia; I certainly didn't. I couldn't imagine that any part of Georgia had not been exposed to the extensive publicity about the missing and murdered children, nor could I imagine any area where picking a jury would be fairer for Wayne Williams.

The judge now prepared to read a list of names, and he wanted to know whether any jurors knew them or their families or were related to them in any way. Slowly, Judge Cooper read off the now-familiar names of the twenty-nine young people on the list of missing and murdered children: Edward H. Smith? Alfred James Evans? Milton Harvey? But for Cooper's voice in this solemn moment, not a single sound could be heard in the hushed courtroom.

Al Binder asked that the names of all potential witnesses be read, in case jurors knew any of them. Gordon Miller stood, unfurled a lengthy computer printout, and rattled off names of nearly five hundred police officers, FBI agents, crime lab experts, family of victims, witnesses to dozens of offenses, and people who, in one capacity or another, might be called as witnesses. The process seemed to take forever as jurors raised hands and identified themselves when they knew someone. The long and tedious process continued uninterrupted until a lunchtime recess.

After lunch, Gordon Miller and I stood at the judge's bench with members of the defense team as each juror who claimed to have a medical problem approached. One woman said, "My husband has health problems and I have to care for him."

"What is his problem?" the judge asked.

"He has emphysema, liver cirrhosis, diabetes, and a failing heart." When the judge said, "I don't think I need to ask anything further," the woman replied, "No. Because he should have been dead in 1970." I couldn't help but smile. One lady wanted to be excused because she was worried about her cats; we let her go. This went on for much of the afternoon. A dozen or more were excused.

The panel of forty-eight had shrunk considerably as we began individual questioning of the remaining panel members. We already had the lengthy questionnaires each potential juror had filled out. Both prosecution and defense asked questions. By the end of the day, we had eleven potential candidates to be jurors. The process continued with this group the next day. Then we started over and repeated the entire process with another panel of forty-eight potential jurors. Many sought to get excused by saying they had "formed opinions" as to the guilt of Wayne Williams. Word had apparently spread that a strong opinion could get you off jury service.

To my great relief, Jack Mallard came by the courtroom and reported that his wife, Jo, was doing much better. He would be rejoining the team.

December 30, 1981, was the third day of questioning jurors, and we were all getting more comfortable with the routine. The crowds of the first day had thinned out; the process of questioning jurors was not the exciting stuff that people had hoped to see. Even members of the press found it boring. It *was* boring, of course. A reporter with the local NBC affiliate created a stir when she slipped and fell in the center aisle of the spectators' area. Her embarrassment was obvious as everyone turned to see the source of the commotion as she was helped from the floor. Wayne Williams created a stir of his own when he didn't like one juror's responses and made a gesture like he was slitting someone's throat.

Sketch artists in the courtroom complained that some of us were wearing light-colored suits; they wanted us in dark colors. One prospective juror was obviously drunk. Judge Cooper released him as he ran out, yelling from the courtroom, "Thank God, I'm free at last!" Another juror, hoping to avoid jury service, admitted drinking before coming to court; he did *not* get excused. As we took a lunch break, a United Press International photographer wanted to take my picture for the newspaper in my hometown of Kankakee, Illinois. A photo of me, seated at my office desk, would appear on the front page of the *Kankakee Journal* the following Sunday, with the headline: "Ex-city man prosecuting Atlanta case." I wondered whether my folks were proud of my notoriety.

After lunch, as the questioning of jurors continued, I watched Wayne Williams as he reacted to certain jurors and to one woman in particular. His foot began tapping and one leg began shaking nervously. He noticed me watching him and began to look from side to side. Something was making him uncomfortable.

Seven jurors were excused because they were friends of family members of the victims. The mother of a convicted armed robber was excused because of her son's upcoming trial on his latest charge, murder.

New Year's Eve, like the preceding days, was consumed by sorting through dozens more potential jurors. Few onlookers remained in the courtroom. For me and the lawyers on both sides, this process was crucial. We took note of every word uttered by potential jurors. One holdout on a jury could mean having to hold a retrial. At 12:45 p.m., we took a break, having found fifty-one jurors who were willing to serve and who could be open-minded and impartial. We had only eight more potential jurors to question before the day was done, so we would not get our sixty jurors as the year 1981 came to an end. We would have to continue jury selection into the new year.

New Year's Day 1982, was not the normal holiday of sleeping late and watching football games. After a quick breakfast at home, I met Wally and Gordon at the office, where we sat in the war room and went through different possibilities for the composition of the jury. A Georgia statute allowed the defense to excuse twice the number of jurors we were allowed. These were known as peremptory challenges—no reason needed to be given for excusing a juror. The defense got twenty such "jury strikes," and we got ten. The defense could reject many jurors we would very much like to have on the jury. We went through the exercise of trying to anticipate who the defense would excuse, who we would excuse, and who we expected would remain as the twelve who would constitute the jury. Having spent most of the day at the office, I got home that evening in time to see the last half of the Rose Bowl game, a mismatch in which the Washington Huskies crushed the Big Ten champion Iowa Hawkeyes, 28–0.

As the new year began, Atlanta would be ushering in a new era—Maynard Jackson had completed his two terms as mayor, and my former congressman, Andrew Young, would begin the first of his two terms.

January 2 and 3, 1982, fell on a weekend, which meant that the trial would resume on Monday, January 4. At 10:00 a.m. on Saturday, January 2, Lewis Slaton joined Wally, Gordon, and me in the war room. Major W. J. Taylor, who had helped us through the Task Force records, arrived a few minutes later. We continued the scenarios that we had practiced the day before as we took turns role-playing and going through the list of jurors. We identified seven or eight on the list that we would strike, regardless of what the defense did. Wally Speed and I left around lunchtime to meet witness A. B. Dean at a Waffle House in Douglasville, Georgia, just west of Atlanta. Dean had seen Wayne Williams talking to a person he identified as Jimmy Ray Payne shortly before Payne disappeared. Dean was sure of his identification but was not likely to come off as a great witness. He was elderly and hard of hearing and had had a limited view as he drove by Williams and Payne talking outside a car stopped along Bankhead

Highway. Wally and I worried that cross-examination would probably rattle him.

After lunch at the Waffle House, Wally and I headed down Bankhead Highway toward another location crucial to our case, the James Jackson Parkway, passing the place Mr. Dean had described. We turned onto the Parkway and drove to the bridge, walking the bridge and checking out the positions where four law enforcement officers had been waiting in silence when they heard a splash in the river below. About ten that evening, I returned to the bridge alone, to see what it might look like in darkness. That visit gave me a new appreciation for the challenges police officers faced on the morning of May 22, 1981.

On Sunday morning, January 3, 1982, our team assembled again at 10:00 a.m. in the war room. Slaton was not there, but Jack Mallard was now resuming his role in the prosecution. We went over a list of our witnesses and began outlining the order in which we would call them to testify. So as not to confuse the jury, it was important to tell a story in a logical order. We would start with the finding of the body of Jimmy Ray Payne. Jessie Clyde Arnold, who was out fishing on April 27, 1981, would be our first witness. We would then proceed with witnesses in chronological order after this first sighting of the body. Before we could call any witnesses, however, we had to complete the process of choosing a panel of jurors.

Jury selection resumed on Monday, January 4, 1982. A contractor wanted to get off jury duty, as did a woman whose mother had high blood pressure. I questioned the woman about her mother and concluded there was nothing preventing her from serving, but Judge Cooper was feeling generous and excused her. By late morning we had our sixty potential jurors. None of them wanted to be there, but none had a good enough excuse to get them out of what could mean a long time locked in a motel room when they weren't performing their duty in the courtroom. Slaton suggested we go ahead and strike a jury (referring to the process in which each side chooses or excuses potential jurors until a jury of twelve remains). Al Binder wanted time to ponder which jurors to strike, and we agreed to start jury selection at 4:00 p.m. that day. Binder mentioned nothing about moving the trial to another county. Apparently, the defense had decided not to invoke their previously filed "reserve" motion for change of venue. They were content with trying the case in Fulton County.

The process of jury selection did not really involve "selecting" jurors so much as eliminating or "striking" people from the list of remaining potential jurors. Those not excused by either side would constitute the jury. The defense could exclude twenty; we could exclude ten. The clerk, who had the list of potential jurors, called the first person on the list, Charles Block. We had to respond whether we accepted the juror or would use one of our ten jury strikes to excuse the juror. Lewis Slaton announced: "The State respectfully excuses Mr. Block." We now had nine strikes left. The defense still had twenty. Claire Gardner was announced as the next person on the list. Al Binder said, "We respectfully excuse her, your honor." Now nineteen strikes left for the defense. The name of Helene Rice was called. Slaton said, "The State is satisfied with Ms. Rice." Al Binder excused her. Now eighteen strikes were left for the defense. Charles W. Harris was called and stood up. We accepted him; Binder struck him. Now there were seventeen strikes left for the defense. Marjorie Rosser stood up to be considered. Slaton struck her; now we had eight strikes left. Not a single person had been selected for the jury yet.

The procedure continued. The defense struck Marvin Mahanay. Then came Julia Wing. "The State is satisfied," said Slaton; "the defense is satisfied," said Binder. We finally had our first juror. We were surprised; in all our role-playing, we had anticipated that the defense would probably strike Ms. Wing. Both sides agreed on the next person, Sandra Laney, and she became the second juror. Binder excused Dorothy Crowson, leaving sixteen strikes remaining for the defense. Then came Edward Derum. Derum was a businessman and a former police officer. We thought he would be an ideal juror. We were sure the defense would excuse him. Slaton announced that we were satisfied. To our great surprise, Al Binder said, "We're satisfied, your honor." We now had juror number three. We later learned that Wayne

Williams and at least one member of the defense team thought Derum would be unimpressed with the evidence and see through what they hoped would be a flimsy prosecution.

We excused Anita Jones, leaving us with seven strikes. Binder excused Phyllis King, Essie Ferguson, and Emma Davis, leaving the defense with thirteen strikes. We agreed on Joelynne Willingham, who became juror number four. Binder excused Sterling Quinn and Charles McGlothlin; the defense now had eleven strikes left. We agreed on the next two: Vickie Lambert and Diane Elaine Brennan. We now had six jurors. Binder excused Ruth Fowler and we excused Jauncye Cosby. The defense now had ten strikes left and we were down to six. We agreed on the next two, Rubye Head and Claryce Jones. We now had selected eight of the needed twelve for the jury. Binder excused the next three, Sallie Mae Smith, Bernice Abel, and Leneve Cann. The defense now had seven strikes left. We agreed on Walter Brown, who was now juror number nine. Slaton excused Larry Simon and Brenda Hurley; we now were down to four remaining strikes. We were beginning to sweat as it was possible we could run out of strikes. We might end up unable to excuse a juror openly hostile to the prosecution.

We agreed on Gail Jones, who would be juror number ten. Binder used another of his strikes on Kenneth Johnson, leaving him with six strikes, then excused Robert Lee Jones, leaving him with five. Slaton excused Raphael Harris, leaving us with three remaining strikes. Binder struck three more; he was now down to two strikes. We agreed on Lonnie Brown; he became the eleventh member of the jury. Binder excused Mary Lackey and he now was down to one remaining strike. Slaton excused Bobby Cook; we now had just two strikes remaining. Finally, we agreed on Dorothy Rucker. We now had our jury.

We continued the process and selected four alternate jurors, who would sit with the other jurors and be available to fill in if a regular juror became ill or had to be excused during what we expected would be a long trial. The alternate jurors would sit through the entire trial and, unless they were needed, would be excused when the case was submitted to the jury. Judge Cooper released the remaining members of the original group of sixty citizens. They were relieved to be leaving the courthouse. We were relieved to have a jury.

The judge gathered the twelve jurors and four alternates in the courtroom and told them to report to the courthouse the next day at 3:00 p.m. with their suitcases and whatever they needed for a long stay. Cooper could not tell the jurors how long the trial might last, as it was impossible to predict. He assured the jurors that everything possible would be done to make them comfortable. They were not to watch TV, listen to the radio, or read newspapers. They were being "sequestered." Now they knew what that meant, and they were not happy.

The judge announced he would start the trial at 9:00 a.m. on Wednesday, January 6, 1982. He wanted us for a pretrial conference in his chambers at 8:30 a.m. Before we recessed for the day, Al Binder and I met with the judge to discuss the protocol for opening statements.

Tuesday, January 5, 1982, was a blur of meetings and conferences with the judge. Gordon and I met with the defense regarding stipulations, which are agreements in regard to evidence. Cliff Bailey and Gordon Miller agreed that we did not need to call witnesses to identify aerial photographs of the bridge and the Chattahoochee River. They also agreed that the Williams family first used the white Chevrolet station wagon in October of 1980, that our large maps were accurate maps of Atlanta, and that our bridge model was an accurate model of the James Jackson Parkway Bridge. We would not need to bring in witnesses to corroborate these facts, and it would speed up the trial. Gordon and I met with lawyers representing a group of newspapers concerned about their access to court records and all proceedings. We would cooperate as much as allowed by the law and by rulings by the judge. We met with Commissioner of Public Safety Lee Brown concerning his testimony and statistics about murders in Atlanta. We met with Al Binder and his investigator to go over the photos we would be offering in evidence. It was a tiring day, but I slept little that night. We were finally ready to begin calling witnesses.

| NAME OF VICTIM | LIST OF MISSING & MURDERED CHILDREN OF ATLANTA | | |
SD = BODY FOUND NAKED/NEARLY NAKED IN SOUTH RIVER/DEKALB CO. CF = BODY FOUND NAKED/NEARLY NAKED IN CHATTAHOOCHEE RIVER/FULTON CO.	AGE	CAUSE OF DEATH	DATE BODY FOUND (VARYING TIMES AFTER DEATH, UP TO YR)
EDWARD HOPE SMITH	14	GUNSHOT WOUND	JULY 28, 1979
ALFRED EVANS	13	ASPHYXIA	JULY 28, 1979
MILTON HARVEY	14	UNDETERMINED CAUSE	NOVEMBER 5, 1979
YUSEF BELL	9	ASPHYXIA (STRANGLED)	NOVEMBER 8, 1979
ANGEL LANIER	12	ASPHYXIA (STRANGLED)	MARCH 10, 1980
JEFFERY MATHIS	10	UNDETERMINED CAUSE	FEBRUARY 13,1981
ERIC MIDDLEBROOKS	14	HEAD TRAUMA	MAY 19, 1980
CHRISTOPHER RICHARDSON	11	UNDETERMINED CAUSE	JANUARY 9, 1981
LATONYA WILSON	7	HEAD TRAUMA	OCTOBER 18, 1980
AARON WYCHE	10	ASPHYXIA	JUNE 24, 1980
ANTHONY CARTER	9	STABBED TO DEATH	JULY 7, 1980
EARL LEE TERRELL	10	UNDETERMINED CAUSE	JANUARY 9, 1981
CLIFFORD JONES	13	ASPHYXIA (STRANGLED)	AUGUST 21, 1980
DARRON GLASS	10	MISSING SINCE SEPTEMBER 14, 1980	
CHARLES STEPHENS	12	ASPHYXIA	OCTOBER 10, 1980
AARON JACKSON	9	ASPHYXIA	NOVEMBER 2, 1980
PATRICK ROGERS	16	HEAD TRAUMA	DECEMBER 8, 1980
LUBIE GETER	14	ASPHYXIA (STRANGLED)	FEBRUARY 5, 1981
TERRY PUE	15	ASPHYXIA (STRANGLED)	JANUARY 23, 1981
PATRICK BALTAZAR	12	ASPHYXIA (STRANGLED)	FEBRUARY 13,1981
SD CURTIS WALKER	13	ASPHYXIA	MARCH 6, 1981
SD JOSEPH BELL	15	ASPHYXIA	APRIL 19, 1981
CF TIMOTHY HILL	13	ASPHYXIA	MARCH 30, 1981
CF EDDIE DUNCAN	21	UNDETERMINED CAUSE	MARCH 31, 1981
LARRY ROGERS	20	ASPHYXIA (STRANGLED)	APRIL 9, 1981
CF MICHAEL MCINTOSH	23	ASPHYXIA (STRANGLED)	APRIL 20, 1981
CF JIMMY RAY PAYNE	21	ASPHYXIA	APRIL 27, 1981
WILLIAM BARRETT	17	ASPHYXIA (STRANGLED)	MAY 12, 1981
CF NATHANIEL CATER	28	ASPHYXIA (STRANGLED)	MAY 24, 1981
JOHN PORTER*	28	STABBED TO DEATH	APRIL 27, 1981

Names in yellow are cases that have remained open since those murders took place, with no evidence implicating Williams. Included are the murders of two girls, which did not appear to have been related in any way to the 24 murders attributed to Williams, who appeared to have killed only males.

Names in blue are cases presented at Williams' trial as related "similar transactions" and part of series of killings attributed to Williams.

Names in red are cases in which Wayne Williams was convicted of murder.

*John Porter was a recent murder not yet on the official "List of Missing and Murdered Children" but because of significant similarity of evidence to the serial murders, was used as a similar transaction at the trial of Wayne Williams.

| NAME OF VICTIM | FIBERS FROM THE WILLIAMS' HOME | | | |
| | NOTE: HOME FIBERS STAY CONSTANT, AS DOES HIS RESIDENCY. | | | |
C = BODY FOUND IN RIVER CLOTHED / N = BODY FOUND IN RIVER NAKED / PARTIALLY NAKED	VIOLET ACETATE BEDSPREAD	WELLMAN CARPET (TRILOBAL)	DOG HAIR	# OTHER TYPES OF HOME FIBERS
ALFRED EVANS	●	●	●	
YUSEF BELL	●	●	●	1
ERIC MIDDLEBROOKS	●		●	1
CHRISTOPHER RICHARDSON				1
AARON WYCHE	●	●	●	3
ANTHONY CARTER	●		●	2
EARL LEE TERRELL		●	●	1
CLIFFORD JONES	●	●	●	
CHARLES STEPHENS	●	●	●	4
AARON JACKSON	●		●	
C PATRICK ROGERS	●	●	●	
LUBIE GETER	●	●	●	1
TERRY PUE	●	●	●	2
PATRICK BALTAZAR	●	●	●	6
N CURTIS WALKER	●			1
N JOSEPH BELL	●			1
N TIMOTHY HILL	●			
N BUBBA DUNCAN	●			
LARRY ROGERS	●	●	●	3
N MICKEY MCINTOSH				
JOHN PORTER	●	●	●	3
N JIMMY RAY PAYNE	●	●	●	3
WILLIAM BARRETT	●	●	●	3
N NATHANIEL CATER	●	●	●	3

Fiber and dog hair associations between Williams' environment and the twenty-four cases cleared by police after his conviction.

FIBERS FROM VEHICLES IN WILLIAMS' POSSESSION

NOTE: FIBERS CHANGE WHEN HIS POSSESSION OF VEHICLE CHANGES AS INDICATED BY SHADING

| 1978 PLYMOUTH | 1979 RED FORD LTD | 1980 BROWN FORD (RENTAL) | 1980 YELLOW FORD (RENTAL) | 1980 WHITE FORD (RENTAL) | 1970 CHEVY STATION WAGON |

F = FIBERS FROM VEHICLE FOUND ON VICTIMS' BODIES.

B = BOTH TRUNK FIBERS AND INTERIOR CARPET FIBERS FROM VEHICLE FOUND ON VICTIMS' BODIES.

JAMES JACKSON PARKWAY BRIDGE

FBI AGENT GILLILAND

COBB COUNTY

Campbell, stationed on the Cobb riverbank, heard a loud splash in the river in front of him. He looked up and saw lights come on through the bridge rail. The lights began moving slowly toward the Fulton County side of the river. He radioed other team members at the bridge.

EXPANSION JOINT

APD RECRUIT ROBERT CAMPBELL

CHATTAHOOCHEE   splash

RIVER

Jacobs, hidden in bushes at the Fulton end of the bridge, heard the radio message and saw the car, starting close to the bridge rail, come toward him. The car passed, made a U-Turn in the parking lot in front of a closed liquor store, and headed back over the bridge toward Cobb County.

FULTON COUNTY

APD RECRUIT FREDDIE JACOBS

LIQUOR STORE

PARKING LOT

APD OFFICER HOLDEN

Holden, in a car hidden near the liquor store, saw Williams' car make the U-turn and followed it back across the bridge, where he joined Agent Gilliland in stopping Williams as he got on I-285.

285

NOTE: MAP NOT TO SCALE

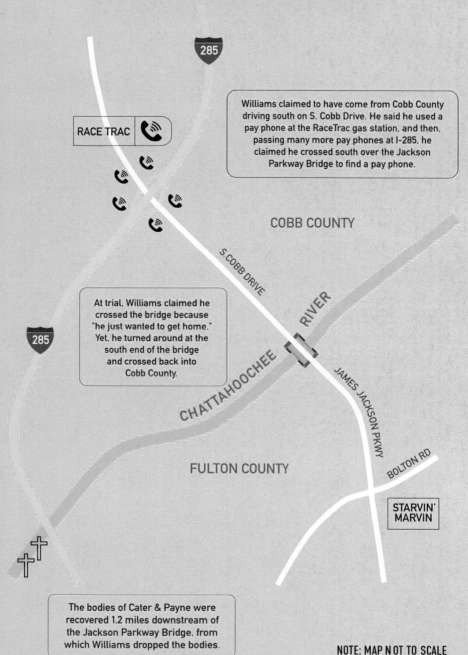

WILLIAMS HAS NEVER BEEN ABLE TO EXPLAIN WHY HE WAS ON THE BRIDGE.

285

RACE TRAC

Williams claimed to have come from Cobb County driving south on S. Cobb Drive. He said he used a pay phone at the RaceTrac gas station, and then, passing many more pay phones at I-285, he claimed he crossed south over the Jackson Parkway Bridge to find a pay phone.

COBB COUNTY

S. COBB DRIVE

RIVER

285

At trial, Williams claimed he crossed the bridge because "he just wanted to get home." Yet, he turned around at the south end of the bridge and crossed back into Cobb County.

CHATTAHOOCHEE

JAMES JACKSON PKWY

BOLTON RD

FULTON COUNTY

STARVIN' MARVIN

The bodies of Cater & Payne were recovered 1.2 miles downstream of the Jackson Parkway Bridge, from which Williams dropped the bodies.

NOTE: MAP NOT TO SCALE

NAME OF VICTIM	VIOLET AND GREEN BEDSPREAD WILLIAMS' BEDROOM	GREEN CARPET WILLIAMS BEDROOM	DOG HAIRS WILLIAMS' DOG	YELLOW BLANKET WILLIAMS BEDROOM	BLUE RAYON LILACS DEBRIS FROM WILLIAMS' HOME	TRUNK LINER 1970 PLYMOUTH	CARPET 1979 FORD	CARPET 1970 CHEVROLET	ADDITIONAL ITEMS FROM WILLIAMS' HOME, STATION WAGON, OR PERSON.
Alfred Evans	X	X	X			X			
Eric Middlebrooks	X		X			X			YELLOW NYLON — FORD TRNK.
Charles Stephens	X	X	X		X				YELLOW NYLON WHITE POLYESTER / BACKROOM CARPET FORD TRNK.
Lubie Geter	X	X	X				X		KITCHEN CARPET
Terry Pue	X	X	X				X		WHITE POLYESTER / BACKROOM CARPET
Patrick Baltazar	X	X	X	X			X		YELLOW NYLON WHITE POLYESTER HEAD HAIR / GLOVE JACKET PIGMENTED POLYPROPYLENE
Joseph Bell	X			X			X		
Larry Rogers	X	X	X	X			X		YELLOW NYLON PORCH BEDSPREAD
John Porter	X	X	X	X	X		X		PORCH BEDSPREAD
Jimmy Payne	X	X	X	X	X		X		BLUE THROW RUG
William Barrett	X	X	X	X	X		X		GLOVE
Nathaniel Cater	X	X	X	X			X		BACKROOM CARPET YELLOW GREEN SYNTHETIC

Chart included with the author's brief filed in the Supreme Court of Georgia showing fiber and hair connections in the twelve cases involved in the trial of Wayne Williams.

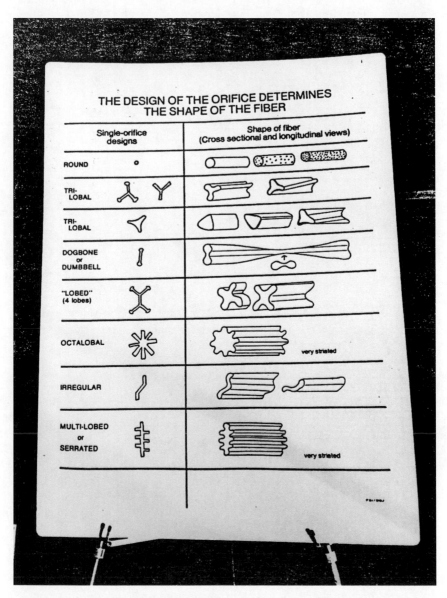

One of the 30" X 40" foam-core presentation boards used to explain fiber evidence to the jury; State's exhibit 1000 shows some of the variety of fiber cross-sections that can be found in man-made fibers.

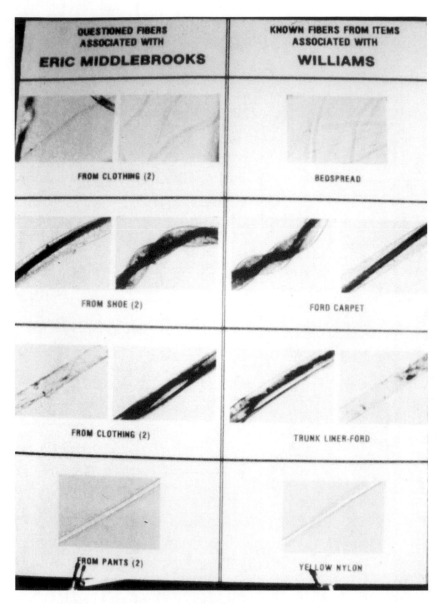

A presentation board comparing fibers found on Eric Middlebrooks with fibers from sources in Williams' environment. In the top left box, green cotton fibers are mingled with violet acetate; in the middle, red trilobal fiber from Middlebrooks shoe next to fiber from the Williamses' Red Ford LTD.

GBI microanalyst Larry Peterson was instrumental in the investigation and served as a key prosecution witness.

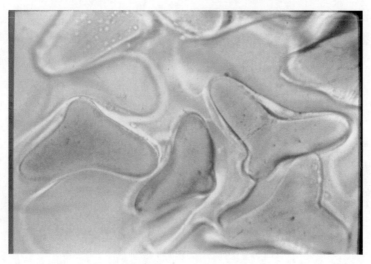

Photo of the cross-section of fibers showing the presence of the very unusual Wellman trilobal fibers with one short leg and two long legs.

Evidence photo of the point where a car was spotted on the James Jackson Parkway bridge. The low bridge rail and very narrow cat-walk can be seen in this view looking toward the Cobb County side of the bridge. The bridge expansion joint can also be seen in the foreground.

Evidence photo of the 1978 Plymouth "detective car" used by Williams, equipped with a police radio, scanner, siren, and blue light. Fibers from the car were found on victim Alfred Evans.

Evidence photo of Wayne Williams' bedroom, showing the bedspread composed of violet acetate and green cotton fibers. On the floor is carpeting containing the rare Wellman fibers.

Evidence photo showing a tuft of red fibers caught in the elastic band of Eric Middlebrooks' shoe; the fibers matched the fiber in the red Ford LTD being used by the Williams family at the time.

STATE'S EXHIBIT NO. LG 23
2751

State's Exhibit LG 23: the artist's drawing from the description given by witness Ruth Warren of the person she saw with victim Lubie Geter at or about the time of his disappearance.

Wayne B. Williams at time of booking in the Fulton County Jail.

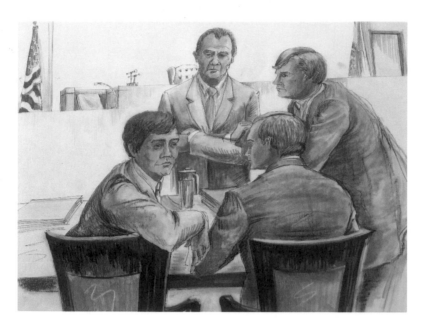

January 1982 drawing from TV network courtroom artist Eleanor Dixon Stecker showing author Joseph Drolet, left in the foreground; Jack Mallard, seated to the right; Gordon Miller, standing at right; and Lewis Slaton, standing, facing artist.

Prosecutors at their counsel table during the trial. Left to right: Lewis Slaton, Jack Mallard, Joseph Drolet, Gordon Miller, and Wally Speed.

Chapter 10

GETTING TO
KNOW ONE ANOTHER

The Trial—Week One

January 6, 1982, was the day the crowds had been waiting for. Hundreds stood in a line that snaked around a full city block. Each person was waiting and hoping for one of the few seats in the spectators' area on the right side of the courtroom. That day the prosecution and the defense would make opening statements, and then witnesses, for the first time, would begin telling their stories. We had the burden to show, beyond a reasonable doubt, that Wayne Williams was guilty of murder.

Gordon Miller and I met with Judge Cooper and Al Binder, agreeing that Wayne's parents could be in the courtroom, even though they might later be called as witnesses. The parents of victims were also allowed to be in the courtroom and sit in one of the front rows, not far from Homer and Faye Williams.

Shortly after 9:00 a.m., Judge Cooper entered the courtroom and gaveled the case to order. The jury, now seated in the jury box, sat in judgment. As the elected district attorney, Lewis Slaton wanted to give the opening statement. He had asked for a theme for the opening statement, and I had come up with it—the case was like a jigsaw puzzle. We didn't have all the pieces. There would be holes in the picture. But the picture would be very clear. Jurors would see that Wayne Williams had murdered Jimmy Ray Payne and Nathaniel Cater. Slaton delivered the statement without incident, making it short and keeping expectations low. It was never wise to promise a jury more than you could deliver.

Al Binder's opening statement surprised us—it was long, going into great detail, and it promised much. When Binder made reference to the bad character of victim Nathaniel Cater, Cater's father erupted in the back of the courtroom. Judge Cooper quieted the grieving father and warned the audience to avoid any such outbursts.

I probably looked calm, but I was not. When starting a trial, anything can happen. A witness might say something inappropriate and cause a mistrial. A witness might freeze on the witness stand. We were feeling out the defense's style, and they were doing the same to us. I was on edge.

Slaton read one of the stipulations of evidence to which we had agreed earlier, in regard to the aerial photographs of the Chattahoochee River and their accuracy. The jury may not have fully understood what this meant, which was that the photographs were now admitted in evidence just as if a witness had testified as to their accuracy.

Slaton called our first witness, a fisherman who had spotted the floating body of Jimmy Ray Payne as it passed under a bridge carrying traffic overhead on Interstate 285. The fisherman, Jesse Arnold, had noticed red shorts and could see the back of a body. He drove his boat to the Cobb County shore and ran to a phone to call the police. Arnold came down from the witness stand to point out where the body was sighted on the large aerial photograph of the river.

Another witness described how he saw the body getting hung up on trees on the Fulton County side of the river, after which he waited there until the police arrived. No one touched the body. Al Binder extensively questioned both witnesses and had them mark, on the aerial photograph, where they had been. Binder seemed to be establishing his style as a slow, thorough, and methodical examiner. There were no "gotcha" moments as Binder went into unnecessary detail and was polite and respectful. This was our first look at Al Binder's cross-examination style. He was good. The jury had to like him and he seemed like a decent guy. And he looked the part, distinguished and fatherly.

Slaton called our next witness, Jim Hallman, an agent with the Georgia Bureau of Investigation. I had known Jim for years and often saw him at the State Capitol, where he was a lobbyist for the GBI, friendly and easygoing. Jim was at the scene when the body of Jimmy Ray Payne was pulled from the Chattahoochee River. He watched officers use a rope to retrieve the body from the river, saw them place the body on a clean white sheet, and zip it into a disaster bag. On cross-examination, Al Binder took full advantage of Hallman's accommodating demeanor, getting Hallman to agree each time Binder suggested that multiple officers were gathered around the body, potentially contaminating the crime scene with fibers from their uniforms. Binder was good at extracting helpful information from witnesses. I could see what Binder was doing, and I tried to show no emotion. Slaton was able to minimize the damage by bringing out the fact that none of the officers were wearing anything that would match the fibers on Jimmy Ray Payne. There were no pieces of carpet nearby, nor bedspreads, nor any dogs.

The next witness was Ruby Jones, Payne's mother, who described a broken home, her son's unemployment, his lack of a car, and his recent release from a three-year sentence in a juvenile detention facility. She last saw her son, who never swam in the river, as he headed to the Omni, the entertainment complex in downtown Atlanta frequented by so many of the victims. Payne's girlfriend, Kathleen Turner, lived with Payne and his mother and had walked with him to a MARTA transit station. She identified the red cotton underwear shorts he was wearing the day he disappeared.

Dr. Saleh Zaki, the assistant medical examiner of Fulton County, had performed the autopsy on the body of Jimmy Ray Payne. The death, Zaki said, might have looked like an accidental drowning, but it wasn't. Zaki's multipage autopsy report concluded that the cause of death was "asphyxia" and that the manner of death was "homicide."

Zaki, during the preceding summer, had discovered that the death certificate, filled out six weeks after the autopsy, mistakenly indicated the manner of death as "undetermined," rather than "homicide," as clearly set out in the autopsy report. Zaki filed an amended death certificate correctly showing the manner of death as "homicide." Even though Zaki had ruled the death a homicide from the very beginning, we knew Binder would hammer Zaki on cross-examination about amending the death certificate *after* Wayne Williams was indicted. We prepared Zaki for the assault. He would be accused of changing the death certificate to correspond to the indictment of Wayne Williams, and his integrity would be challenged. And if we couldn't prove Payne was murdered, we obviously couldn't convict Wayne Williams of murdering him.

As expected, Binder calmly asked if the death certificate was a solemn public document. He asked if the death might have looked like a drowning. Despite Zaki's protestations, Binder intimated that Zaki had changed the certificate to "homicide" so that we could use it against Wayne Williams. Zaki explained why he considered the cause of death a homicide: there was no mud or water in the airways, no mud or water in the stomach, and no muddy fluid in the sinuses. The weather was not yet warm, and there was no evidence that Payne had gone swimming, and there were other similar cases of bodies found in the river, nearly naked. Those cases were clearly not from accidental drowning, with many of the related cases showing more obvious signs of choking or strangulation.

Binder moved for a mistrial after Zaki had mentioned the "other cases" of missing and murdered children. There had been no ruling allowing evidence of the other murders to be discussed. But there was no way Zaki could explain his finding of homicide without doing so in the context of the other similar murders. Cooper denied the motion.

Al Binder now wanted to offer a police report in evidence in an attempt to contradict Zaki and make it appear that Payne's death was accidental. Jack Mallard objected, and I approached the bench with what would become a scourge to the defense team: my three-inch-thick, black, three-ring binder of Georgia law. It contained notes I had compiled and indexed over the years from cases in the Georgia Supreme Court and the Court of Appeals. I provided the court with three Georgia cases that prohibited the use of a police report to impeach testimony such as that of Dr. Zaki. The judge took the matter under advisement, and the next day Binder conceded that my cited law was correct. In the coming days, Binder would grow more familiar with my black ring binder as I repeatedly carried it to the bench to cite Georgia law.

Zaki was exhausted after surviving a grueling cross-examination, and I was relieved to see him leave the witness stand. Slaton was exhausted as well, and he relinquished the role of questioning witnesses. He had demonstrated that he was the chief prosecutor, and now the rest of the team took over.

Lee Brown, the commissioner of public safety, had been the public face of the Task Force investigation for many months. Prompted by Jack Mallard's skillful questioning, Brown provided a history of the investigation of the missing and murdered children. Brown explained how the pattern of the killings had changed when word got out, in February of 1981, that significant fiber evidence was being found on the bodies. Brown explained how the police were staking out the James Jackson Parkway Bridge and twenty-three other bridges because bodies had been showing up in rivers. Binder objected repeatedly, claiming we were getting into cases of murders for which Wayne Williams was not charged. Mallard explained that the evidence was provided only to explain the thinking of the police in setting up a Task Force and staking out the bridge where Wayne Williams was stopped. Without that context, there would be no explanation for why an FBI agent, a police officer, and two police recruits were hanging around a bridge at three in the morning.

Al Binder became frustrated. Lee Brown, ever the professional, was calm and confident in the face of Binder's cross-examination.

At the end of Al's questioning, Al asked an innocuous question about small phone booth–sized police kiosks that had been set up around the city to increase police visibility. Specifically, Al asked Lee Brown what the "little houses with the blue lights were for." Brown did not understand what Binder was asking about. It had been a long day, and the frustrated Binder asked again, saying: "You can understand English, can't you?" The courtroom was quiet. "I have for a number of years, yes, sir," Brown calmly responded.

The first day of trial was finally over. It had been agonizing, but we had survived the first-day jitters. There had been rough spots, like Zaki's cross-examination, but we were putting in place the first few pieces of the puzzle.

On the second day, January 7, we all arrived at court early to help set up the bridge model the FBI had made. We assembled it and placed it parallel to the jury box, about seven or eight feet in front of where the jurors would be seated. Major W. W. Holly had coordinated the stakeouts of the various bridges and, starting in late April 1981, arranged to man the bridges with stakeout teams from 8:00 p.m. until 6:00 a.m. Mallard referred to a large map of the Atlanta area as he asked Holly to come down from the witness stand and show the jury where the bridges were located and where bodies were found. Holly found the Chattahoochee River on the map and marked where three bodies had been found.

Jack asked Holly to point out where Bankhead Highway was located, so jurors would have a point of reference. Holly looked at the map. And he looked at the map some more, his eyes roving from place to place in frustration. I was shifting in my seat, tempted to jump up and say, "There it is, right there!" I sat quietly and showed no emotion. Binder, realizing Holly's frustration, objected to anyone helping him. Jack decided to save Holly by switching to a different question. "How about Route 166?" That was no help as Holly said, "As soon as I get my bearings where we are." Then Jack said, "To make it easier, Major, let's start with I-20 and, if you would, identify the major arteries shown on the map." Holly looked in vain for I-20 and finally said, "Well, one of the major arteries is Gordon Road." Then Holly found Route 166. Binder added to Holly's nervousness, asking: "Has he found it?" Jack mercifully asked Holly to return to the witness stand. This wasn't the way we wanted to start the day.

Benjamin J. Kittle, a respected scientist from the Army Corps of Engineers, was chief of the Hydraulic Section and an expert on river currents. The Corps had recreated the river conditions existing on May 22, 1981, and a thick hydrology report had been prepared based on tests of the river's currents. Kittle explained how a body would hit the water at an angle, with the current, and how the warm water temperature on May 22, 1981, would cause the body to decompose, slowly drag along the bottom of the river, and then rise to the surface as gases formed in the body. Based on where Cater's body was found, he said, it had most probably entered the river from the James Jackson Parkway Bridge. A second hydrology report conducted by the Corps showed that a certain current, about a mile downstream from the bridge, would carry a body over to the Fulton County side of the river, where the body had been discovered.

In cross-examination, Binder brought out the fact that David Dingle, from the National Weather Service, had assisted Kittle on the first hydrology report. Binder would later call Dingle as a witness for the defense. Kittle conceded that the water at seventy-seven degrees would be warm enough for a person to swim in the river and that the water temperature in the river had risen from sixty-seven degrees on May 21, 1981, to seventy-seven degrees on May 24, 1981. Binder was trying to suggest that Cater had been swimming. Kittle came across as professional, exhibiting no bias for the prosecution or for the defense. Detective Frank McClure followed Kittle's testimony by explaining how the James Jackson Parkway Bridge was the only place from which the bodies of Jimmy Ray Payne and Nathaniel Cater could realistically have gotten into the river.

After a short lunch break, we were ready to tell the jury about what happened on the bridge on the morning of May 22, 1981. Freddie Jacobs, a police recruit at the time, had been hiding at the end of the bridge on the Fulton County side of the river. Since the bridge incident, Jacobs had completed training and was now a full-fledged Atlanta police officer. He explained how recruit Robert Campbell had radioed him from below the bridge, saying: "I heard a loud splash, is there a car on the bridge?" He looked out from the bushes and saw a car coming toward him from the Cobb County end of the bridge. The car was close to the bridge rail and approaching slowly from a parked position. Jacobs watched as the car passed by him, turned around in a parking lot right behind him, and headed back across the bridge toward the Cobb County side of the river and Interstate 285.

When the car first approached, Jacobs had heard no sound from the heavy steel expansion joint that connected two parts of the bridge close to the Cobb County side. As cars passed, they normally made a loud noise as wheels went over the steel joint. Jacobs had seen no lights from the vehicle prior to Campbell's radio message, and there had been no traffic on the bridge for more than twenty minutes before the vehicle in question, later determined to belong to Wayne Williams, appeared. After Williams' car crossed back over to the Cobb County side, there was no more traffic until a truck crossed the bridge ten minutes later.

When Mary Welcome cross-examined Jacobs, he repeated for her what he had already said. Mary accused Jacobs of materially altering his story since he first testified months earlier when he said Campbell mentioned a "loud splash." He now described it as a "big loud splash." Jacobs was unfazed by Mary's questioning and failed to see what the change in his testimony was supposed to be. Campbell, he said, had radioed him about a big loud splash. Jacobs proved unflappable as a witness, and we ended the day with his testimony.

A trial can be much like a theatrical performance, full of surprises. We had made it through the second day with only minor embarrassment. We never knew what might happen, who would botch lines, who would be sick, or who might give a poor performance. Back in the war room we critiqued the day and went over our plans for the next day, when the jury would hear more about what happened on the bridge. I slept a comfortable six hours that night, as the trial was now unfolding and more pieces of the puzzle were falling into place.

On Friday, January 8, we kicked off the day with Robert Campbell, the recruit who had heard the loud splash in the river. Campbell had been on the riverbank on the Cobb County side of the river, about eight feet from the water's edge. When he heard the splash, he shined his flashlight on the water, where he saw concentric circles of waves on the surface. As he looked up, he saw a car's headlights directly above where he had seen the splash. As the headlights started moving slowly toward the Fulton County side of the river, he radioed Jacobs to see whether Jacobs could see the car.

I looked over at Wayne Williams, seated at the defense table to my right. He was fidgeting and appeared agitated by the testimony. During a recess, his mother joined him as he looked over bridge photos we had just introduced in evidence. He rebuffed his mother's assistance and told her to "shut up." A strange family relationship, I thought.

Binder cross-examined Robert Campbell, thoroughly questioning him on every detail. He suggested the splash could have been made by a beaver, questioned whether Campbell was asleep when something hit the water, and implied that Campbell was an alcoholic. After Campbell left the witness stand, Binder explained to us why he had suggested Campbell was an alcoholic—a witness Binder interviewed had made the allegation. Later in the trial, we would learn the identity of that witness, another recruit who had been asked to resign. In any event, Campbell was unwavering in his testimony, despite the withering cross-examination.

Under questioning from Jack Mallard, Carl Holden, one of the four officers stationed near the bridge, explained how his unmarked police car was hidden near an old liquor store at the Fulton County end of the bridge. He heard the radio traffic about the splash and then saw Williams' station wagon pull into the liquor store parking lot, right in front of him, and make an immediate U-turn. The car never stopped but headed immediately back over the bridge toward the Cobb County side of the river. Holden followed the car across the bridge, and he and FBI Agent Greg Gilliland continued to follow it onto I-285, at which point they turned on their blue lights and stopped the car. In additional testimony, Holden described how he later helped in an experiment with the expansion joint on the bridge, driving over it at different speeds as Gordon Miller and Atlanta police officers listened from the riverbank.

Jack Mallard had one last question for Carl Holden: "Can you lift a 150-pound person over your head?"

"Yes, sir, I believe I could."

"Have you done it? "

"Yes sir, I have." A slight smile came across Mallard's face; Jack had been in the Grand Jury room when Holden demonstrated lifting me over his head. We took a lunch break.

Binder cross-examined Holden, who admitted that Wayne Williams was cooperative when he pulled his car over. Holden also acknowledged that he had noticed no blood or skin on the railing of the bridge. Atlanta Police Officer Terry Cook described how he and other officers dropped varying weights of concrete blocks off the bridge in an effort to recreate the sound of the splash. Recruit Campbell was on the riverbank, listening. The sound of the last weight, 130 pounds, most closely resembled the splash that Campbell had heard on the morning of May 22, 1981.

FBI Agent Greg Gilliland, the fourth member on the bridge stakeout, had been hidden on a side road on the Cobb County side of the river. Gilliland, a tall young agent, had heard the radio transmissions and, along with Holden, pulled in behind Wayne Williams' station wagon as it headed for I-285. Williams brought his car to a stop, and as Holden checked out his driver's license, Williams asked Gilliland, "What's this all about?" Gilliland said he wasn't at liberty to say. Williams responded: "I know, this is about those boys, isn't it?"

Gilliland chatted briefly with Williams, who told him that he was out looking for Cheryl Johnson, who lived at Spanish Trace Apartments. She had left a phone number, which he provided to the officers. Williams claimed he had picked up boxes at the liquor store and gone down to the Starvin Marvin store a half mile past the bridge. There, he said, he tried to call Cheryl Johnson again and picked up more boxes.

As they spoke, Gilliland noticed that Williams was initially nervous and excited, but then seemed to become more placid and cooperative. Williams' car was a mess, with dog hair evident, and Williams explained that his family owned a German shepherd dog. Williams had no objection to Gilliland's looking in the car, where Gilliland noticed a pair of long pants in the rear area. Williams explained that he had been playing basketball, saying that he was on the "Schlitz" beer team and that they played in long pants. He denied stopping or slowing on the bridge and asked Gilliland if he had seen the two white Purolator trucks that had been on the bridge the same time he was. Gilliland had seen no other vehicles, only Wayne Williams' white station wagon. Williams claimed he was getting onto I-285 because he was going to pick up some musical equipment.

FBI Agent Mike McComas arrived on the scene and asked Williams to sit in his car with him. Williams was wearing a black baseball cap, a sweater, blue slacks, and black loafers. Williams told McComas he was the owner of two businesses, Southern Media and Nova Entertainment, and was out looking for two sisters named Cheryl and Barbara Johnson who lived in Spanish Trace Apartments and were scheduled for an interview at 9:30 or 10:00 a.m. that same morning. Williams said that he had left his house at 12:30 or 1:00 a.m., and he claimed that his attempts to call the sisters had been unsuccessful; he guessed that he had been given a bad number.

Williams had consented to a search of his car, and McComas noticed a pair of suede gloves with fleece lining and a flashlight on the front seat, right in the middle of the seat. On the center hump in the back seat was a white nylon braided ski rope, about twenty-four inches long. Williams said he picked up the cardboard boxes in the back of his car at a Starvin Marvin store and at the Racetrac gas station on Cobb Parkway. McComas noticed dog hair in the back area of the station wagon.

Al Binder began his cross-examination of McComas as he had with other witnesses, gently lulling the witness into a comfort zone before pouncing with what he hoped would be an embarrassing question. Gordon Miller had earlier provided the defense with the statement McComas had taken from Wayne Williams. Binder must not have noticed it among his papers. Other than the statement he had taken from Williams, McComas had made no other report. Binder thought he had. Binder went through a series of questions about FBI reports, how important they were, and how important it was to put all the details in the report. Binder prepared to pounce, asking, "Would you tell this jury whether you wrote down in your report anything about finding a twenty-four-inch nylon cord?"

"Yes, sir," responded McComas.

Caught off guard, Binder said, "You did?"

"Yes, sir, second paragraph, first page."

Binder asked to approach the bench, where Gordon Miller explained, "We furnished that as the statement, the various statements your client made."

Binder returned to his counsel table, apologized to McComas, and said, "You told the jury the truth." The jury seemed impressed that Binder acknowledged his mistake, and Binder, regaining his footing, ended his cross-examination by asking if McComas had quizzed Williams about being homosexual. McComas had asked, and Williams had denied it.

As Friday afternoon wore away, we called someone who probably seemed an innocuous witness. Gene Nichols was an identification technician for the Atlanta Police Department—he took pictures and made measurements at crime scenes. Nichols identified photos of the bridge and explained measurements he made along the bridge rail where Wayne Williams' car had been seen. The distance from the road surface to the top of the concrete rail was four feet and one inch. There was a narrow sidewalk on that side of the bridge, just fourteen and a half inches wide. The distance from the sidewalk to the top of the railing was only thirty-two inches. Nichols also identified pictures of four pay phones at the Exxon gas station right up from the bridge at I-285, the highway Wayne Williams had turned onto after crossing back over the bridge.

Nichols' testimony was vital to our case. The bridge was a perfect place from which to drop a body, with its low concrete railing and narrow catwalk sidewalk, allowing a car to stop close to the low railing. In other words, a person would not need to carry or lift a body over his head to dump it off the bridge. And late at night, when there was almost no traffic on this particular bridge, there was no need to head across the bridge to use a telephone. There were plenty of phones on the Cobb County side of the river, including those at the gas station at I-285. Al Binder had no questions.

Atlanta Police Detective Sergeant Henry Bolton explained how he had borrowed a car just like the Williamses' Chevrolet station wagon and made more measurements. Jack Mallard asked if Bolton had used the car to do a reenactment of events. Binder erupted, claiming this was not based on facts and was an attempt to inflame the jury. The judge called a fifteen-minute recess. As he did, I approached the bench with my black three-ring binder. I asked if the court "would like some law on it; I've got some cases right here." I then showed the judge's law clerk, Michael Smith, two recent cases on the validity of conducting experimental tests. Judge Cooper wanted to discuss the matter in his chambers. Al Binder was under the impression that we had reenacted dropping a body off the bridge, which we had not done. Judge Cooper read my cases and indicated that our testimony would be allowed if we could show a justification for what we did. Because it was late on a Friday, and we were already on our nineteenth witness of the day, the judge recessed the trial until Monday morning, January 11, 1982.

We had made it through three full days, and the case was beginning to flow well. We were gradually filling in at least a corner of the puzzle. What had happened on the bridge was becoming clear, and Williams' first two statements were before the jury.

I was feeling more comfortable with our progress, and I was getting more sleep. Over the weekend, Gordon, Wally, and I met in the war room and reviewed witness testimony, telephoned witnesses, double-checked the evidence we would need the following week, made sure our exhibits had the right labels, and discussed strategy as we moved forward.

Chapter 11

SNOW COMES TO ATLANTA

The Trial—Week Two

Sergeant Bolton resumed his testimony on Monday, January 11. Bolton described how he had taken measurements of a car identical to the Williamses' 1970 Chevrolet Concours station wagon, in an effort to show the jury that moving a body from the car to the top of the bridge rail would not be difficult. Bolton explained that the tailgate on the station wagon was twenty-four inches above the road and only thirty-one inches from the top of the bridge rail. Other officers had taken photographs of Bolton holding a tape measure, showing the short distance from the tailgate to the top of the bridge rail. The photos were admitted in evidence.

Bolton also measured the distance to the two gas stations at I-285 and Cobb Parkway, just north of the bridge on the Cobb County side of the river. The Exxon station was less than a mile into Cobb County, and the Racetrac station was another half mile or more beyond it into Cobb County. Bolton counted other pay telephones visible at night on the approach to the James Jackson Parkway Bridge from the Cobb County side. There were twenty-five pay phones easily visible from Cobb Parkway before one would get to the James Jackson Parkway Bridge. Williams had claimed to have stopped at the Racetrac station to call the elusive Cheryl Johnson. If that were true, by the time Williams got to I-285, there was no need to continue south across the bridge to find a telephone. And, coming south on Cobb Parkway, he could have gotten on I-285 to head home, if that was where he was headed.

On the Fulton County side of the bridge, Bolton's measurements showed that the Starvin Marvin store was a half-mile to the south of the bridge. Bolton's testimony provided more pieces to the puzzle, pieces that would loom large later in the trial.

FBI Agent Bill McGrath described Wayne Williams' third statement about what happened at the bridge. McGrath and FBI Agent John Benesh visited the Williamses' home at 1817 Penelope Road at about 10:30 a.m. on the morning of May 22, 1981, just hours after Wayne Williams had been stopped near the bridge. Homer and Faye Williams, his parents, were at home but did not participate in the interview with Wayne. Nathaniel Cater had not yet been reported missing, and no bodies had yet washed up downriver. Williams was advised of his rights and signed a written consent form, agreeing to an interview. He said he was out looking for a person he now identified as Cheryl J. Johnson, with whom he had had a lengthy conversation by telephone on Wednesday, May 20, 1981. Williams described offering to help develop her entertainment talent, and she was to get back in contact with him later. Williams claimed his mother, Faye, had a later contact, on May 21, 1981, the afternoon before he was stopped on the bridge. Mrs. Williams, he said, took down Cheryl Johnson's address: "2300 Benson Road, Marietta Road, Marietta, Georgia." Williams showed McGrath and Benesh the note he claimed his mother had written, which also included a phone number. This was the first mention of a note of any kind. When stopped near the bridge, Williams had not shown anyone a note, nor had he ever mentioned the existence of such a note.

Williams explained that before he went looking for Cheryl Johnson, he had gone to the Sans Souci lounge on West Peachtree Street to pick up a tape recorder he had loaned the lounge manager, Gino Jordan. Jordan was not there, he said, and he had spoken to a Black female in her forties who was working the front door of the lounge. Williams said he then headed toward Smyrna, Georgia, to look for Cheryl Johnson's address. He searched on Church Street but couldn't find Benson Road, so he headed south on South Cobb Drive, which later becomes James Jackson Parkway. He claimed to have made a phone call at the liquor store at the south end of the bridge (where Carl Holden had watched him make a U-turn). He said he called the phone number he'd been given, and someone answered and said "She ain't here" and hung up. He then picked up some cardboard boxes for his mother and headed back across the bridge. He claimed to have seen a small pickup truck on the bridge with blue lettering on the side. He claimed to remember part of the license plate: WD 1.

After the interview with Wayne Williams, McGrath returned to the FBI office and called the phone number Williams had given him. A recorded message said the number had been changed. McGrath called that number, which turned out to belong to a Merle Norman cosmetics store.

Al Binder cross-examined McGrath and asked to see his notes from the interview. Jack Mallard objected. I approached the bench with my black binder, pointing out cases from the Georgia Supreme Court and the Court of Appeals. The cases were directly on point; Binder could not see the notes. Judge Cooper sustained our objection.

Gino Jordan, manager of the Sans Souci Lounge, was questioned by the newest member of our team, Wally Speed, who was now taking on a larger role in the case. Jordan was a musician and had recorded tapes with Wayne Williams' help. He had been paid a few times, not by Wayne, but by Homer Williams, Wayne's father. Jordan thought Wayne Williams was a police officer, based on his "costuming and demeanor," and Jordan had seen Williams with police radios in what looked like police vehicles. Williams had come in to retrieve a tape recorder, not on a Thursday evening as he had claimed, but on a Friday evening in late May, before 11:00 p.m. Jordan remembered Annie Smith being there, as was Jordan's brother. His brother worked only on Friday and

Saturday nights, and Annie Smith worked only on Mondays, Fridays, and Saturdays. No woman, Jordan stated, would have been working on Thursday evening. Wayne Williams had claimed to have gone to the Sans Souci to get his tape recorder on Thursday evening before going out to look for Cheryl Johnson. Annie Smith confirmed that no other woman works the door at the Sans Souci and that she was *not* there on Thursday, May 21, 1981. She was there on Friday, the evening *after* the bridge incident, and that was when she saw Wayne Williams at the club looking for Gino Jordan.

Thus far in the trial, we had covered the discovery of the body of Jimmy Ray Payne, testimony about his cause of death, and the basics about the bridge incident and Wayne Williams' first three statements. We now turned to the death of Nathaniel Cater.

As we had done with Payne, we began with the finding of Cater's body. Alan Maddox discovered Cater's body while canoeing on the Chattahoochee River on May 24, 1981, a little more than two days after the bridge incident. It was nearly noon, the weather was "sweltering hot," and the body was caught on the Fulton County side of the river among fallen trees and logs just south of the I-285 bridge, in the same area where Jimmy Ray Payne's body had been found a month earlier. The bloated body was naked, floating facedown. The nearby bank of the river was inaccessible, and nothing indicated that the body could have entered the river from that location. A Cobb County police lieutenant, arriving from the Cobb County side of the river, rode in Mr. Maddox's canoe over to a clearing on the Fulton County side, to make sure no one touched the body. Atlanta Police Detective Frank McClure, wearing surgical gloves, helped lift the body from the river and place it on a clean white sheet, which was then placed in a disaster bag. Cater's body was pulled to the shore at the very same spot from which Payne's body had been pulled from the river earlier. After crime lab fiber expert Larry Peterson removed fiber from the body, Identification Technician Willard Ford fingerprinted the body and determined that it was Nathaniel Cater.

Seventeen witnesses testified that Monday, January 11, 1982.

Our case was flowing well, and Al Binder only rarely objected to the admission of evidence. Photographs were identified by each witness as he or she testified, and Binder wisely did not haggle with us over photographs, knowing there was no legal basis for an objection, and that, by being agreeable, he could appear magnanimous and transparent.

Tuesday, January 12, started quietly as we were all settling into a comfortable routine. As usual, court convened at 9:00 a.m. The weather was chilly, and some forecasts suggested there might be a dusting of snow flurries later in the day.

Fulton County Chief Medical Examiner Robert Stivers had performed the autopsy on Nathaniel Cater. Stivers educated the jury about the role of a forensic pathologist, explaining that he had a medical as well as an investigative function. For a forensic pathologist, the autopsy is only about one-quarter of the inquiry. The rest involves an investigation of the circumstances under which a body is found. Stivers explained how a body in water would rise as it decomposed. The warmer the water, the faster it would rise. Nathaniel Cater, like Jimmy Ray Payne, had died of asphyxia—in Cater's case due to strangulation, there being visible marks on his throat. Stivers ruled the death a homicide and explained how a chokehold could inflict the injuries on Cater's neck. He also explained how a victim, being choked from the rear, might grab at the assailant's arms, possibly inflicting scratches on the forearms.

Nathaniel Cater was likely intoxicated when he was murdered, given that at the time of the autopsy, his blood still contained a high alcohol content. Stivers, who had performed more than six thousand autopsies, explained that changing a death certificate, as Zaki had done, was not unusual. He also explained that asphyxia was a rare form of homicide. Since 1963, there had never been more than three asphyxiation deaths per year in Fulton County. And in some years, there were none.

Vicki Snipes said she had seen Cater when he came into her blood bank to sell his blood, on May 21, 1981, the afternoon before the bridge incident. Lyle Nichols, the desk clerk at the downtown

Falcon Hotel where Cater lived, had seen him that afternoon near the hotel. Cater had no car, drank a lot, and hung out at two local bars, the Cameo and the Silver Dollar lounge.

Outside the courtroom, two of our witnesses who were waiting to testify wanted to go home. They were nervous about the deteriorating weather. We accommodated their requests and got them on the witness stand as soon as we could. Frank Wright worked at the Gulf station across from the Starvin Marvin store at Bolton Road and James Jackson Parkway, a half-mile south of the bridge. Wright pointed out Wayne Williams as the man he had seen at his gas station about a week before the incident on the bridge, the second time in a few weeks he had seen Williams in the area. Eighteen-year-old Grady Summerour was walking near the Omni downtown when Williams drove by in a white station wagon and then came back and offered him "a lift." Williams offered Summerour twenty dollars to pass out a bundle of flyers that said, "Can you sing, dance, act, or play an instrument?" The flyer had a phone number to call. Summerour identified one of the flyers, which was admitted in evidence.

Isaac Taylor, the manager at the Pizza Palace in the Omni, said a man who looked like Wayne Williams had been there a few times. But as he looked at Williams in the courtroom, he decided "the guy was taller than Mr. Williams." This would happen from time to time during the trial as a person who thought he recognized Wayne Williams from TV would come to court and then not recognize Wayne Williams. It didn't really hurt the case, but it was always mildly embarrassing. All we could do was say "Thank you for coming in" and excuse the witness. For the next witness, this was not a problem.

Margaret Carter knew Nathaniel Cater and had seen him with a man she believed she could identify. It was about a week before Cater's body was found, and Ms. Carter was in a park near her Verbena Street apartment. Nate, as she referred to Cater, came over to Ms. Carter and asked, "Where's Slim?" a nickname for Ms. Carter's niece, Janet. Ms. Carter watched as Nate and the man sat at a picnic table and talked. The man sat on top of the table and had his feet on the seat. A station wagon was parked nearby. A German shepherd dog was close by and seemed to belong to the man, who had glasses, an afro, and gray slacks. That man was Wayne Williams, Ms. Carter said, and she was sure that Williams was the man she saw.

Al Binder nibbled away at Margaret Carter's testimony but could not shake her. He implied that she had changed her story from previous versions she had given. He quibbled about her description of a shirt Williams had been wearing and whether she knew the sex of the German shepherd dog she had seen. He suggested that her daughter, Gwinnett, would contradict her testimony. But Margaret Carter held firm.

Meanwhile, Michael Smith, Judge Cooper's law clerk, had been monitoring the weather. Snow flurries were visible through the windows of the courthouse. Al Binder wanted to recess and have another shot at Margaret Carter the next morning. Jack Mallard insisted we finish with Ms. Carter's testimony. We knew that Binder couldn't have that many more questions. He didn't. In a few minutes, Binder was finished with his cross-examination. It was only 3:00 p.m., but snow continued to fall, and Atlanta does not handle snow well. Judge Cooper decided to recess court for the day.

The snow turned from flurries to large snowflakes. The roads grew treacherous as panicked motorists packed expressways and major streets trying to get home. People began abandoning their cars on the impassable roads as several inches of snow piled up. Atlanta was unaccustomed to measurable snowfall. By 5:00 p.m., Lewis Slaton, Gordon Miller, and Wally Speed had all returned to the courthouse after unsuccessful attempts to get home. They would all sleep in their offices that night.

Things got worse. The temperature quickly began to drop. Freezing rain fell on top of four inches of snow, as the entire region became littered with snowdrifts and abandoned cars. Mobility in Atlanta was shut down, as the storm that would become known as "SnowJam" held Atlanta in its grip.

I used the time to catch up on research in my office. At around

8:00 p.m., when the snow finally stopped falling, I decided to try to get home. I lived close by, in the Inman Park neighborhood, just two miles east of the courthouse. With no one on the abandoned streets, I was able to slowly make my way home on the slippery streets.

The temperature dropped until it was below zero, a highly unusual event in Atlanta. Pipes burst as they froze behind the uninsulated walls on the back of my house. I had just enough plumbing experience to work into the night and slowly make crude repairs to the copper pipes. By midnight, it was obvious that we would not resume court the next day. Atlanta was paralyzed by snow, ice, and bitter cold. I continued my plumbing repairs the next day, on my own home and the homes of neighbors who had heard that I had the equipment needed to get their water flowing again. I also received a distressing phone call from the Task Force—someone had tried to kill Margaret Carter, the last witness we called before the snow hit. Unfortunately, we were never able to determine if this incident was related in any way to Carter's appearance as a witness.

After a day of being snowed in, I ventured downtown on Thursday, January 14. Usually bustling, Atlanta was quiet with iced-over streets and closed businesses. From the courthouse, I walked the two blocks to the State Capitol, which was open but virtually deserted. Returning to my equally deserted office, I prepared legal arguments I knew would be coming up and mapped out where various victims of the killer had been found. Soon, I knew, I would be called upon to make a presentation to the court, a request to allow us to bring in evidence of other murders.

Atlanta was still frozen and deserted on Friday, January 15. I made it to the office, where I could work without distraction.

By Saturday, January 16, 1982, the weather was improving, and I spent the afternoon at the State Crime Lab, meeting with two of our fiber experts, Larry Peterson from the Georgia State Crime Laboratory and Hal Deadman, the fiber expert from the FBI lab. We discussed what they could expect to be asked by the wily Al Binder. The fiber experts would be explaining to the jury how fibers got on the victims and how those fibers would reflect the victims' environment at the time of death.

If a victim's body was on the floor of Wayne Williams' car before being placed along a roadside, that victim would likely have fibers from that floor carpeting and whatever other fibers or hairs had been tracked into the car from the Williamses' home. The experts referred to this as the transference or exchange principle. The question I knew Al Binder would ask was this: if fibers from Williams' environment wound up on the victim, why weren't fibers from the victim found on Williams or in his car? To my surprise, when I asked Larry Peterson that question, he said, "Well, we *did* find evidence from Jimmy Ray Payne. In Williams' car, we found fibers matching the red cotton shorts he was wearing when he was pulled from the river." I asked why he hadn't mentioned this before. He explained, "Red cotton is not an unusual fiber. We don't consider fiber matches significant unless the fiber is unusual, like the rare carpet fibers from the Williams house or the violet acetate from Wayne Williams' bedspread." I looked forward to Al Binder's surprise if he asked that question.

The next day, Sunday, January 17, I returned to the crime lab, where I spent time with three more people who would help explain fiber evidence to the jury. Herb Pratt was an expert from DuPont, which was the preeminent pioneer in creating new fibers for carpeting. He would explain how fiber was created and how it was made into carpet. Henry Poston, from the Wellman Company, was the inventor of the rare trilobal fiber found in the Williamses' green carpet. Gene Baggett, from West Point Pepperell Company, had purchased much of the fiber and dyed it various different colors before weaving it into carpet that matched the carpet found in the Williamses' house. My weekend at the crime lab gave me a new appreciation for the significance of the fiber and hair evidence.

The single most important fiber was the rare Wellman 181b, Nylon 6,6 fiber with the odd trilobal cross-section. Only a small amount of the fiber was ever produced, and only a fraction of that small amount was dyed English Olive, the color of the fiber found in the wall-to-wall carpeting in the Williamses' home. Few homes in the southeastern United States would have that fiber, and even fewer would have that fiber dyed English Olive. Finding that one rare fiber on a victim would create a strong link to Wayne Williams. As it happened, that same fiber had been found on fifteen victims.

Another significant fiber found on victims was made of acetate dyed a specific shade of violet. On some victims, the violet acetate fiber was interwoven with a particular green-dyed cotton fiber. And Wayne Williams' bedspread was composed entirely of the violet acetate fiber interwoven with green cotton fibers. Twenty-one victims had the violet acetate fiber clinging to their clothing or caught in their hair.

Fibers from Williams' cars were also found on victims. As Williams changed cars, the fibers found on the victims would vary accordingly. When he got rid of a car, its fibers would no longer show up on subsequent victims. A host of other fibers from the Williamses' home matched fibers found on various victims.

And then there was the dog hair found on eighteen victims. It appeared to match the hairs from Williams' dog, Sheba. Head hairs from Wayne Williams appeared to be the same as two head hairs found inside the shirt of twelve-year-old victim Patrick Baltazar.

The fiber and hair evidence promised to be powerful indeed.

Chapter 12

BACK ON TRACK

The Trial—Week Three

After five days, the snow and ice were finally melting, and we resumed the trial. The jury had been locked away in their hotel for six days without hearing any testimony. I worried that the break would disrupt the flow of the trial. We had presented forty-two witnesses in five days, and we would try to pick up where we left off.

We recalled Bill McGrath, the FBI agent who had interviewed Williams at his home on May 22, 1981, hours after the bridge incident. McGrath had interviewed Williams a second time, on June 3, 1981, when Williams was brought to the FBI office in response to a search warrant for samples of his hair. There, Williams told McGrath a new version of events, saying he spoke to Cheryl Johnson at about 4:00 p.m. on May 21, 1981, and that she lived at the Spanish Trace Apartments on Church Street in Smyrna, Georgia, in Apartment F-4. These new details were very different from what Williams had said during the interview at his home just two weeks earlier.

In this new version of events, the interview with Cheryl was for 7:00 a.m. on May 22, 1981. Williams said he came south from Cobb

County and stopped at a phone booth on South Cobb Drive to call Cheryl Johnson using the phone number 934-7766. He said the line was busy. He picked up some boxes and called again. This time there was no answer. This all happened, he claimed, in Cobb County, long before he got to the bridge. He then headed south and crossed over the bridge toward Atlanta. Williams now claimed he saw three other cars on the bridge. He added details about the cars and the drivers, details different from any previous versions of events. In this version, he pulled into the liquor store parking lot near the Fulton County end of the bridge to check the phone number and then continued south to the Starvin Marvin convenience store a half mile farther south, at Bolton Road. There, Williams said he called the number again, and the person who answered said, "There's nobody here by that name." Williams claimed he then drove back over the bridge toward Cobb County.

Williams also told McGrath he had played basketball on the Schlitz beer team at the Ben Hill Recreation Center the day before the early-morning encounter on the bridge. During his visit, Williams seemed to be enjoying all the attention and was in no hurry to leave the FBI's Atlanta headquarters.

After speaking with McGrath, Williams spoke with Richard Rackleff, the FBI polygraph examiner, who administered a lie-detector test. Georgia law did not allow the results of polygraph tests to be entered as evidence, but we could use the statements Williams made to Rackleff. Williams told Rackleff he *never* spoke to Cheryl Johnson. This was the opposite of what he had just told Agent McGrath. Someone else, Williams said, had taken the phone call.

After returning home from his visit to the FBI offices, Williams did something strange—he held a press conference. A reporter from the CBS affiliate in Atlanta was one of a few dozen people present for the June 4, 1981, "press conference" in the living room of the Williams home. Al Binder vigorously objected to the reporter, Dan Keever, playing a recording of the press conference. Binder claimed it could only be used to impeach Wayne Williams in the event he later testified. Jack Mallard and I argued at length with Binder in Judge Cooper's chambers. This was Williams' own press conference, in his own words, in his own home. It was completely voluntary and a public event. He should be accountable for his own actions.

At the press conference, Williams admitted that he "had flunked the polygraph examination." We offered to redact that portion of the press conference transcript and recording, although I argued that voluntary public statements by inept criminals often included admissions of embarrassing and incriminating topics. Judge Cooper agreed to admit the recording of the press conference but would not allow the jury to hear about the polygraph. Each juror got a redacted copy of the transcript and listened attentively to a tape of the press conference. They were hearing the voice of Wayne Williams for the first time.

During his press conference Williams passed out copies of his résumé for the reporters and launched into a rant about his interviews with the FBI. He just wanted to "clear the air," he said. He explained that he was a performing arts manager and had agreements with a Los Angeles producer, Wade Marcus, to produce record deals for his young performers. To say Williams was exaggerating would be an understatement. The Los Angeles music producer Wade Marcus, who had produced records for the likes of Stevie Wonder, had no relationship with Williams.

Williams claimed the police were just trying to embarrass him because he made them look bad when a police car had an accident while "tailing" him.

Williams told the assembled reporters what happened on the bridge. He had stopped to pick up boxes on South Cobb Drive before he got to the bridge and had "used the telephone once at a gas station there." Then, he claimed, he crossed to the Fulton County end of the bridge for a few seconds to check the phone number on the sheet of paper he had, and he continued a half mile south to use the telephone at the Starvin Marvin store. When he called the phone number from the Starvin Marvin store, the person who answered said, "She's not here." Williams said he then "decided to go home," and crossed back over the bridge into Cobb County, where he was stopped by police.

In regard to conversations with Cheryl Johnson, Williams said, "I did not take the telephone call. One of my workers took it, and they were not sure of the exact telephone number that she gave them."

As for the missing and murdered children, Williams said, "Some of these kids are in places they don't have no business being at certain times of the day and night. Some of them don't have no kind of home supervision, and they're just running around in the streets wild."

The jury had now heard, in six different versions, Wayne Williams' explanations of his presence on the James Jackson Parkway Bridge:

1. The first version, to FBI Agent Gilliland when Williams was initially stopped after crossing the bridge.
2. A more detailed version to FBI Agent McComas, who interviewed him near the bridge right after Gilliland.
3. Another version just hours later when Agent McGrath interviewed Williams at his home.
4. A fourth version, given to McGrath a couple of weeks later on June 3, 1981, at the FBI office in downtown Atlanta.
5. A fifth version shortly thereafter at the FBI office to Agent Rackleff.
6. Wayne Williams' own press conference, held on the morning of June 4, 1981, just hours after he had spoken to McGrath and Rackleff.

In each version, details came and went, and in more than one version, Wayne Williams said he had never even spoken to Cheryl Johnson. In some versions, he had driven to the Starvin Marvin convenience store, a half mile south of the bridge. In other versions, he made phone calls on the Cobb County side of the bridge, while still on South Cobb Drive. In each version, he said he had stopped by the Sans Souci lounge immediately *before* going to look for Cheryl Johnson's apartment. We now presented evidence that described the actual events at the Sans Souci lounge, events that had taken place the evening *after* Wayne Williams was stopped on the bridge. Williams probably thought the folks at the Sans Souci would get the two nights confused and confirm that they saw him on Thursday night, rather than Friday. They didn't.

The jury heard from phone company representatives that the number 934-7766 could not have been answered as he said it had. Phone company employee Diane McCook explained that 934-7766 had not been an active number for over three years and that a caller would get a message saying the number was not in service or that it had been changed to a new number. She also noted that there were no numbers in the Atlanta area with a 934 prefix. They also checked out 434-7766 at the request of the GBI. That number was issued to a person named Steven Edelstein.

Renate Haley confirmed that she was the person who had previously had the number 934-7766 for her business in Tucker, Georgia. That phone number had been changed, and she had the phone company add a message advising callers of the new number. She later sold her business location to Merle Norman cosmetics, which still had the number. Williams' statements regarding the phone calls had been completely fabricated.

Three witnesses from apartment complexes in Smyrna and Marietta testified that there was no one named Cheryl Johnson living there. Cheryl Johnson, if she had ever existed, would never be found.

Williams had initially told Greg Gilliland, the FBI agent, that he had seen two Purolator trucks on the bridge at the same time that he was there. David Henry, from Purolator Company, testified that they operate no pickup trucks and had had no vehicles at all in the South Cobb area in May of 1981. Williams had also mentioned to Gilliland that he was on the Schlitz beer basketball team. Phoebe Simon of Premium Beverages, the Schlitz beer distributor, said there was no Schlitz basketball team, and Mary Welsh, from the Ben Hill Recreation Center, explained that no Schlitz basketball team played at the center on Thursday, May 21, 1981. In fact, that was Ladies Exercise night, and Wayne Williams could not have been there playing basketball with a Schlitz team.

More pieces of the puzzle were falling into place. The picture was emerging more clearly. And almost everything Wayne Williams said was a fabrication.

AN EDUCATION ON FIBER EVIDENCE

As the day dawned on Tuesday, January 19, we were about to shift gears. We had called forty-six witnesses so far. We would now introduce fiber evidence, which required testimony from several experts.

Herb Pratt, the expert from DuPont, took the witness stand as if he were a professor teaching a class. He was there to explain how fibers were made and how they were turned into carpeting. DuPont was the pioneer in patenting nylon in 1937, and the company held most of the patents for carpet fibers made from nylon. They produced ten billion pounds of fiber each year and jealously guarded their patents for one of their most popular fibers, the trilobal nylon fiber, which they had patented in 1960. Pratt gave what amounted to a chemistry class lecture, explaining how molten combinations of chemicals, known as polymers, were forced through thirty-four tiny holes in a circular-shaped piece of steel called a spinnerette. To make a trilobal fiber, the tiny holes were shaped like propellers, with three spokes sticking out from the center. The minuscule fibers that oozed out of the spinnerette would have this same shaped cross-section if viewed under a microscope. The trilobal fiber was very popular in carpeting; it didn't show dirt.

Pratt's daylong tutorial was extensive, as he handed exhibits up to the judge and requested that they be passed around. Pratt had charts, photos, and flowcharts showing the process for making fiber and then attaching it to backing to turn it into carpeting. He explained how six to seven thousand commercial dyes were used to make different colors of carpets, how fibers could be "crimped" or bent to add bulk to the carpet, and how fibers could have different thicknesses and shapes. A particular color and shape of fiber would be very identifiable. Pratt also explained the extreme rarity of acetate fiber.

Months earlier Pratt had been shown a fiber that had been found on victims in Atlanta's missing and murdered children case. It was a highly unusual fiber. Although he kept tabs on fibers produced all over the world, Pratt had never seen this one before. He could recall no manufacturer of it anywhere in the world. An associate finally recognized it as coming from a small company called Wellman in South Carolina.

Henry Poston was the director of technical services for Wellman, Incorporated, the South Carolina company that produced the unusual fiber. Poston had designed the fiber in an attempt to circumvent the DuPont trilobal patent. The fiber had been produced only from 1969 to 1974, and no one else made such a fiber. Wellman gave up on the fiber design in 1974 and changed to a DuPont style fiber, DuPont's patent having expired that year. The company made only a small amount of the odd fiber during the brief period of production. They sold much of it to the West Point Pepperell Company in West Point, Georgia. Poston recognized the fiber being found on the victims. It was his design and what he called the "Wellman 181b, Nylon 6,6 fiber." The "18" referred to the thickness, or "denier," of the fiber, and the "1" following meant that it was crimped. The "b" meant it was bright and would reflect light. The "6,6" indicated the fiber was made by combining two types of chemicals, each containing six carbon atoms. The fiber was indeed rare.

Gene Baggett, from carpet manufacturer West Point Pepperell, explained how the company had purchased fiber from the Wellman Company and dyed it sixteen different colors. One of those sixteen colors was called English Olive, and that fiber was made into what they called their Luxaire and Dreamer lines of carpeting. They sold some of their carpeting to Rich's department stores in Atlanta. Given the limited amount of the Wellman fiber in existence and the small portion of it dyed English Olive, finding the carpet in a particular home would be a rare occurrence.

After a break for lunch, we called FBI fiber expert Harold Deadman to the stand. Al Binder claimed we couldn't present Deadman's testimony because the defense expert Charles Morton had not been allowed sufficient time to examine our fiber evidence. Binder also claimed that we had failed to turn over written reports of laboratory tests on fibers in a timely fashion. I recited for the judge a list of all the reports we had provided the defense, including when we had provided them and how many times we had permitted Mr. Morton access to the fiber evidence. Judge Cooper allowed Deadman to testify but ordered that Mr. Morton be allowed extra time at the crime lab.

Harold Deadman did not disappoint. He was an objective, well-educated chemist with years of experience not only with the FBI but also with DuPont. Deadman had a doctorate and worked in microscopic analysis of fiber and hair at the FBI lab. He also taught hair and fiber analysis at the FBI Academy in Quantico, Virginia. Al Binder had no objection to the court's declaring Deadman an expert in fiber and hair analysis.

Deadman, like DuPont expert Herb Pratt before him, delivered what amounted to a lecture on fiber analysis. He showed charts on mineral fiber, like asbestos; plant fiber, such as cotton, jute, and kapok; animal hair, such as wool, horsehair, and silk; and man-made polymers, such as acetate, acrylic, nylon, olefin, polyester, and rayon. He explained how man-made fibers can appear in hundreds of different and identifiable forms, and he showed how cross-sections of minuscule fibers can vary within a wide range of shapes.

As Deadman explained the significance of fiber evidence, I glanced over at Wayne Williams, seated nearby to my right. He was agitated and hurriedly writing notes to Al Binder and to his parents, who were seated behind him in the first row of the spectator area.

Deadman explained the "exchange principle," the phenomenon that occurs when a person comes in contact with either loose fibers or fibers from fabric. Some of the fibers will be deposited on the person's clothing or body. Most of those fibers will be knocked off as the person moves about and comes in contact with other environments. When a person is found dead, the fibers found on the body will likely reflect the victim's last environment.

Using tweezers, the tiny fibers can be removed from a person's clothing or hair, placed on glass slides, and analyzed under various kinds of microscopes. The color, coarseness, shape, and cross-section can be used in making comparisons to other fibers. Other characteristics can be viewed using a variety of specialized microscopes such as a polarized light microscope, a fluorescence microscope, or a microspectrophotometer. Some fibers are common and therefore insignificant in making identifications; other fibers are rare and, thus, noteworthy. As I looked over at him, Wayne Williams was more nervous than usual.

Al Binder cross-examined Harold Deadman, but there was little he could do to weaken the impact of his testimony. Deadman maintained his professional demeanor as he explained how fiber evidence can be significant in making connections between a victim and his killer, in much the same way that fingerprints can corroborate such associations.

Larry Peterson was our next witness, and he was on the stand all day on January 21. As with Harold Deadman, Binder did not challenge Peterson's qualifications as a fiber expert. There was nothing to challenge as Peterson explained how he retrieved hair and fibers, using tweezers, from the body and red shorts of Jimmy Ray Payne and the body of Nathaniel Cater. Peterson also recovered fibers from the Williamses' station wagon, and he had accompanied the search team to the Williamses' home on Penelope Road on June 3, 1981. There, he collected fiber samples from each room in the house and returned on June 22 to recover other items and samples, including a violet-and-green bedspread from Wayne Williams' bed. Peterson also took hair samples from the Williams' dog, Sheba. Each of the items Peterson identified were admitted in evidence.

On Payne's red shorts, Peterson found Wellman carpet fibers

that matched those found in the carpet in Wayne Williams' bedroom, violet acetate fibers like the fibers in Williams' bedspread, and fibers matching the carpet fiber in the Williamses' Chevy station wagon, which Williams had been driving. Payne's shorts also had fibers from the yellow blanket found under Williams' bed, fibers from a blue bathmat in the Williamses' home, and dog hairs matching the hairs from Sheba. In all, there were seven different types of fibers or hairs on Payne's body that matched items from Williams' environment.

Peterson went through the same process with fibers found on Nathaniel Cater. Six different fiber matches came from the Williamses' home, including the dog hair, the unique Wellman carpet fiber, and the unusual violet acetate fiber from the bedspread. Peterson explained how the microspectrophotometer confirmed, with precision, the exact color of the fibers found. Binder objected to the jury seeing the microspectrophotometer graphs, but under Georgia law, the graphs were admissible. The jury would see them.

Peterson ended his testimony by explaining the significance of the fiber and hair comparisons. "In my opinion, it is highly unlikely that any environment other than that present in the Williams home and car could account for the combination of fibers and hair I recovered, examined, and compared from Mr. Cater and Mr. Payne."

Binder tried to weaken Peterson's testimony by implying that the fibers could have come from the clothing of police officers who had carried the bodies of Cater and Payne. Peterson responded that the clothing of police officers would contain no carpet fiber, bedspread fiber, or dog hairs. Binder suggested that the fibers may have come from the river water in which the bodies were found, but Peterson had tested the river water and found no fibers like those he had used for his comparisons. Binder observed that there were hundreds of fibers found on the victims, and Peterson agreed, explaining that most of the fibers found were cotton or other common materials and would have little significance in making comparisons.

Binder thought he had a "gotcha" moment when Peterson admitted that Wayne Williams' bedspread was made from interwoven violet acetate and green cotton fibers. Peterson had said nothing about finding green cotton fibers on Payne or Cater. Binder assumed Peterson would have said something if he had also found green cotton fibers of the same type found in the bedspread.

In his booming voice, he asked, "How many green cotton fibers did you find on Mr. Payne?"

Larry's answer wasn't what he expected: "There were a significant number of green cotton fibers observed in the questioned material from Mr. Payne, but because cotton in itself is a fairly common fiber, I did not proceed heavily into the examination comparison." In other words, both types of fibers from the bedspread were found on victims, but Peterson preferred to understate the significance of all but the most relevant fibers. Rather than diminish the credibility of Peterson's testimony, Binder's question had enhanced it.

Binder continued to try to nibble away at Peterson's testimony. Soon he was ready to pounce again. Deadman had testified about the "exchange principle," how fibers can be picked up from the environment. Binder had heard evidence only about fibers from the Williams home being found on the victims, but nothing about fibers from the victims being found in Williams' environment. Binder led Peterson along: If Williams' fibers were found on the victims, shouldn't fibers from the victims be found on Williams? Binder followed with more questions about the exchange principle and then asked: "There's one thing I need to ask you . . . tell the jury, in the Williams house, in the automobile, in the sweepings, in the carpet cleaner, did you find a hair, a fiber, or anything there that pertained to Jimmy Payne?"

Binder expected the answer to be no. Peterson calmly said, "In examining the vacuum sweepings of the floorboard of the Concours (Williams' station wagon) I found a red cotton fiber which, in my opinion, had the same microscopic characteristics of the red cotton of Mr. Payne's shorts. The microspectrophotometer also indicated that the dyes involved were similar." Larry explained that because of the common nature of cotton, he did not consider this fiber significant in making his comparisons. Cater was naked, so there was no item of his clothing available for comparison. I smiled when Larry explained this. This was the same question I had asked Larry the weekend before when we were preparing for his testimony. Al Binder, like me, had assumed that there was no exchange of fibers, and he saw that as a weakness in the case. In fact, it was an example of Larry Peterson's not wanting to overstate evidence. To me, the fact that fibers from Jimmy Ray Payne's underwear were found on the floor of Wayne Williams' car was a bombshell. I hoped the jury had the same reaction.

Now we were close to the point where I would be asking Judge Cooper to allow us to bring in evidence from other murders, evidence that would show that Wayne Williams was the serial killer who had terrified Atlanta for over two years.

I was ready, but I was also anxious. I knew the law, and I knew what facts I had to work with. Generally, in a criminal prosecution, you can't just show that someone is a bad person or has committed a criminal act totally separate and unrelated to the crime on trial. But the exception to that rule, honored in the courts of various states and federal courts, allows other "extrinsic" acts to be admitted in evidence if the acts of the defendant were logically connected or similar to the crimes on trial and thus showed plan, scheme, pattern, and identity. I spent the evening going over my notes and the law. For each of the ten murders I would offer in evidence, I had a single sheet from my yellow legal pad, filled with relevant information. Sleep was difficult, but I finally dozed off.

When the chilly morning of Friday, January 22, 1982, dawned, I was up, going over notes and legal authority once again. Later this day I expected to be on stage, making one of the biggest presentations of my life. I tried my best to act calm.

We began court that morning by recalling Harold Deadman, the FBI fiber expert, to go into further detail about the fiber evidence linking Wayne Williams to the deaths of Jimmy Ray Payne and Nathaniel Cater.

Deadman explained how he had compared carpet from the Williamses' home with identical carpet samples from the West Point Pepperell company. The pile, the yarn, the spacing, the backing, and the adhesives were the same. Deadman reviewed records from West Point Pepperell and found that the Luxaire line of carpeting dyed the English Olive color was "extremely unusual," having been produced using the Wellman fiber for only one year, from December 1970 to December 1971. Approximately 820 rooms of carpeting sold in the ten southeastern states could have contained the odd Wellman fiber dyed English Olive. The amount sold in Georgia would have been only a fraction of that total, and the amount sold in Atlanta would be even less, probably fewer than eighty-two rooms of carpeting.

Deadman recovered samples of many of the fibers in the Williams home during the June 3, 1981, search of the house. He cut a sample from the yellow blanket under Wayne Williams' bed, and he collected hair from Sheba, the family dog. He retrieved the vacuum sweepings from inside the Regina vacuum cleaner found in the room next to Wayne Williams' bedroom. Among those vacuum sweepings, Deadman found an unusual blue rayon fiber. Another of the blue rayon fibers was found on Wayne Williams' bedspread. A similar such fiber had dropped from the body of Jimmy Ray Payne onto the sheet that had carried his body from the Chattahoochee River.

Deadman found other fibers, including some from a blue throw rug in the Williamses' home, that matched a fiber found on Payne's shorts. Deadman went through the fiber associations that Larry Peterson had gone through and explained again the "exchange principle" and how the fibers on a dead person "will normally reflect the environment in which that person was either shortly before or shortly after his death."

Deadman concluded with his expert opinion about the significance of the seven different fiber associations between Wayne Williams and Jimmy Ray Payne and the six different fiber associations between Williams and Nathaniel Cater. In his words: "I would consider it virtually impossible to obtain these findings and not have the two victims in this case have some contact or some other association with the home and/or automobiles of Wayne Williams." Deadman agreed completely with Larry Peterson that the more different fiber associations you have, the more significant are the findings.

The jury got to look closely at the two pieces of carpet, one from the Williams home and one from West Point Pepperell. The carpet pieces slowly moved from one juror to the next as each juror compared the two hunks of green carpet. Binder had repeatedly attempted to undermine Deadman's testimony, but Deadman had remained calm and professional.

OFFERING EVIDENCE OF SIMILAR CASES

It was my turn to drop a bombshell. I stood and announced, "Your honor, at this time we have a matter that should be taken up outside the presence of the jury." The bailiff escorted the jury out of the courtroom.

Judge Cooper asked me and Al Binder to approach the bench. "It's now 11:02. Is this a matter we ought to take up after lunch?"

I was ready to go—the anticipation was killing me. But I responded, "Either way, your honor." The judge then recessed court for lunch. We were to return at 1:00 p.m.

I felt like a field goal kicker who gets all ready to kick, just as the other team calls a time-out to mess with his mind. But I would wait. I tried to eat lunch, but I had no appetite.

Finally, one o'clock came. We waited at our counsel table as the jury was brought into court by the bailiff. The judge then entered the courtroom and turned to the jury. He explained that there was a matter that the court must take up "outside your presence." He then went on: "Because of the nature of the matter and not knowing how long it may take—that is to say it may take one hour, two hours, three hours, four hours, or it may extend over to tomorrow—the court is going to excuse you at this time so that you can return to your hotel."

I waited impatiently as Gordon Miller tied up some loose ends from Hal Deadman's testimony, offering in evidence the fiber and carpet samples Deadman had identified. That completed, Judge Cooper turned to me: "Mr. Drolet? We're now ready to proceed."

I could not help but notice how quiet it was in the courtroom. I rose, stepped to the podium, put my papers where I could refer to them, and opened my mouth to speak. My mouth was suddenly dry, but words came out: "Pursuant to your pretrial order that set out the procedure for doing this, the State at this time is prepared to begin offering evidence in regard to other transactions which there is evidence connecting the defendant. This evidence is being offered for a limited purpose, the limited purpose being that it tends to prove plan, scheme, pattern, bent of mind, and identity." The "other transactions" were the ten other similar murder cases.

I cited the Court to the most recent case from the Georgia Supreme Court authorizing what I was doing. Then I began to list the names of the ten victims whose murders we were offering in evidence. The first was Alfred Evans. In Evans, and in each subsequent case that I listed, I enumerated the elements that were similar and likely tied to the cases of Jimmy Ray Payne and Nathaniel Cater. I described the background and vulnerable circumstances of each victim. None had a vehicle, all were poor, all were male, all were Black, they came from broken homes, they were relatively small in stature, and all frequented the streets of Atlanta.

I described the crimes. Each victim disappeared, and there was no evidence of forced abduction and no apparent motive. Each victim was dumped or placed not far from access to a major expressway. Those victims whose bodies were found on land were usually laid out on their backs, and some of their clothing was missing. Asphyxia was the common cause of death, as it had been for Nathaniel Cater and Jimmy Ray Payne. Some of the victims had stab wounds or had been struck in the head with a flat blunt object. In each case, fibers like those found on Cater and Payne were found on the bodies. Additional fibers from different automobiles were found on victims, and those fibers corresponded to the times when Wayne Williams had access to those automobiles. As Wayne Williams changed cars, the fibers found on the victims would change.

I explained how the early victims in the murder spree were found laid out on land, and how, after news reports of fiber evidence came out in February of 1981, the bodies began to be dropped in rivers, absent their clothing. I had chosen cases from the earliest murder to the most recent. This was the serial killer we had been looking for.

I went through the names: Alfred Evans, Eric Middlebrooks, Charles Stephens, Lubie Geter, Terry Pue, Patrick Baltazar, JoJo Bell, Larry Rogers, John Porter, and William Barrett. I added that in some of the cases there were witnesses who could place Wayne Williams with a victim shortly before death, and I added that blood found on the back seat of the Williamses' station wagon matched victims, Porter and Barrett.

As I was making my presentation, I was unable to see Williams' reaction, but I expect it was making him uncomfortable.

The court recessed for twenty minutes to allow Al Binder time to get his argument together. When we resumed, Binder started his argument by saying he wouldn't "refer to these deceased as street hustlers" as I had done. The evidence would show that victims were often on the streets, searching for ways to make money. Binder was trying to score points by showing his sensitivity and compassion for the victims. Binder claimed that the only similarity among the victims was that they were poor. He also argued that we couldn't offer this type of evidence until we proved the corpus delicti, meaning we had not proven homicidal deaths in regard to Cater and Payne. Judge Cooper interrupted, saying, "It's your contention that the state has not shown foul play in either the death of Cater or Payne. Is that correct?"

"Yes, sir," responded Binder. "No one saw Wayne Williams kill anyone."

Binder argued that I had not cited a single case in my presentation. Cooper reminded him that I would present appropriate case law after Mr. Binder had argued. Binder replied, "He's going to cite some, I'm sure, when I get through."

I rose to respond, and I was no longer nervous. I noted that Binder had referred to Cater and Payne as street people, and I pointed out that other victims had come from similar backgrounds. In regard to the corpus delicti argument, I noted that two medical examiners had given their expert opinions that the deaths were murders. I cited cases from the Georgia Supreme Court supporting our position that this evidence was enough to prove the cause of death beyond a reasonable doubt. I conceded that our case was based on circumstantial evidence, and I explained how circumstantial evidence, such as fibers or fingerprints, can be just as powerful as direct evidence from a witness.

I corrected Al's assertion that the cases we offered had to be very similar or identical to be admissible. The cases needed only to be similar *or* logically connected—our cases were similar in many ways *and* also logically connected. I also showed that in the similar cases, we only needed to provide evidence of Wayne Williams' culpability; we did not need to prove each case beyond a reasonable doubt. It would be up to the jury to determine the weight they gave to the similar cases.

I finished by concluding that "the logical connection runs through these cases unmistakably. The pattern was so obvious that it caught the attention of virtually the entire western world." I then quoted from an older Georgia case, ironically titled *Williams v. State*, that said: "Evidence may be admitted to prove other like crimes by the accused so nearly identical in method as to earmark them as the handiwork of the accused."

Al Binder insisted on having the last word. Despite my objection, the judge allowed it. Binder said the only thing that caught the attention of the world was "the inability to find out what was happening and why these people were being killed."

Cooper called Binder and me to the bench and asked if we could give him a list of all the cases we cited. The judge asked what would happen if he didn't rule until Monday. I told him that all the witnesses we had lined up were witnesses in the ten similar cases I had just presented. Binder scoffed at my assertion and muttered that surely we had other witnesses. Judge Cooper said he would try to rule by Sunday and asked for our home phone numbers so that he could reach us.

Thus ended a hectic week of trial. I was relieved. My presentation had gone well, and as I gathered my files and prepared to leave the courtroom, a half dozen courtroom artists wanted me to sit down so they could sketch me. I quietly enjoyed the brief respite from an emotionally exhausting day. As sketch artists scribbled, photographers from the *Atlanta Journal* and the *Atlanta Constitution* snapped pictures.

Reporters were perplexed by one of the ten similar cases I presented. They had never heard of John Porter, who was not on the list of missing and murdered children. Porter had been murdered recently, and the circumstances of his death bore a strong resemblance to Nathaniel Cater's case. Porter was covered with some of the more significant fibers discussed in earlier testimony, and his body had been placed on his back, near abandoned apartments where he had been squatting.

The next morning, Saturday, I went outside to pick up my newspaper and was surprised to see my picture staring back at me on the front page. Expanding the murder trial from two murders to twelve was big news, and a clear indication that we were trying Williams as the Atlanta Child Murderer.

In the days to follow, I saw that same picture many times. The story had been picked up by news organizations all over the country, all using the photo taken by the *Atlanta Constitution* photographer. My mailbox began to fill with copies of newspapers and magazines sent by distant relatives and friends. I even made appearances in *Jet* magazine and *Stars and Stripes*, the newspaper for American servicemembers overseas. A cousin in Colorado I had never met sent me a sweet note saying: "Every 'cousin,' no matter how distant, is singing your praises now and claiming the relationship. You look wonderful on the evening newscasts where we've seen you 'live,' not just sketched, several times." My quote about the pattern being "so obvious it caught the attention of the entire western world" appeared in *Newsweek*, the *New York Times*, and other publications.

Not all my mail was friendly. One anonymous letter, from "the Wayne Williams Defense Committee," suggested that I "get the fuck back up to where [I] came from." (I had moved to Georgia from Illinois in 1971.) Many more such letters would follow during the trial and for thirty years thereafter.

The attention buoyed my spirits, but that Saturday, January 23, 1982, as our team gathered in the war room to prepare for Monday's proceeding, the big question remained: Had my presentation been successful? Was Judge Cooper going to grant my request and allow us to bring before the jury ten additional murders?

Jack Mallard, Gordon Miller, Wally Speed, and I went over evidence and discussed the order in which to present upcoming witnesses. But we still needed to know whether the judge was going to rule in our favor and allow evidence of other similar murders. I called Michael Smith, the judge's law clerk. He said the judge had not yet decided his ruling, and we would have to wait.

I began researching other issues we knew the defense would raise, such as a claim that the prosecution was motivated not by the evidence, but by political pressure from the governor.

We met again on Sunday morning and discussed our strategy in the event that Judge Cooper denied our use of the similar cases. Our different scenarios depended on how the judge ruled. We had notified witnesses to be ready to go on Monday, but we weren't sure which witnesses we would actually be calling. I researched more issues until about 4:30 Sunday afternoon and still had had no word from the court. Our whole team was feeling uneasy and depressed. Were we going forward with everything we had, or would we be prevented from telling the jury what I had just told Judge Cooper about ten more murders tied to Wayne Williams?

Chapter 13

IS HE A SERIAL KILLER?

The Trial—Week Four

Early on Monday morning, January 25, 1982, Judge Cooper's law clerk called my office. The judge wanted to see me and Al Binder in his chambers. From my seventh-floor office, I catapulted down the stairwell to the fourth-floor courtroom. In his chambers, the judge announced his ruling. Cooper was ruling in our favor—the similar cases would be allowed. I rushed back to the office to spread the word.

We hurriedly let anxious witnesses know when they would be needed, and we headed for the courtroom, knowing that we were now starting a new phase of the trial. We would be reinforcing our argument that Williams was indeed a serial killer.

PROVING TEN MORE MURDERS

As we sat waiting at our counsel table, the judge took the bench. He read his ruling into the record: "In light of the contentions of the State and considering the authorities, the court will admit evidence of other alleged independent crimes for the limited purpose of showing plan, scheme, pattern, bent of mind, and identity to the extent that a fact issue is raised to be determined by the jury. Bring the jury in." Al Binder rose and moved for a mistrial. I responded with the cases I had cited on Friday, which confirmed that Binder was not entitled to a mistrial. Cooper denied the motion.

Jack Mallard resumed his role as the examiner of witnesses. In recent days, Gordon Miller had presented all the fiber evidence witnesses, and I had argued the legal issues.

Our first witness that Monday was Dr. Timothy Benich, a dentist who could identify the dental records of victim Alfred Evans. Benich had done dental work on the young man and had his dental charts and X-rays of Evans' mouth. Homicide Detective Mickey Lloyd found Evans' body in July of 1979—it had been dumped down an embankment in a wooded area near Niskey Lake Road in southwest Atlanta. The decomposing body was wearing only black slacks. No shirt, socks, or shoes. There were maggots around the nose, eyes, and mouth as Evans' body was placed on a white sheet and taken to the medical examiner's office. No signs of a struggle and no other clothing were found in the area.

Alfred Evans' mother provided a vest that matched the slacks being worn by her thirteen-year-old son. But Ms. Evans refused to accept the fact that her son was dead. She denied that the body was Alfred. A neighbor from the East Lake Meadows housing project knew the thirteen-year-old and remembered that he was often out on the streets at night.

Dr. John Feegel, associate Fulton County medical examiner, performed the autopsy on Evans. Feegel explained the role of the medical examiner in uncovering the cause of death in criminal cases as well as in accidents and unexplained deaths. As a forensic pathologist, his role was medical as well as investigative, like a detective. A hospital pathologist, by contrast, would simply determine a cause of death from the autopsy. Feegel, like medical examiners Zaki and Stivers, was qualified as a forensic pathologist. Alfred Evans, he said, died of asphyxia, most probably from strangulation.

Binder tried to get Feegel to say he was just guessing about asphyxia being the cause of death. Feegel artfully responded about his expertise and his years of education and experience: "It is the best-educated guess, and the amount of education employed in the so-called guessing is how we define 'expertise.' So, as a forensic pathologist, my diagnosis here is asphyxia." Binder shifted gears and suggested that many people could have touched the body in the morgue; Feegel agreed. Binder was trying to undermine any fiber evidence found on the body. Feegel responded that before anyone was near the body, the slacks and underwear Alfred Evans was wearing had already been bagged up and sealed to go to the crime lab. No one else had touched it, and it would be from that clothing that fibers and dog hair would be recovered.

When we reconvened after lunch that day, Judge Cooper wanted us in chambers. A drawing had been found in the area of the hotel room where the jurors ate breakfast. The drawing was the outline of a male face in profile, and underneath, the word "GUILTY." A deputy sheriff had noticed the drawing and did not know how many jurors might have seen it, although at least one juror had commented to the deputy that she saw the drawing. The judge called the deputy sheriff, Sergeant Bussey, to his chambers to explain what had happened. Bussey explained to us that as jurors were coming in to sit down for breakfast, Juror Derum, the former police officer, saw the drawing taped to a chalkboard and tore it down.

As I listened, I fully expected Al Binder and Mary Welcome to ask for a mistrial. They did not. The fact that Juror Derum had torn down the drawing may have reassured them that the incident did not hurt the defense. Binder asked that the drawing be marked and made a part of the record. The judge agreed. We returned to the courtroom and continued the trial.

We moved to the next murder, that of Charles Stephens, but before we did, Judge Cooper wanted the defense to know that he was going to instruct the jury, on each of the similar cases, that they should consider the evidence only to the extent it showed plan, scheme, pattern, bent of mind, and identity, and it would be up to the jury to decide if the evidence showed that. Binder approved the instruction.

Sonny Lowrey, a detective with the East Point Police Department, had investigated the murder of Charles Stephens, a twelve-year-old who had been found along a roadside laid out neatly on his back, with one arm off to his right side and bent at the elbow. Stephens was missing his T-shirt and belt. There were no signs of a struggle, and it was apparent that he had been carefully placed at this location. Stephens lived five miles from where he was found and had been reported missing the day before, on October 9, 1980. Lowrey noticed fibers visible in Stephens' hair.

Stephens' grandfather, Reverend Burrus Gibbs, identified his body and reported that Stephens was from a broken home and lived in public housing. Neighbor Kevin Risby remembered that Stephens hung out on the street a lot. With this witness, Al Binder began referring to victims with great respect. Stephens was now "Master Stephens."

Dr. John Feegel was the medical examiner on this case, as he had been on Alfred Evans. Stephens had petechial hemorrhages on the eyelids and the heart, signs of asphyxia. He died from some form of suffocation, and his death was clearly a homicide. Binder unsuccessfully tried to get Feegel to say that there was no pattern in the types of asphyxia among the missing and murdered children.

The judge again repeated his admonition to the jury in regard to the "similar transactions," and we proceeded to the murder of fourteen-year-old Lubie Geter. Geter was reported missing on January 3, 1981, and was found a month later, laid out on his back, in a wooded area of south Fulton County. Geter was identified from fingerprints compared to fingerprints found on his schoolbooks, provided by his mother. Some of Geter's clothes were missing, and some were found scattered nearby. Binder objected to Jack's offering gruesome photographs of the scene where Geter's body was found. Judge Cooper was sympathetic to Binder's argument, so I joined Jack and cited cases that permitted the admission of evidence of multiple horrible crime scene photos. The Georgia Supreme Court had ruled as follows: "Pictures may be gory, but murder is usually a gory undertaking." Cooper was unimpressed and limited us to just a few photographs to be viewed by the jury.

Dr. Robert Stivers, chief medical examiner of Fulton County, had testified earlier in regard to the death of Nathaniel Cater. He now returned to testify regarding Lubie Geter. Family members had identified Geter's body in the morgue, as portions of his disfigured face and the lower portions of the body were covered when family members viewed the body, small animals and birds having left their marks during the month the body lay in the woods. Stivers found petechial hemorrhages on the heart and the lungs and inside the brain. "We knew we had an asphyxia death." As there was trauma to the neck, Geter had probably been strangled, perhaps by a chokehold, Stivers said.

Al Binder tried to undermine Stivers' testimony based on statements Stivers had made at a medical examiners' conference. Stivers admitted that the total number of murders of young people was not out of the ordinary over the past year. This opened the door for Jack to ask how many *asphyxial* deaths of persons under thirty years old there had been since Wayne Williams was arrested. The answer was zero. Since the time Williams had been jailed, the bodies of asphyxiated young men were no longer being found along roads and in rivers. Stivers had checked records going back nearly twenty years and found that deaths of young people by asphyxiation were rare. Yet they had spiked in 1980 and during the first half of 1981. After that, and the arrest of Wayne Williams, they had returned to normal.

We recessed for the day, and no mention was made by Al Binder or Mary Welcome about the drawing found in the jurors' breakfast area.

When we resumed the next day, Tuesday, January 26, Al Binder began complaining about an upcoming witness. Binder said Ruth Warren was not on the list of witnesses we provided the defense. He was wrong; we had provided the name. Binder also complained that I was trying to change Georgia law in order to pursue the prosecution of Wayne Williams. He suggested that I had taken a slightly different position on similar transactions in a brief in the Georgia Supreme Court in a totally unrelated case. I responded that "we'd be pleased for the court to read" my brief. Judge Cooper compromised regarding the witness list, by permitting Binder and Welcome to interview Ruth Warren before she was called to testify. Moments later another argument ensued when we started to call I. B. Hood, Geter's uncle. Binder complained that his witness list did not contain Mr. Hood's name. Binder was using the wrong witness list. I had given an updated list to defense team member Clifton Bailey the week before we started the trial. Binder said he didn't intend to use that list, and I responded that "the law doesn't give the defense the option to choose which witness list they're going to use."

Mr. Hood was permitted to testify. He said he identified the body of Lubie Geter in the morgue. Assie Geter, Lubie's mother, said her son had gone off to sell car deodorizers on the day he disappeared. She identified the shirt he was wearing when he left home. FBI clerk Robert Swabe found the blue T-shirt about three hundred yards from where the body was found, hanging on a small tree branch. Thirteen-year-old Michelle Spann had seen Lubie a lot at the Omni downtown, where they would hang out at the game room and go to the movies. She was supposed to meet him there on Sunday, January 4, 1981, but Geter had disappeared a day or two earlier.

Geter's friend Eric Conway often hung out at the Omni with Geter and went with him as he sold car deodorizers and air fresheners. He last saw Geter on Friday, January 2, when Franklin Jordan, Lubie's half brother, had dropped Lubie and Conway off near the Stewart-Lakewood shopping mall. Conway had later caught a ride with Jordan, but Geter was nowhere around, and Conway never saw him again.

We again tried to call Ruth Warren as a witness, but Al Binder said they had not yet had a chance to talk to her. Court recessed to allow that opportunity. During the recess, I read into the record the dates on which we had given names of witnesses to the defense. Ruth Warren's name had been provided on November 12, 1981, nine weeks earlier, and the name of Darryl Davis, who was also about to testify, had been given six weeks earlier, on December 3, 1981. I listed fifteen more witnesses we were about to call, names we had provided to the defense five months earlier.

Ruth Warren had been shopping for a mattress at the Stewart-Lakewood mall on Friday, January 2, 1981, when she saw a man standing and talking to a young boy about twenty feet away. She recognized the young boy, who had earlier tried to sell her an air freshener for her car, and she heard him tell the man, "I'd like to go with you but I've got to sell these," referring to a box he carried under his arm. After buying her new mattress, Ms. Warren saw the man and the boy walking together toward a nearby jewelry store. The man, who had what looked like scratches on the left side of his face, was wearing a red baseball cap. Ms. Warren identified a photo of the boy, Lubie Geter. She then looked around the courtroom and said she saw the man who had been wearing the red cap. It was Wayne Williams. Williams showed some discomfort, shifting in his seat a few times.

At the time of Geter's disappearance, Ms. Warren had described the person she saw to a police sketch artist. She identified the sketch, and it was admitted as evidence for the jury to consider. The drawing looked very much like Wayne Williams.

Al Binder tried to get her to say the sketch didn't look like Wayne Williams. But the drawing *did* look like Williams, and she said, "It's very, very similar, yes sir!"

We broke for lunch and got an update on the issue of the drawing with the word "GUILTY" that had been found in the jury dining area. Sergeant Bussey reported that deputies had secured the room where breakfast was served and that they would check it each morning before the jury went in. Binder asked Bussey if jurors could see newspaper boxes, which might display news of the case when jurors went through the food line in the cafeteria. I reminded him that the newspaper racks had been removed, so the jurors would never see them. Binder replied: "Then I have nothing further." Nothing further was said about the drawing.

Now another issue arose as Juror Vickie Lambert mentioned to a deputy that her uncle worked for the East Point police department. The judge called Ms. Lambert into his chambers and questioned her about her relationship with her uncle. She had not mentioned her uncle during jury questioning, and she did not recall anyone asking her about it. He was not close to the family and would not influence her in any way, she said. Al Binder was satisfied and had no objection.

We called another witness who was sure to create a stir. Darryl Davis was fifteen years old. To protect his identity, his full name was not revealed in open court. He was simply addressed as "young man." Davis was working on a loading dock at a carpet store at the Stewart-Lakewood mall, and he saw Lubie Geter get in a car with Wayne Williams. Davis recognized Williams from months earlier when Williams picked him up in the middle of the night on Stewart Avenue, south of downtown.

On that earlier occasion, Davis rode around with Williams, who asked if he wanted to make some money working at a car wash. As they rode around, Williams became more inquisitive, asking if Davis played a musical instrument or had any brothers or sisters. He asked if Davis had any money and reached over like he was feeling his pocket, but instead was feeling Davis' penis. Williams then drove to an area near a dump and some woods, where he asked if Davis had ever had sex with boys. Williams asked Davis to take his penis out of his pants. Williams then got out of the car and said he had to get something out of the trunk. Davis jumped out of the car and ran to the nearby Village Apartments. In the courtroom, Darryl Davis pointed at Wayne Williams, identifying him as the man who picked him up.

Darryl Davis knew Terry Pue, one of the missing and murdered children, and while at Pue's funeral with his court services officer, Davis saw Williams again and pointed him out to a friend, Eric Thompson. Williams left the funeral, he said, in a white station wagon.

Darryl Davis had a juvenile record, and Al Binder exposed his background as a petty thief. He made Davis look bad, but we hoped that the jury would see that Davis could have ended up like many of the victims—except Darryl Davis had gotten away. A TV reporter for one of the network affiliates told me later that day that when Davis testified, "It was like you lit a fire in the Press Room."

Byron Dawson, the medical examiner at the Georgia State Crime Lab, had performed the autopsy on the next victim, Terry Pue. Pue's body was found on January 23, 1981, laid out along a road in Rockdale County, twenty-five miles east of Atlanta and about a half mile from Interstate 20. Fifteen-year-old Pue was clothed but for his undershorts, which were missing. There were three separate ligature marks on his neck, with damage to his voice box. The ligature marks left a braided impression on Pue's neck, likely resulting from a rope of some kind wrapped around his throat. Pue had also been struck on the top of his head, and there was traumatic hemorrhaging under the scalp. Dawson concluded that Pue died from strangulation, a form of asphyxia.

Pue's sister, Pamela Terrell, testified that her brother had lived in Hollywood Courts, a public housing project near downtown Atlanta. He hung out at the Omni game rooms downtown, in the West End area just west of downtown, and at Tri-City Plaza in East Point. Pamela had identified Pue's body, and she described how he did odd jobs for money and was dependent on the bus for transportation.

Eric Thompson attended a special school for troubled youth, the "Challenge School," with victims Terry Pue and Darryl Davis, the young man who had jumped out of Wayne Williams' car. Fifteen-year-old Thompson had attended Pue's funeral and met up with Darryl Davis as the funeral ended. Davis poked Eric and said: "There's the man that grabbed me!" Thompson had seen Wayne Williams before, and he watched as Williams got in a white station wagon after the funeral was over.

On cross-examination, Al Binder sparred at length with Eric Thompson, who argued with Binder and refused to answer some questions.

On Wednesday morning, January 27, H. B. Starr, a former

deputy sheriff in Rockdale County, explained how he helped set up a perimeter around the body of Terry Pue. After Dr. Dawson and Larry Peterson from the crime lab arrived, Starr helped keep people away from the crime scene. At one point he was approached by a Black man with a ruddy complexion, who wanted to take pictures of the scene. He believed it was Wayne Williams. Mike Leathers, another former Rockdale County deputy sheriff, was at the crime scene with Starr and saw Starr talk to the man and check his driver's license. In the courtroom, Leathers pointed to Wayne Williams as that man.

At this point in the trial, we had presented eighty witnesses in thirteen days of testimony. The jury had heard about the murders of Nathaniel Cater, Jimmy Ray Payne, and four others: Alfred Evans, Charles Stephens, Lubie Geter, and Terry Pue. We had educated the jury about fibers, hairs, and carpet construction. Larry Peterson and Harold Deadman had explained the significance of the fiber evidence against Wayne Williams. Based on that evidence, Cater and Payne had to have been in contact with Wayne Williams.

After spending four weeks together in the courtroom, we had all gotten to know one another. We were familiar with every item of clothing the jurors wore, and we knew which seat each juror would take in the jury box, and who would sit together. We knew who paid attention, and who didn't. The jurors had seen every suit I owned and nearly all my favorite ties. They knew the defense team and how Al Binder started every cross-examination, calmly introducing himself to each witness and saying: "I just have a few questions I'd like to ask you." They knew when Al was setting a witness up to make him look bad, as Al would uncharacteristically raise his voice, frown at the witness, and say, "And the truth of the matter is . . ." At this point, Al would point out some fact or admission he had been trying to drag out of the witness.

Binder knew that Jack Mallard was unflappable, with his down-home country style, and that he could elicit what he needed from witnesses. Binder had become familiar with my practice of responding to legal questions with my thick, black ring binder in which I had been keeping track of every relevant decision in Georgia's appellate courts for more than a decade. I expect Al was sick of my popping up to the judge's bench, ring binder in hand, when a matter was in dispute, and saying, "Judge, I have a case on that!" Everyone knew Gordon Miller would be involved whenever there was mention of fiber evidence, that Wally Speed could back up Mallard when needed, and that Lewis Slaton, as district attorney, was there because this was the biggest case his office had ever prosecuted.

Court reporter Susan Northington was now a fixture in the courtroom, unobtrusively sitting at her stenograph machine quietly taking down every word spoken and accepting each item of evidence as it was marked, identified by a witness, and offered in evidence. Judge Cooper was respected by everyone and served as a calming influence in the courtroom—low-key, rarely raising his voice, and fairly considering any issue raised by lawyers for either side. We joked with the defense team that Cooper was so fair that he alternated how he ruled, one ruling for the prosecution and the next one for the defense. But Cooper was keeping the trial going and doing a great job of not letting anything get out of hand.

Late that Wednesday morning, January 27, we turned our attention to the murder of Patrick Baltazar, the fifth similar transaction we were offering in evidence. On February 13, 1981, Ishmal Strickland had found twelve-year-old Patrick Baltazar's body partway down an embankment near Corporate Square, an office park just off an exit from Interstate 85 in DeKalb County. The body had been deposited there shortly after the DeKalb police chief was quoted as saying that if the cases had been happening in DeKalb County, he would have solved them by now. The choice of this site seemed to be a response to the boast by the chief.

DeKalb Detective B. W. Humble said Baltazar hung around near Foundry Street, where he lived, and near the Omni complex in downtown Atlanta. His mother was in Louisiana, and Baltazar lived with his dad. David Breeden knew Patrick, noting that he kept late hours and would do just about anything to make money.

Dr. Joe Burton had gone to the scene where Baltazar's body was found. He noticed that Baltazar's shirt was unbuttoned and that he wore gym shorts over his underwear. Burton later performed the autopsy, noting that there were ligature marks on Baltazar's neck, and hemorrhages in the eyes, the lungs, and the area of the Adam's apple. Baltazar died from asphyxia due to ligature strangulation, and Burton concluded that someone had probably held the ligature around his neck from behind.

Next came the murder of JoJo Bell. Fifteen-year-old John Laster and his twenty-one-year-old brother, Lugene, knew Bell, and they also knew Wayne Williams. JoJo Bell lived with his mother on Lawton Street, in the West End area near downtown Atlanta. Both brothers had seen Williams in a white station wagon near where JoJo lived, and JoJo told John Laster he had called Wayne Williams, apparently after seeing one of Williams' flyers seeking young people who could sing or play an instrument. In early March of 1981, Lugene Laster saw JoJo Bell get into a sky blue station wagon with Williams.

Al Binder tore into Lugene Laster, accusing him of saying only what FBI agents told him to say, berating his memory, and pushing him on his testimony about seeing Wayne Williams. Lugene Laster was irritated by Binder but did not back off from his identification of Williams.

Twenty-four-year-old Kent Hindsman met Wayne Williams after seeing one of Williams' flyers soliciting young people with musical talent. Hindsman was trying to form a musical group of his own. In December 1980, Williams picked up Hindsman in a white station wagon, asking Hindsman if he was a bum, if he was gay, and if he ran the streets all the time. Williams took Hindsman to Atlanta Studios, a recording studio in a house on Shadowlawn Avenue in northeast Atlanta, where Hindsman watched as Williams auditioned some young boys. The next week Hindsman returned to the studio and met John Laster and JoJo Bell, who were there with Williams, and a woman named Carla Bailey. Williams told Hindsman he was going to "sign JoJo Bell to a contract" and gave both Hindsman and JoJo Bell a ride back to downtown Atlanta in the white station wagon.

Hindsman later returned to Atlanta Studios with other performers and ran into Williams. They talked about the missing and murdered children, and Williams, referring to the victims, said, "They ought to keep their damn asses at home!" Then Carla Bailey, who was sitting next to Wayne Williams, handed Hindsman a note. The note said, "I could be a president, I could be a mayor, or I could even be a killer." Carla Bailey then grabbed the note back, and she and Williams laughed about it.

Hindsman saw Williams in three different station wagons, a white one, a blue one with a primer spot on it, and a green one that looked like it had been repainted. On one occasion, Williams picked Hindsman up in one of the station wagons, and they went to the Omni, where Williams handed out his flyers, soliciting young people to call him. Williams called this "stargazing" and said he was looking for potential stars. Williams also bragged about how he flew airplanes and had been suspended from the Air Force for flying under a bridge.

During a fifteen-minute recess in the trial, we met a friend of Al Binder's from Mississippi. Jim Kitchens, a fellow lawyer, was passing through town and dropped by to visit Al. Al said Kitchens would probably just be sitting behind him for the day. During the break, Al moved for a mistrial, claiming the note described by Hindsman was damaging to his client and should not have been allowed. We disagreed, and so did the judge. Jack continued his questioning of Kent Hindsman, who said Williams had bragged about having a black belt in karate and having worked for a law enforcement agency.

Al Binder was obviously concerned about the testimony. Three witnesses had reported seeing Wayne Williams with JoJo Bell. Al accused Kent Hindsman of being a failure and a jealous competitor to Williams. Al also accused him of trying to destroy Williams, saying: "Oh, come now. Haven't you made it known to everybody that you were going to get him today?" Al scored what points he could, but Hindsman did not wither under cross-examination. Like other witnesses before him, Hindsman stepped off the witness stand feeling as if he had been through a storm.

Dr. Joseph Burton, who had performed the autopsy on Patrick Baltazar, also did the autopsy on JoJo Bell. Fifteen-year-old Bell was one of the first victims found nearly naked in a river, after word got out that identifying fibers were being found on victims. On April 19, 1981, Bell's body was pulled from the South River, in DeKalb County near the Rockdale County line, downstream from a bridge crossing the river. Bell had been missing since March 2, and his body was found caught in some branches. He was facedown and wearing only jockey shorts. Hemorrhaging in the neck showed he died of asphyxia. Bell had not drowned. There were no fluids found in his airways. This was another homicide.

Thursday, January 28, 1982, began with a meeting in chambers. Binder announced that Jim Kitchens, who had visited court the previous day, was going to be joining the defense team. The judge had to approve his participation, as he was not a member of the Georgia bar. The judge asked if we had problems with Kitchens being involved. Jack said, "No problem." I wanted to hear more about Kitchens and he complied, explaining that he had been a lawyer in Mississippi for fifteen years and had served as district attorney of his county. I raised no objections and Kitchens was now on the case.

I then brought up another matter. We had a new witness who might have seen Wayne Williams with Nathaniel Cater. We had just learned about the witness.

I also asked if we could substitute a husband for his wife, who was now unavailable. They both were neighbors to one of the murdered young people. Binder went off on a tirade about how our witnesses wouldn't talk to him. I explained that we did not instruct witnesses not to talk to the defense, but we did tell them it was their choice as to whether they spoke to the defense lawyers or investigators. I took the opportunity to bring up the tricks being used by Defense Investigator Durwood Myers to make witnesses think I had sent him to talk to them. Jack Mallard then chimed in on the question of witnesses refusing to talk, and he reminded the court that we had no idea who the defense would be calling as witnesses. They were under no obligation to tell us. I also brought up a threatening letter I had received, supposedly from the Wayne Williams Defense Committee.

Binder explained that he, too, had gotten a threat, by telephone. All of these issues were manifestations of the complexity of the case, and few of them could be resolved there in the judge's chambers. I could see that the usually calm Judge Cooper was losing patience. We were all tired and irritable, and Cooper soon dispersed our rambling meeting.

We resumed our familiar places in the courtroom—we were waiting for a witness from the Terry Pue case who was unable to get to court. As it turned out, we would have to take that witness, Charmaine Kendrick, out of order when she arrived. We moved on to the next case, and Cooper again instructed the jury about the limited purpose of the similar transactions.

On April 9, 1981, the partially clothed body of twenty-one-year-old Larry Rogers was found by an Atlanta police officer checking out an unattended car in the parking lot of an abandoned apartment building in northwest Atlanta. The officer had noticed the distinctive odor of a decomposing body coming from the building. Rogers had learning disabilities and had been missing for ten days. His body was clothed only in blue shorts, with yellow stripes down the sides. An identification technician from the Fulton County Police Department confirmed that the body was that of one of the missing young people. Rogers' fingerprints were on file, as he, like other victims, had been in trouble as a juvenile. Rogers had lived with his foster father, George Hood, and he had no job and no car, and he did odd jobs around the neighborhood.

Tilbert Bynum was a petty criminal, known on the street as "Cool Breeze." He had seen Larry Rogers with Wayne Williams a few days before Rogers disappeared. Cool Breeze thought Williams might be a "narc" (an undercover police officer). Bynum was getting a joint of marijuana for Rogers, and he watched Williams closely because of his suspicions. Williams was clean-cut and well dressed, and he saw him with Rogers two more times that same day. Cool Breeze provided some light moments in court as he admitted smoking marijuana and volunteered that he had, that very morning, smoked some "herb" before coming to court.

Nellie Trammel was a sweet matronly neighbor of Larry Rogers who had known him since he was a young child. She last saw him on March 30, 1981, in a car with Wayne Williams. The car driven by Williams had cut her off as she made a turn. It was then that she noticed Larry Rogers, a passenger in the car. She called out Larry's name, but he was slumped over in the car and did not respond.

She had seen Williams before. She thought he was a cameraman from a news crew. She had noticed him earlier when the "bat patrol" had been organized by residents of Techwood Homes. On that occasion, he had parked his station wagon, a white one, and gotten out with a camera over his shoulder.

When we resumed after a break for lunch, Al Binder announced that Jim Kitchens would be handling the cross-examination. Kitchens introduced himself to the jury and said he lived in Crystal Springs, Mississippi. The judge explained, "Mr. Kitchens is now part of the defense team, so you'll see him quite often." Kitchens asked a series of questions that confused Ms. Trammel. Ms. Trammel said she thought she had identified a picture of Wayne Williams a few weeks after Larry Rogers went missing. It had actually been about six weeks later, after Williams became a suspect. Kitchens thought he was on to something and that Ms. Trammel must have identified someone other than Wayne Williams *before* Williams was stopped on the bridge and became a suspect. In fact, the only person she ever identified was Wayne Williams *after* he became a suspect. Kitchens was convinced that shortly after Larry Rogers disappeared, one of us had shown Ms. Trammel pictures of a suspect other than Wayne Williams, and that she had identified that other person. He and Binder demanded the picture of that other person. But there was no such picture. No one else had ever been identified by Ms. Trammel. Kitchens and Binder would bring up this nonissue again and again.

Charmaine Kendrick, who had been unavailable earlier, took the stand in regard to the murder of Terry Pue. As often happens in trials, a witness can't show up exactly when you need them, and it can make a smooth presentation difficult, as you shift your focus from one subject to another. Now we were back to the murder of Terry Pue.

Kendrick knew Terry Pue from her job at a Church's Fried Chicken on Lee Street in the West End area of Atlanta. Pue would often come in the store, and he was always trying to sell something. Pue had assured Ms. Kendrick that he was not afraid of becoming a victim of the killer who was snatching children off the street. He boasted that if anyone tried to get him, he would stab them. She saw Pue a week before his death walking toward a green station wagon that had "mud and stuff on it." Wayne Williams was the driver. She did not recall the date.

In cross-examining Ms. Kendrick, Al Binder prefaced each question with a reference to the month of April, suggesting that that was when Pue disappeared. Ms. Kendrick barely noticed until Binder asked, "If he was missing on the twenty-third of January, '81, it would be difficult for you to see him in April, wouldn't it?" Jack short-circuited Binder's ploy, reminding Ms. Kendrick that she last saw Pue a week before his body was found. She didn't remember the month or date. Binder protested that Jack was trying to impeach his own witness, saying, "She's already said April too many times." The jury would be left to determine the truth.

We returned to the Larry Rogers murder with Dr. Stivers, who had already testified in regard to two other murders. Rogers had a scratch line on his neck, blood and hemorrhaging around the voice box, and cracked bones in his neck. He had died of asphyxia due to strangulation. He had also been struck on the right side of his head, which produced a hemorrhage over the temporal bone.

The eighth of the similar cases was the murder of John Porter, a twenty-eight-year-old victim who never made the list of missing and murdered children. Detective Bob Buffington testified Porter's body was found on April 12, 1981, in the Capitol Avenue area near Atlanta–Fulton County Stadium, just south of downtown Atlanta. Porter was lying on his back on a retaining wall with one foot dangling just above the sidewalk. The body appeared to have been placed there deliberately, as there was dirt in the rear waistband of Porter's trousers, indicating that the body had been dragged to its final resting place.

Porter was homeless and had been sleeping in an abandoned building nearby. He was unemployed and on drugs, and had no vehicle or other means of transportation. There were stab wounds to his body, but there was no blood at the scene. Two stab wounds had gone through his shirt, while four others were inflicted without making holes in the shirt. This suggested that Porter had been stabbed four times with his shirt off and twice while he wore it.

Dr. Stivers returned to the stand and described Porter as being about five feet, ten inches tall, and weighing 123 pounds. The stab wounds on his body were all horizontal, less than a half-inch across, about two to two and a half inches deep, and all inflicted on the lower chest and upper abdomen area. A single stab wound had penetrated Porter's heart and most likely caused his death.

Judge Cooper recessed court briefly to take up the issue raised earlier by Jim Kitchens in regard to witness Nellie Trammel. Kitchens maintained that Ms. Trammel had identified someone other than Wayne Williams, and he wanted to see the photo of that person. Jack assured Judge Cooper that there was no photo and that he had never been to her house. I noted for the judge that Ms. Trammel was obviously confused about when she spoke to different people. Her only identification had been of Wayne Williams, and that was after he became a suspect. Since there was no photo of some other suspect, we had nothing to turn over to the defense.

We moved to the murder of Billy Barrett, whose body was found dumped along a roadside near Interstate 20 in DeKalb County in early May of 1981.

An identification technician was about to identify a group of photographs of the scene where Barrett's body was found when Jim Kitchens rose from his chair and objected, claiming the photos should have been provided to him prior to trial. Judge Cooper overruled the objection and noted that as provided by Georgia law, the defense would be given an opportunity to look at the photos when they were presented.

Al Binder wanted to raise another objection: "We don't believe your honor has jurisdiction over this particular crime, and we object to you admitting evidence ... for crimes allegedly committed outside your jurisdiction." Cooper clearly had jurisdiction over the evidence in the case, and he promptly overruled the objection. We were all exhausted and getting testy, and given that it was 4:30 in the afternoon, Judge Cooper took the opportunity to recess for the day.

On Friday morning, January 29, Sam Hudgins, a special education teacher in DeKalb County, identified photos of Barrett, whom Hudgins knew from the four times Barrett had faced problems in juvenile court. Donna Martin, Barrett's juvenile court caseworker, said Barrett failed to report to her, as he was supposed to, on May 11, 1981. Barrett's mother didn't know where he was, and he was never seen alive again.

James Barrett, a twenty-three-year-old cousin of Billy Barrett, said Billy had no job and no car and had just been released from a juvenile facility. Not long before he disappeared, Billy and two friends had come by to visit James at his mother's house, wanting to borrow ten dollars. One of the two people with him was Wayne Williams. James Barrett's mother, Mary Harris, remembered that visit, and she, too, pointed out Williams, as he sat calmly at the counsel table to my right.

Dr. Joseph Burton returned to the stand for the third time, to explain the ligature marks on Barrett's neck and the two postmortem horizontal stab wounds in the abdomen, near five other small stab pricks in the same area. Only two holes were found in Barrett's shirt and, apparently, he had also been stabbed with his shirt off, similar to the wounds found on the body of John Porter and on victim Eric Middlebrooks. Burton thought the wounds looked ritualistic, noting that Barrett had been strangled elsewhere and his body deposited where it was found. Burton also observed that Barrett's clothing was loose on his body, his shirt was unbuttoned, and his pants were almost falling off.

Dr. Burton showed the jury how a victim of strangulation would instinctively grab at the arms of the person trying to strangle them, often leaving the attacker with scratch marks down the arms. Al Binder's cross-examination of Burton failed to present any significant challenge to his earlier testimony.

A few days earlier, Dr. Burton had testified in regard to the murders of Patrick Baltazar and JoJo Bell, but he had a conflict the next morning, and Al Binder hadn't had a chance to cross-examine him about those cases. Binder was now given that chance and asked that the court recess early for lunch so he could refresh his memory on what he wanted to ask.

As the jury left the courtroom, Lewis Slaton wanted to confirm that we would not be having court the next day, a Saturday. The jury was getting impatient with the length of the trial, and Slaton was worried that Cooper would say something to the jury suggesting that the State was to blame. When the jury returned after lunch, Cooper explained to them that it was best to let all the lawyers make preparations over the weekend and resume trial on Monday morning. Cooper assured the jury that "by not holding court tomorrow, the case will move along at a much faster and smoother pace."

Meanwhile, testimony resumed for the afternoon, as Binder questioned Dr. Burton about victims Baltazar and Bell. Binder spent most of his time trying to get Burton to say things that would differ from what Dr. Stivers and Dr. Zaki had said. Nothing significant emerged from the questioning.

Now medical examiner John Feegel returned to the stand to testify about the tenth, and final, similar transaction, the murder of fourteen-year-old Eric Middlebrooks, who had died from a blow to the right side of his head and had postmortem horizontal stab wounds to the upper chest area. Feegel thought Middlebrooks had been struck by a flat object, possibly a slapjack-type weapon, and he had been laid out where he was found, along with his bicycle.

Al Binder tried to get Feegel to say that Middlebrooks was killed where his body was found, since there was some blood at the scene. Feegel responded that Middlebrooks may well have been struck elsewhere and dumped, unconscious, to die at that location.

Detective Bob Buffington, who had earlier testified in the John Porter case, returned to the stand and explained that Middlebrooks appeared to have been dumped, and his bicycle, which had two flat tires, looked like it had been thrown where it was found. Middlebrooks was found about seventy-five yards from Interstate 20 and about a mile from where John Porter had been found. Buffington also noticed a significant piece of evidence caught in the elastic band that encircled the edge of Eric Middlebrooks' left tennis shoe, a tuft of red fiber. The tuft had to have gotten stuck in the band near the time of his death, for if Middlebrooks had walked on that shoe, the tuft would easily have been dislodged. Jim Kitchens cross-examined Buffington and suggested that Middlebrooks may have been robbed since his pockets were turned out. In Buffington's opinion, as a homicide detective, this was no robbery.

Kerry Middlebrooks, Eric's half brother, was an Atlanta police officer. He took the stand in his police uniform, explaining how he and Eric had never lived with their real parents. Eric had been given up by his mother when he was four months old and lived in a foster home, a situation that allowed him to be out at night a lot, and he did whatever he could to make money. The entire courtroom fell silent when Kerry was shown a photo of Eric and said, "That's Eric Middlebrooks, my brother!"

Al Binder announced, "No questions!"

This concluded the tenth case demonstrating similar transactions, and Judge Cooper gave his tenth and final instruction to the jury about these cases, which had been admitted to show pattern, scheme, and identity. At this point, we had presented 105 witnesses and provided evidence and witnesses relating to ten murders in addition to the killing of Jimmy Ray Payne and Nathaniel Cater.

THE FIBER EVIDENCE BEGINS TO CONNECT ALL THE VICTIMS

We moved to our next phase in the trial, when the jury would hear a host of facts about Wayne Williams, his cars, his carpet, and the fibers and hairs found on the additional ten murder victims. The jury would also hear from other witnesses who had encounters with Wayne Williams.

Gordon Miller read a stipulation of evidence: the defense and the prosecution had agreed that certain facts were not in dispute and therefore there was no need to call a witness. The stipulation was that in October of 1980, Wayne Williams' uncle, Ralph Barnhart, loaned his 1970 Chevrolet station wagon to the Williams family, and they had been using the car since that time.

Detective M. F. Jones now explained how some of the vehicles used by Wayne Williams had been located. He identified the red Ford LTD that the Williams family had purchased in 1979 and that had been repossessed in December of 1980, after the Williams family began using Ralph Barnhart's white station wagon. We assumed Williams was using the red Ford LTD until at least October of 1980, but later in the trial, we would find out otherwise.

Detective Jones and a GBI agent found the red Ford LTD in Alabama and took samples from the interior carpet and trunk liner. Jones also found a blue 1978 Plymouth Fury that Wayne Williams had purchased, fashioned to appear like a police car, with the title in the name of his Southern Media Communications company. This car had been repossessed after eighteen months, with sixty thousand miles on it. Williams had also driven a silver 1975 Plymouth Fury (another car typically driven by police at the time) and a brown 1976 Plymouth Fury. Unknown to us, Homer Williams had rented various cars—just how many we didn't know. It was obvious that Williams borrowed cars frequently, as various witnesses reported seeing him in three different station wagons and several other vehicles.

Another week had ended, and the jury, we knew, was growing impatient to go home. The trial was tiring, at times boring, and it was wearing us down as well.

Jack, Gordon, Wally, and I met in our war room on Saturday and planned out the remaining twenty to twenty-five witnesses we planned to call. We all agreed that Sharon Blakely should be our last witness before the State rested. She was a friend of Wayne

Williams and had information we were sure the jury would find interesting.

On Sunday, I spent most of the day at the State Crime Lab with our fiber experts — Larry Peterson, from the GBI, and Hal Deadman, from the FBI. Both had already testified about the fiber matches found on the bodies of Nathaniel Cater and Jimmy Ray Payne. They would now be matching fibers found on the ten other murder victims. Barry Gaudette, an expert on loan from the Royal Canadian Mounted Police Laboratory, would be joining them and explaining additional significant fiber matches that we had recently discovered.

While at the lab, we inspected the thirty-by-forty-inch foam-core presentation boards mounted with photos of fibers, enlarged to show detail. Fibers found on each of the twelve victims were compared, side by side, with the corresponding source of the fibers from Williams' home and automobiles. Hal Deadman had directed the creation of the presentation boards at the FBI lab in Washington, DC, and we would use them to continue educating the jury about the significance of the fibers and hairs.

Chapter 14

MORE PIECES
OF THE PUZZLE

The Trial—Week Five

$\mathfrak{T}$he month of February started with a brief legal battle in Judge Cooper's chambers. Al Binder moved to suppress all fiber and hair evidence relating to the ten similar cases, claiming that defense expert Charles Morton had not been allowed to examine the fibers from the ten additional cases. He was mistaken, as there had never been a motion to allow Morton to examine the fibers and hairs, and more important, Morton had been given an opportunity to examine the evidence and had declined to do so. In addition, prior to trial, we had provided the defense with all the laboratory reports in compliance with the law. We returned to the courtroom, and Judge Cooper denied the motion.

Crime lab analyst Richard Ernest identified gloves found in the glove compartment of the white station wagon, and he also identified the rear seat that had been removed from that car. Lieutenant John Cameron explained to the jury how he kept track of the evidence taken from the bodies of victims, and then delivered the evidence to the crime lab, making sure in each case that he had marked bags of evidence with his initials. He was a "chain of evidence" witness, the person who can show that the items analyzed at the lab were the actual items found at the crime scene. Witnesses in the chain of evidence may have seemed inconsequential to the jurors, but they were essential for confirming that the evidence we presented was directly relevant to this case.

Now it was time for the final fiber presentation, bringing together all the fiber evidence from Nathaniel Cater, Jimmy Ray Payne, and the ten similar murders. Gordon Miller called Hal Deadman, the FBI expert, back to the witness stand. Deadman explained again about the rare fiber combination found in Wayne Williams' bedspread, an unusual violet acetate fiber interwoven with green cotton. He talked about the extremely rare Wellman 181b, Nylon 6,6 carpet fiber found in Williams' bedroom, and he described the dog hairs and the blanket fibers from the yellow blanket found under Wayne Williams' bed. There were fibers from three of the automobiles Williams had been driving and, as Deadman pointed out on one of the large foam-core charts, fibers from other sources, including a blue throw rug, polypropylene carpet squares, and vacuum sweepings found in the Williamses' own vacuum cleaner, which the Williams family had used to vacuum the station wagon. The charts made clear the connections between the murder victims and either Wayne Williams' home or one of his automobiles.

Deadman explained how trunk fibers in automobiles are made from undyed junk fibers that are "felted" together and crushed with an adhesive into a pad placed in the trunk of a car. Williams' 1978 Plymouth contained crushed white polypropylene fibers, and the red Ford LTD had forty to fifty different types of fibers crushed together with adhesive into the black feltlike pad in the trunk of that car.

Deadman explained about the red trilobal fibers from the carpeting in the red Ford LTD and fibers from a second bedspread found hanging in the carport at the Williams home. Brown woolen and brown rayon fibers were recovered from the cuffs and waist area of Williams' leather jacket. A gray glove recovered from the Chevy station wagon was composed of two types of acrylic fiber, and Deadman showed pictures of the two fibers on one of the charts.

Deadman explained how all these fibers were tied to the various victims. Cater, Payne, and all ten of the other murder victims had the violet acetate fibers from the bedspread. On some of the victims, the violet acetate was still interwoven with the green cotton of the bedspread. The Wellman 181b, Nylon 6,6 green carpet fiber was found on Cater, Payne, and eight of the other murder victims. Every victim but JoJo Bell (who had been in the river for over a month) had hairs matching those of Sheba, the Williamses' dog. Cater, Payne, and four of the other victims had fibers from the yellow blanket found under Williams' bed. Cater had a total of six different fiber types associated with Williams' environment. Payne likewise had six associations, in addition to fiber from the Chevy station wagon that Williams had been driving on the James Jackson Parkway Bridge. Patrick Baltazar's body had nine different fiber types found in Williams' home, plus fibers from the Chevy station wagon. The jury watched closely, and I hoped they were grasping the significance of what they were hearing and seeing.

As a lunch recess was called, Cliff Bailey, one of Williams' lawyers, asked to see any of Wayne Williams' business records among the evidence in our possession. I took Bailey to my office on the seventh floor of the courthouse and showed him records and color slides taken during the search of the Williams home on June 22, 1981. I had no idea what he was looking for. Apparently, Williams had told his lawyers that we had something that would be helpful to them. Whatever it was, Bailey didn't seem to find it. We resumed court and took up the subject of hair evidence.

Hal Deadman explained the process of comparing questioned hairs with hairs from a known suspect. Unlike man-made fibers, hairs have far fewer different colors, are all the same shape, and are all composed of the same natural material, keratin. Deadman had a chart showing all the various characteristics that hairs display, such as scales and pigments, and variation in the parts of the hair called the medulla and the cortex. Deadman had taken hair samples from Wayne Williams in June of 1981 and compared them to two hairs found inside the shirt of Patrick Baltazar. They displayed the same microscopic characteristics as Williams' hair. That hair, in addition to the ten different types of fibers from Williams' environment found on Baltazar, further substantiated our belief that Williams was in close contact with Baltazar at the time of his death.

Fiber evidence from Williams' house would inevitably get tracked into the cars Williams was using. Vacuum sweepings from the Chevy station wagon contained most of the types of fibers from the house. Every time Williams left the house, his shoes would carry fibers from wherever he had been walking in the house. Fibers from the bedspread, the Wellman carpet, and the yellow blanket could all be found in the car. When asked his opinion on the significance of all the fiber and hair associations he found on the twelve murder victims, Deadman said that for at least eleven of the twelve cases he reviewed, the victims had to have been in contact, directly or indirectly, with the home or automobiles of Wayne Williams.

Deadman's testimony was powerful, and Al Binder couldn't ignore it. Binder's usual polite, low-key demeanor gave way to a much more combative style. He accused Deadman of changing his testimony, now saying that the fibers could have come from the car, not just the house. He got Deadman to admit that he didn't know whether the carpets or trunk liners in two of the cars had been replaced after the Williams family got rid of those cars. Deadman also conceded that there were some Caucasian hairs found on two of the twelve victims. Binder suggested that Ford trunk fibers from the red Ford LTD couldn't have been found on Charles Stephens because that car was in the shop and the Williams family didn't have access to the car in October of 1980, when Stephens was murdered. Binder did everything he could to undermine confidence in the fiber evidence.

Deadman held his own and, on occasion, enhanced his testimony by expounding on significant fiber characteristics.

Deadman also explained that he had taken samples from the trunks of eleven Ford automobiles, and that the junk fibers Ford used were different from those used by other automobile companies and even varied slightly among different Ford models. Al suggested that fibers from the victims should have been found in the Williams house, but Deadman explained that the victims may not have been in the house, and in any event, they were normally clothed in common materials like white cotton or cotton from blue jeans, fibers that were too common to have any significance in demonstrating an association. Binder tried to make Deadman look biased, saying, "The real truth of it is that you didn't mention that to this jury . . . because that points the way to innocence, doesn't it?" Deadman explained again why common fibers are insignificant in showing association.

Binder should have stopped his questions at that point, but he insisted on asking one more: "Have you found anything in those sweepings [from the Chevy station wagon] relating to any of the deceased?"

Deadman responded that there were "two associations; there was a red cotton fiber in the vacuum sweepings of the automobile consistent with coming from a pair of shorts that Jimmy Payne had on," and that in the debris from the gray acrylic glove found in the station wagon, there were some "white acrylic fibers that were consistent with the white acrylic fibers in William Barrett's socks."

Binder, stung by the evidence, accused Deadman of bringing up these two fiber associations to "have some effect on this jury."

Deadman said he simply sought "to answer your question."

Binder questioned Deadman's impartiality, suggesting that the vice president of the United States was interested in this case, and that Deadman was expecting a big promotion or other reward. There was no big promotion or reward, the vice president was not involved, and Deadman's testimony remained firm.

Gordon Miller asked a few questions on redirect examination. Deadman explained that Williams' environment was unique to his living situation, and that finding the fibers from this particular environment on eleven of the victims he examined "linked" them "positively to the Williamses' environment." I thought Binder might come back with more questions, but he wisely chose not to. Gordon offered in evidence all the fibers and other items that had been identified by Harold Deadman, and they were admitted without objection from Binder.

The fiber presentation continued with Barry Gaudette, the civilian fiber expert from the Royal Canadian Mounted Police. Gaudette was the scientific advisor for hair and fibers for Canada's Crime Detection Laboratory System. Binder objected to any testimony from Gaudette because Gaudette had submitted no written report. I rose to remind the judge that Georgia law required reports to be turned over *only* if a report had actually been prepared. After a fifteen-minute recess, Cooper overruled Binder's objection.

Gaudette explained that, before Wayne Williams became a suspect, he had been invited to the June 13, 1981, conference at the Georgia State Crime Laboratory. At that conference, he reviewed some of the fiber evidence. Later, in November 1981, Harold Deadman asked Gaudette to conduct an independent assessment of the evidence. Gaudette spent more than ten days examining evidence in the Cater, Payne, and Baltazar cases.

Gaudette offered to do a demonstration for the jury to explain the exchange principle. Gaudette had with him a sweater with fibers dyed fluorescent so they would show up under ultraviolet light. A deputy cut the lights off in the courtroom, and Gaudette showed how the sweater lit up under ultraviolet light. Gaudette had Gordon Miller step forward, and he pointed out that Gordon's suit did not light up; it lacked fluorescence. With the lights back on, Gaudette had Gordon handle the sweater and then place it back in a bag. Again the lights went out. The ultraviolet light showed fibers shining brightly on the front of Gordon Miller's suit, where the sweater had come into contact.

The test was repeated with a piece of carpet, treated so as to be fluorescent. Gordon got down on the floor with his head on the piece of carpet. The ultraviolet light easily revealed a half dozen of the carpet fibers visible in Gordon's hair. The jury was riveted by the presentation. Gaudette concluded by endorsing the methodology used by our experts, Larry Peterson and Harold Deadman. At that point, it was late in the day, and Judge Cooper recessed court.

The next morning, Groundhog Day 1982, we had gathered in our war room and were preparing to walk up to the fourth-floor courtroom together when an Atlanta police officer rushed into the room laughing. He couldn't wait to tell me something that had happened a few minutes earlier. As a courtesy to Wayne Williams' parents, the Atlanta police department would escort Homer and Faye Williams to and from court each day. On this day, as the police car they were riding in was coming around the block by the courthouse, I happened to be crossing the street from my parking garage. According to the officer, Homer and Faye yelled to the police officer driving the car: "Run him down! Run him down!" Fortunately, the amused Atlanta police officer disregarded the suggestion, and my life was spared.

In the courtroom, Barry Gaudette bored the jury with long explanations about the characteristics of human and dog hairs. Then he got to the important part, as Gordon Miller asked him the significance of the fiber and hair associations on Cater, Payne, and Patrick Baltazar. Gaudette responded: "If we consider the total number and combination of hairs and fibers in these cases and the unusual nature of some of them, the possibility that they could have originated from alternate sources would be so remote as to be not worth considering, and I can form no other opinion than that it is nearly certain that there was some form of association between the victims and the environment of Wayne Williams."

Al Binder spent forty-five minutes asking questions, with few responses that helped the defense. Gaudette confirmed that a degree of judgment is involved in making hair and fiber comparisons. Binder implied that Canada was a White country and that Gaudette knew nothing about the hair of Black people. In his folksy style, Al said, "Now, Mr. Gaudette, you don't know a blooming thing about Black hair, do you, and that's the truth of it, isn't it!?" Gaudette disagreed and described his experience with all types of hair. Binder suggested that Gaudette had only been shown fibers that Deadman and Peterson wanted him to see and that perhaps the fiber collection efforts had been contaminated. He ended by using his usual phrase, "The truth of the matter is," followed by the suggestion that Gaudette had been brought here just to back up Harold Deadman. Thus concluded the three hours Barry Gaudette was on the witness stand.

During a lunch break, I met with defense team members Jim Kitchens, Cliff Bailey, and an investigator as they followed me to my office to again look through evidence boxes for some records. I watched as they looked through everything we had. I was curious what they were looking for. They never said, and they never seemed to find whatever it was.

Our Georgia fiber expert Larry Peterson was now back on the witness stand to identify evidence he had recovered from the victims of the ten additional murders we presented. Peterson went through each case, as Deadman had, and explained the individual fibers and hairs he found. First Alfred Evans, and next came Eric Middlebrooks, Charles Stephens, Lubie Geter, and Patrick Baltazar. Then Larry Rogers, Terry Pue, John Porter, William Barrett, and JoJo Bell. In each case, Peterson noted the connections with items found in Wayne Williams' environment. Peterson directed the jury's attention to many of the large foam-core charts with photos of the items found on victims and the sources of the fibers in Williams' environment.

Peterson explained how in January of 1981, he was aware of the unusual Wellman 181b, Nylon 6,6 green carpet fiber, the rarest among the unusual fibers in the case. This was five months before Wayne Williams was stopped near the James Jackson Parkway Bridge. Peterson was unsuccessful in finding the source of the fiber until June 3, 1981, when he accompanied a search team to the Williams' home on Penelope Road.

Peterson identified the head hairs found inside Patrick Baltazar's shirt, which displayed significant similarities to the head hairs combed from the head of Wayne Williams. He went on to say, "In my opinion, it would be virtually impossible due to the fiber combinations for eleven of these victims discussed not to have been in contact with the home and/or automobiles of Mr. Wayne Williams."

Al Binder complained that Peterson and Deadman had collaborated to use the same terminology in describing the significance of the fiber associations. Peterson was calm and professional and explained that he used language to describe his conclusions that appropriately described those conclusions. He further explained how he continued to find the unusual fibers as each new victim was found and as the pace of the killings increased in the spring of 1981. Binder tried to discredit the foam-core charts being used, but this gave Peterson a chance to explain in greater detail how conclusively the fibers matched. Binder picked at every item he could—variations in the color of fibers, whether more photographs might have been useful, and specks of debris on some of the fibers.

Al Binder again brought up the fibers found on Charles Stephens. Peterson had assumed that the red Ford LTD had been in Wayne Williams' possession in October of 1980 when Charles Stephens' body was found, and Binder again pointed out that it was not possible for the fiber to have come from the red Ford LTD because the Williams family did not have the car at that time. Peterson explained that the microscopic and optical properties of the fibers recovered from the victim were the same no matter which car the Williams family was using. Neither the prosecution nor the defense could have known then that later in the trial, Wayne's father, Homer, would provide a damaging explanation for what seemed, at the time, to be evidence supporting Wayne's innocence.

Binder's final assault on Larry Peterson accused him of picking only fibers from victims that led to Wayne Williams and ignoring significant fibers that might have shown that someone else was the killer. Peterson explained that no fibers from victims escaped their scrutiny.

On redirect examination, Gordon Miller asked, "With regard to the unusual fibers that you were looking for from January on, which did you have first, the fibers or Mr. Williams?"

Peterson responded, "I first associated the victims together through questioned fibers which I recovered from their bodies or clothing." In other words, Peterson knew exactly which fibers were significant, and until the search of Williams' home, he had been unable to pinpoint the source of either the unusual Wellman carpet fiber or the unique combination of fibers being found on victims.

BLOOD EVIDENCE

We now began acquainting the jury with bloodstain evidence, as Connie Pickens, a forensic serologist from the Georgia State Crime Lab, explained that she had received blood samples from the body of John Porter. His blood type was international blood type B, and she turned the blood samples over to her associate John Wegel. Linda Tillman, another serologist, performed the same function in analyzing the blood of William Barrett, who was blood type A. She also took blood from Wayne Williams, who was blood type O.

Ms. Tillman had also analyzed the rear seat of the 1970 Chevrolet station wagon, the car Wayne Williams had driven onto the James Jackson Parkway Bridge. Blood, not easily discernible to the naked eye, was found to have seeped into the seat. Tillman made small incisions in the seat and found blood there, with faint reddish stains still visible. Two small stains were type A blood that still had active blood enzymes of the type PGM 1, which stood for type 1 Phosphoglucomutase. Another stain was type B blood, and it also contained active enzyme PGM 1. The blood types matched the blood types of John Porter and William Barrett and could not have come from Wayne Williams, who had type O blood.

Forensic serologist John Wegel reviewed the samples and noted that blood type B with PGM 1 is found in only 7 percent of the population, while blood type A, with PGM 1, is found in about 24 percent of the population. More importantly, the enzymes in the blood remain active for only a short time after the blood begins to dry, and *the enzyme known as PGM 1 remains active for up to eight weeks*. Thus, the blood found on the back seat of the car was relatively fresh, having been shed sometime during the eight weeks before it was analyzed. John Porter and William Barrett suffered stab wounds and were found murdered in May of 1981, less than eight weeks before the station wagon was searched in early June of 1981. In short, these were fresh bloodstains, matching the blood of victims Porter and Barrett. And no one in the Williams family had any explanation for how those bloodstains got there.

The next witness established that the Williamses' 1970 Chevrolet station wagon had 89,469 miles on it when it was inspected on October 20, 1980, shortly after the car came into the possession of the Williams family. This would be important later in the trial to show how many miles Williams drove, cruising the nighttime streets of Atlanta.

W. C. Clay, the final witness of the day, identified photos he had taken inside the Williams house on June 22, 1981. Clearly visible in one of the photos was a baseball cap, just like the one Ruth Warren said Wayne Williams was wearing when she saw him with victim Lubie Geter. Clay also identified burned remnants of black and white photographs he had recovered in a barbecue pit in the backyard of the Williams home. Al Binder jumped to his feet, accusing us of wanting to put those remnants in evidence as a way to prejudice the jury. Only the edges and corners of the burned photos remained. Judge Cooper promised to rule on the burned photos the next morning, and he did so, sustaining Binder's objection. The jury had learned about the pile of burned photos in the barbecue pit but would not get to see them.

During the period when the first victims were disappearing, Wayne Williams was driving a 1978 Blue Plymouth Fury. In December of 1979, Detective M. C. Cox had received a call from Georgia Auto Recovery, an auto repossession service on Stewart Avenue, south of downtown Atlanta. They had repossessed a car that appeared to be a police detective car. Cox inspected the car, which had a police scanner, a four-channel police radio, a siren, and blue lights—everything but the police radio worked. The scanner picked up police calls from the Atlanta and DeKalb County Police departments as Cox sat in the car, which could pass as an actual Atlanta detective car. The owner of the car was Wayne Williams.

At the time, Cox had spoken with Williams, who claimed the equipment was already in the car when he got it and that he had never used it. Williams claimed he was president of a news-gathering agency called Metro News Production and that he had a permit for the amber light found in the trunk of the car.

GETTING TO KNOW WAYNE WILLIAMS

In our presentation of evidence, we now turned to witnesses who had encountered Wayne Williams in a variety of settings. Andrew Hayes was sixteen years old, lived with his grandmother, and had known Williams for three years. He met Williams in a game room at the West End Mall just west of downtown Atlanta and sometimes rode with Williams to the Omni and to the Rialto and other downtown theaters. He described a Buick Skylark that Williams drove, and said he had seen a police radio in one of Williams' cars. On one occasion, while in Williams' car, Williams had offered him twenty dollars to suck his penis. Binder pressed Hayes on his testimony and challenged his memory of events, try-ing to get him to say that he had told others that he had never met Wayne Williams. Hayes fidgeted on the stand and didn't seem to like answering the questions, but he never wavered on the basic facts of his testimony.

Joe Graham was another young man Williams befriended. Graham was a budding singer and had already cut one record. Williams wanted to take some "promotional" photographs of Graham. Williams, along with Willie Hunter, picked Graham up at a MARTA transit station. Williams was driving a faded green station wagon. At Williams' house, Graham used the bathroom and noticed children's T-shirts and shirts on the floor.

Jim Kitchens questioned Graham, who acknowledged that Williams had produced the photographs he promised, and that at the time nothing seemed sinister or unusual.

Billy Pittman, a twenty-two-year-old aspiring singer, had met Williams in 1979 at Atlanta Studios, where Pittman had recorded a song. Williams claimed he was going to make Pittman a star and even called him at 2:30 in the morning and said, "Pack your bags, you are on your way to stardom." Nothing came of it. Pittman later saw Williams in what he thought was a police car, with a police radio and blue lights. He saw Williams two or three times a week at the Omni, a place frequented by many of the victims on the list of missing and murdered children. In her cross-examination, Mary Welcome tried, without success, to help her client. Pittman slammed Williams' schemes involving recording contracts, saying, "It was bullshit, all of it!" Judge Cooper admonished him not to use profanity, and he apologized. Pittman concluded that "Wayne Williams was not what he said he was, who he said he was." And he added that he had never seen Williams with a female date, only with young men.

James Thompson traveled from South Carolina for the trial and was shy and nervous about testifying, preferring that his name not be spoken aloud. He was seventeen years old and wanted to be a recording star. When he was a few years younger, Wayne Williams had come to South Carolina and invited him to Atlanta, where Williams claimed to be a music producer. In June of 1979, Thompson, along with his parents, came to Atlanta and accompanied Williams to a recording studio. Neither Thompson nor his parents were impressed. Williams told Thompson's parents they couldn't be in the studio. Once in the studio, Thompson simply sat in a control room for a time—there was no audition and no recording made. Thompson and his parents immediately returned to South Carolina.

Later, in January of 1981, Williams called and left a phone message at Thompson's school, claiming he "had something down here that I think you would like." He wouldn't say what it was, but he sent Thompson a bus ticket to Atlanta, where Williams picked him up in a white station wagon and dropped him off at Willie Hunter's house. Williams told Thompson that Willie Hunter was "like a psychiatrist." Hunter asked personal questions and wanted to know if Thompson had ever had sex. When Williams returned to pick James up, he said they were going to a studio. Instead, Williams drove to a bridge over the Chattahoochee River, and then slowly drove across the bridge. After that, they went to Williams' house, where Thompson met a man named Nathaniel. He did not get his last name, but he thought it might be Cater. This person was an adult and had hair parted in the middle, the same way Nathaniel Cater parted his hair.

Al Binder tried hard to undermine James Thompson's testimony. He suggested that Thompson's parents must have trusted Wayne Williams if they let him come to Atlanta. Thompson replied, "They didn't want me to go!"

Binder tried to get Thompson to say the man he saw with Williams was not named Nathaniel but was named Broderick Burns.

Thompson said, "I don't remember anybody by that name."

Binder suggested to Thompson that the police took him to a bridge they chose. Thompson said no, that he directed the police to the bridge that Wayne Williams drove him over. Thompson acknowledged that Wayne Williams had not tried to strangle him.

Binder berated Thompson, saying, "The truth of the matter is, when it comes to singing, you just choke up, don't you?"

Thompson responded, "The fact is, Wayne's not a producer!"

Our next witness was a surprise to the defense. His name was not on our original witness list, but we added the name as soon as we learned about the witness. Two days earlier, a citizen had alerted police about what the witness, Robert I. Henry, claimed to have seen. Henry was a friend of Nathaniel Cater's, whom he knew as Silky. They had worked together at a labor pool and hung out at the same bars, the Cameo and the Silver Dollar Lounge near downtown. Henry saw Cater on a Thursday night, just six or seven hours before Wayne Williams was stopped on the James Jackson Parkway Bridge. Cater was near Forsyth and Luckie Streets "coming right across from the Rialto Theater," and Henry remembered that it was a Thursday because that was the only night that week he wasn't working. He was on his way to a Huddle House diner. It was about 9:00 p.m., and Silky was with three other people. Silky and a man were walking together, and two others were walking behind them and appeared to be men dressed as women.

When Cater saw Henry, he stopped to talk. It was then that Henry noticed Cater was holding hands with the man he was with. Jack Mallard asked Robert I. Henry to look around the courtroom to see if he saw the man Nathaniel Cater was holding hands with. Henry responded, "Sitting right there! The gentleman with the gray suit, three-piece suit, and a blue shirt and the glasses."

Jack asked if Henry was sure that Wayne Williams was that man. "That is the man!" he replied.

Henry had tried to avoid getting involved, but a patron at the Miami Bar told the police about him, and when confronted by a detective working the case, he admitted what he had seen. He explained, "I got it off my chest. I told him."

Binder tried to salvage what he could from the devastating testimony. Robert I. Henry had just put Wayne Williams with Nathaniel Cater hours before Cater was strangled. Binder asked if Henry and Cater drank together and how the detective came to find Mr. Henry. Henry explained that a man who worked with him at the labor pool had told the police about him. Henry admitted that the two people behind Silky and Wayne Williams may not have been with them; they had continued on when Henry stopped to talk to his friend. Binder accused Henry of suggesting something bad about Wayne Williams based on the fact that he and Cater were holding hands.

Henry did not bite: "I'm trying to tell the jury they was holding hands!"

Binder wanted details about which hands they were holding—and Henry demonstrated.

Al Binder now asked Robert I. Henry if he had ever been in trouble with the law.

"Oh, yes," he readily admitted.

Jack Mallard objected to the line of questioning. By law, Binder could only impeach the witness with a certified copy of his convictions, which Binder did not have. As Al Binder continued his cross-examination, he brought out the fact that Henry had seen Williams before—at the Cameo Lounge, one of the places known to be frequented by Nathaniel Cater. Al hammered at Mr. Henry, trying, without success, to confuse him about dates and the people he had confided in about what he had seen.

By this time, Al Binder and Jack Mallard were exchanging sarcastic remarks. Jack wanted the judge to instruct Binder on the proper way to impeach a witness. Binder shot back, "I don't want him to instruct me on anything!"

The judge intervened, saying, "Thank you, Mr. Binder. I'll do the instruction."

Mallard came right back, "That's what I requested!" We had all been locked in this trial for five weeks, and tempers were on edge.

Meanwhile, members of the defense team had found copies of Robert I. Henry's various convictions. Binder, in an attempt to show that Henry was not a credible witness, dramatically read off some of his convictions. The dramatic reading fell short. The convictions were not particularly serious—larceny, for example, and disturbing the peace.

Al asked about other arrests, and Henry gave a disarming answer, saying, "I don't know, I've been in jail a lot of times," explaining that he knew he had been arrested for talking back to a police officer and cussing out a bus driver. But he'd never been held in any jail for more than three or four days. Henry had not volunteered to be there, was not ashamed about who he was, and was unfazed by having to discuss his somewhat checkered past. Nor had he made any judgments about Wayne Williams. All he knew was that he saw Williams holding hands with his friend Silky on the night before Silky was murdered.

Our next witness was an elderly White gentleman named A. B. Dean. Wally Speed and I had interviewed Mr. Dean at a Waffle House diner in Douglas County, Georgia, and we knew his testimony would be shaky—he was hard of hearing and easily confused.

When Jack asked Mr. Dean if he was hard of hearing, Mr. Dean responded, "How's that??"

Dean had passed a station wagon parked along Bankhead Highway in northwest Atlanta in April of 1981, about a mile from where Bankhead Highway crosses the Chattahoochee River. He saw two men talking nearby. When the muffler on Dean's car backfired, the two men turned and looked toward Dean. The next day he drove by the same area and saw one of the men getting in the same white station wagon. Days later Dean saw a picture of Jimmy Ray Payne in the newspaper, and he tore it out and saved it. Payne was one of the two people he had seen talking near the station wagon. Jack asked Dean if he saw the other man in court.

He looked around the courtroom and then said, "That's him sitting right in yonder," pointing at Wayne Williams.

Al Binder was ready for A. B. Dean. Al asked Dean his age, which was eighty-one. Al noted that he wore bifocals. A month earlier Binder had sent two investigators to talk to Dean. Binder now had a third investigator, Durwood Myers, stand up in the very back of the courtroom. He then asked Mr. Dean if he remembered talking to this investigator that Binder had sent to Dean's home. Dean assumed that it was one of the investigators.

Binder then said, "Are you as positive of that as you are that this is the defendant here that you saw?"

"Yes," Dean responded. Binder then told Dean that Durwood Myers had never been to his house.

Dean said, "I've seen that man, I've seen him somewhere." Belatedly, Jack Mallard objected to Binder's testifying. Binder then pulled one more trick. "Mr. Dean, you're as mistaken about that as you are about sitting in a car and identifying two Black males while you traveled down the highway?"

"Yes, sir," was Dean's response. Jack then asked if Mr. Dean understood the last question he was asked.

Dean said, "Not exactly, but he asked if I seen two Black males standing beside a car when I was coming down the highway, and I said 'yes, sir.'"

"And you did, didn't you?" Mallard asked.

"Yes, sir."

I talked to Mr. Dean after he got off the witness stand. He had good reason to recognize Durwood Myers, the defense investigator. Myers had interviewed Mr. Dean in the courthouse hallway and in the witness room. Myers had told Dean that he had been with the investigators who came to his house. The defense team had tricked Mr. Dean.

Denise Marlin worked for Southern Ambulance Company and knew Wayne Williams. Williams used to come around their offices and go on calls with the ambulances. She testified that she had seen him in an old police car, a silver one, and that he usually had some teenagers in the car. She said he used the N-word when referring to Black people. Binder jumped from his chair and objected, saying this was not relevant and was only being introduced to bias the jury. Jack and I argued that the information revealed his bent of mind and motive for killing young Black males, for whom he showed contempt. We told the judge there would be a series of witnesses who would establish this. An animated Al Binder loudly protested the relevance. Judge Cooper said he wanted to think about it and recessed court until the next morning.

We expected to wrap up our case on Thursday morning, February 4, 1982. The day began with Judge Cooper ruling that Denise Marlin could *not* testify that Wayne Williams frequently used the N-word in referring to Black people. Denise Marlin resumed her testimony, and without using Williams' actual words, described Williams' contempt for Black street kids.

Jack Mallard asked Ms. Marlin if she had been out on the bench with other witnesses when A. B. Dean was waiting to testify. She had, and she explained what took place between defense investigator Durwood Myers and the elderly Mr. Dean. Binder objected, claiming this was hearsay. Jack wanted to rebut the trick the defense had pulled on Mr. Dean and to explain Mr. Dean's conduct. Lewis Slaton chimed in, adding, "And maybe Mr. Binder's!"

Judge Cooper allowed us to pursue the matter.

Denise Marlin then explained how she saw Durwood Myers

approach Mr. Dean before Dean testified, and say repeatedly, "Do you remember me, I was at your home?"

We now had seven witnesses remaining to be called before we would rest our case. Eustis Blakely was next. We were saving his wife, Sharon, for last. Lewis Slaton questioned Eustis Blakely.

Eustis and Sharon Blakely sponsored talent shows at high schools and hoped to recruit talent for the entertainment industry. A sixteen-year-old from one of the talent shows told the Blakelys he had met a producer and was supposed to go to the man's house for an interview. Eustis and Sharon gave Aaron Daniel a ride to that house—it was Wayne Williams' house. Wayne was the producer who wanted to see the young man.

When they got there, Williams called to another young man, a fourteen-year-old named Stewart, who came walking out of Wayne Williams' bedroom. Over time, Williams and the Blakelys became friends. Wayne seemed to know a lot about the entertainment business and would come by the Blakelys' Decatur jewelry store and hang out. Sometimes he would bring his friend Willie Hunter. One day Eustis asked Williams why he never seemed to work—didn't he have a job? Williams said he was in the Air Force reserves and "I go up once a month and fly F-4s." Eustis Blakely had been in the Air Force and found that strange. Williams wore thick glasses—there was no way he could be a pilot. Eustis Blakely soon discovered that Wayne talked a lot but never produced any results—and he lied a lot.

Eustis heard Williams boasting about his knowledge of electronics, and he challenged him with some questions. Eustis Blakely was an electrical engineer, and through his questioning, he exposed Wayne's lack of knowledge. Williams reacted by changing completely, hyperventilating, becoming flushed, and pacing back and forth. Williams recovered somewhat and said, "I'll bet I know more about anatomy than you do."

Eustis had been impressed with how strong Williams was after he saw him pick up a seventy-pound jewelry display case with one arm. He also recalled Williams' disparaging attitude toward lower-income Black children. He had a negative term for them:

"street gruncheons."

Al Binder cross-examined Eustis Blakely very respectfully. Al praised Mr. Blakely for his work with young people and attempted to elicit some favorable comments about Wayne Williams. Some of it backfired. He tried to get Eustis Blakely to say that Williams was an expert in the music business. Blakely responded that Williams was not and really didn't know what he was doing.

Jack Mallard next questioned Nick Marlin, from Southern Ambulance Company, who often saw Wayne Williams at accident scenes. Williams frequently came by the ambulance offices in East Point, and Marlin noticed police scanners in Williams' car. He also wrestled occasionally with Williams and said, "Wayne holds his own pretty well!" Marlin, like his wife, had heard Wayne Williams make derogatory statements about poor, Black kids, and like his wife, Marlin had heard defense investigator Durwood Myers try to trick the elderly A. B. Dean, suggesting to Dean that he, Myers, was among investigators who had previously been to his home.

Bobby Tolin was an ambulance driver for Southern Ambulance and had bought an old Plymouth from Wayne Williams. The Plymouth was a former police car, and Tolin rode with Williams to the East Lake Meadows housing project to pick up the car. Williams was driving another car, a blue Plymouth Fury that also looked like a police car, and Williams used the siren on the car to get through traffic. Tolin, like his boss, Nick Marlin, had tussled with Williams, and though Tolin was six feet two and weighed 290 pounds, Wayne Williams could hold his own against him and was strong for his size.

He testified that Williams seemed ashamed of lower-class Blacks, and he once asked Tolin if he had ever considered "how many Blacks could be eliminated by doing away with one male Black child." Except Williams had not used the word "Blacks," he had used the N-word. Judge Cooper was disturbed by the use of the N-word in court and asked Jack to instruct the witness not to use it anymore. Tolin continued his testimony, saying that Wayne Williams had statistics on reproduction and explained to Tolin how killing one male would stop the increase in numbers in the future. I noticed a stir behind me in the courtroom—Faye Williams, Wayne's mother, was leaving the courtroom, soon followed by Wayne's dad, Homer.

Tolin also described an incident in the ambulance company office that involved horsing around with mace. Williams said he had chloroform, and he threatened to use it on anyone who sprayed him with mace.

Al Binder asked for an early lunch recess so that he could prepare to cross-examine Tolin. Judge Cooper accommodated his request, and court recessed shortly after 11:00 a.m.

When court resumed at 1:00 p.m., Binder was loaded with questions for Bobby Tolin. Al accused Tolin of treating Williams disrespectfully and taunting him, even embarrassing Wayne in front of his mother by holding him in a bear hug. Tolin remembered no such incident. Tolin admitted that given his size, he could probably beat Wayne Williams in a fight. On the whole, Binder made no serious inroads challenging Tolin's testimony.

Kathy Andrews operated Atlanta Studios, where Wayne Williams would take young singers to audition. On some of his visits, she noticed that Williams had scratches on his arms, scratches that were severe and went from his elbows to his wrists. The scratches looked like they must hurt, and when she asked what happened, Wayne just said, "I fell."

Al Binder could do little with Kathy Andrews after trying to get her to say the scratches she saw were on Wayne Williams' hands. He would substitute "hands" for "arms" when asking about the scratches, and she kept correcting him and saying the scratches were down his forearms, from his elbows to his wrists, not his hands. Al also tried to suggest that there was nothing unusual about Williams inviting young men to the studio for "auditions."

She explained that the studio was a "demo" studio. People did not come there for auditions, as Al Binder suggested. They came there simply to make demo (demonstration) tapes.

Now we were down to our last three witnesses. Two of those witnesses, eighteen-year-old Andrew Barber and fourteen-year-old Dennis Bentley, had been recruited by Wayne Williams to join singing groups. Barber was in Wayne's so-called Gemini group. While riding with Williams in his Plymouth police car with the radio and the blue lights, Barber noticed the scratches on Williams' right arm and on his face. He couldn't see Wayne's left arm because Wayne was driving at the time and Barber was in the passenger seat. Al Binder got little traction on cross-examination, although he did elicit that Wayne had never made sexual advances toward Barber.

Dennis Bentley, a fourteen-year-old, had seen the scratches on Williams' arms and a wound on his thumb. Bentley asked Williams about the scratches on his arms, and Williams said his dog bit him. It didn't look like a dog bite to Bentley. He asked Williams about the wound on his thumb, but Williams wouldn't answer. Bentley rode with him several times after Williams became a suspect. Bentley told the jury that when news came on the car radio about the missing children, Williams would always turn to another station.

Mary Welcome questioned Bentley and brought out the fact that on one occasion, when riding with Williams after he became a suspect, Williams kept looking back to see if anyone was following him, saying, "They ain't gonna catch me—I wrote the book."

Now we were ready to call our last witness, Sharon Blakely. From the first time Jack Mallard and I interviewed Sharon, in late summer of 1981, we felt sure she would be a powerful witness. She liked Wayne Williams, and she considered him a friend. She didn't want to testify against him, but she had things to say that the jury needed to hear.

Sharon Blakely was a petite Black woman, probably in her thirties, and her emotions were obvious when she talked of Wayne Williams. A hush fell over the courtroom as she took the stand. She was mildly hostile, and not particularly cooperative. Her answers, at first, were as short as she could make them. Did she know Wayne Williams?

"Yes."

When did she meet him?

"1980."

She began to loosen up a bit and repeated much of what her husband Eustis had talked about earlier in the day. They had met Wayne Williams while recruiting young musical talent. Like her husband, she had noticed Williams' strange résumé. He seemed to know a lot, but he was peculiar. Williams was obsessed with auditioning a young man he saw near their shop, but the young man was not interested. Williams kept watching the young man and wouldn't let it go.

Sharon Blakely seemed tense on the witness stand. We took a recess, and I spoke to her as she came down from the witness chair.

"You're mad at me, aren't you?" she began. She had received what she believed were threats, she said, from a friend of Wayne Williams. Al Binder, she said, had also sent investigators to her jewelry store, and they had tried to get her employees to say bad things about her. She was angry. I asked her to relax. We had spoken numerous times, and she seemed comfortable with me.

"Just tell the truth," I told her, "you're doing great." She seemed to calm down.

The jury returned, and Sharon stepped back up to the witness chair. She described seeing Wayne pick up a heavy jewelry case, and it amazed her. He didn't look that strong. One day when Williams dropped by to visit, he had just passed what he considered a low-class street kid. He began pacing and making comments about street kids. "They need to be off the street." Sharon Blakely warned him about messing with such kids, saying they "might beat you up." Wayne said he wasn't worried, that he "could press against their neck" a certain way and could "knock them out within seconds!" She testified how Wayne put his hand on his throat to demonstrate.

Sharon Blakely remembered a phone call from Williams after she heard he had been stopped near the James Jackson Parkway Bridge. He wanted to talk about auditions, and Sharon Blakely said to him, "Just stop the shop talk and you tell me why you were on the bridge!"

Williams said, "I was throwing garbage off the bridge!" She pressed him on the issue, and Wayne said he could "throw garbage wherever he wanted." Wayne said he was going to sue the news media and become rich from the proceeds.

Sharon Blakely concluded that there really was no Gemini group (the singing group Wayne claimed to be organizing) and that Wayne was just leading kids on. She explained how he didn't like poor kids, and he called them "Grungeons" or "Gruncheons," she wasn't sure exactly what the word was.

Sharon Blakely had been on the witness stand for nearly an hour. Al Binder asked for a brief recess before he began his cross-examination. After the break, quiet returned to the courtroom as the jury members returned to their seats. Sharon Blakely waited for Al Binder's first question.

Binder started as he had with just about every witness: "Ms. Blakely, my name is Alvin Binder. I represent Wayne Williams, and I want to ask you a few questions." First Al asked about how heavy the jewelry chest was that Wayne had lifted with one arm. Al seemed to mock the idea that it was heavy. Sharon Blakely knew that it had been weighed and that its weight was sixty pounds. She commented that something that heavy would be pretty hard to lift with one arm. Al accused her of not liking Wayne.

She disagreed, saying, "I like Wayne."

Al pressed her, asking, wasn't she ashamed to know Wayne Williams?

"No!" she responded emphatically, and she explained that she didn't think Wayne would lie to her.

Al Binder now walked Sharon Blakely through all the cooperative efforts she had participated in with Wayne Williams and the music business. Al tried to get Sharon Blakely to agree that Wayne had told her "Black people from lower-income areas tend to have more drive and initiative toward show business than upper-class Blacks."

She responded immediately, "I've heard Wayne say that Blacks from lower-class—lower and poor neighborhoods—didn't have any initiative at all!"

Al returned to his theme that Sharon Blakely disliked Wayne Williams.

Blakely responded, "I really do like him. I don't like what's happening, but I really do like him!" She went on to say, "I don't think that people understand that Wayne is weird and he has a split personality."

Now Al Binder asked a question that Wayne Williams had apparently urged him to ask, "Are you trying to intimate to the jury that you think Wayne Williams killed somebody? Is that what you're trying to tell this jury?"

Sharon Blakely paused and looked at Wayne Williams. Tears welled up in her eyes. A hush fell over the courtroom. She stared at Wayne. After a long pause, she said, "Do you actually want me to say?"

Al Binder, apparently apprehensive about what her response might be, rephrased the question, saying, "Why certainly, madam, because if you feel that way, tell them. That's what you're here to do. Do you *know* that he's killed anybody?"

"You know I don't!" she replied.

Al Binder had had enough. He said, "Thank you," and hurried to his seat at the counsel table.

Jack Mallard, seated next to me, leaned over. "What do you think? Should I ask her to answer the question?"

"Absolutely," I responded.

Sharon Blakely was struggling with her loyalty to Wayne Williams. Wayne was counting on her. Al Binder was nervous about it and had not given her a chance to answer the question when she hesitated and looked at Wayne.

Jack now rose and said, "Do you want to answer his first question, before the last one?"

"Yes, what was it?" she responded. Jack asked that the question be read back by the court reporter. The court reporter, Susan Northington, read back the question.

Sharon Blakely sat quietly in the witness box. "Now what was the question again?" she asked.

Jack said, "I believe Mr. Binder's question was, do you think he killed somebody, or words to that effect."

Sharon Blakely did not move. There was utter stillness in the courtroom. No one seemed to be moving, or even breathing. Seconds passed. Sharon Blakely sat staring at Wayne, tears trickling down her face. Jack asked again, "Do you want to answer it?" More moments of silence passed. It seemed like forever.

"Are you asking me do I think Wayne Williams killed somebody?"

Jack repeated, "Do you want to answer that question?" Jack waited as the jury leaned forward in anticipation. Not a muscle moved in the courtroom. The pause seemed interminable.

Judge Cooper now interrupted the silence, saying, "Ma'am, that's the question Mr. Binder asked you. Do you want to answer that question?"

Sharon Blakely leaned forward and slowly opened her mouth, as tears poured down her face. "Yes, I do. I really feel that Wayne Williams did kill somebody, and I'm sorry!"

A universal gasp echoed through the courtroom. She had agonized over it, but she finally said it.

After a few moments, Jack softly asked her, "Did you want to come down here and testify?"

"No, I didn't!" she sobbed, before Al Binder could object. Then Jack asked her again what Wayne Williams said about being on the bridge. She said, "He threw some garbage over!"

More than two years after the trial, Sharon Blakely would tell me that Wayne Williams had said more. He had said that Nathaniel Cater was "garbage."

After Sharon Blakely stepped down from the witness stand, Judge Cooper said, "Mr. District Attorney, call your next witness."

Lewis Slaton calmly rose from our counsel table. "We rest, your honor, the State rests!"

Al Binder, not surprised, was ready with some motions. The jury was ushered back to the jury room. Al then said, "The defendant, Wayne Williams, moves this court for a directed verdict."

This was a moment I relished. There was no way Judge Cooper was going to stop the trial and declare the defense the winner—that's what a motion for directed verdict would mean. We were well beyond that. Sensing that the judge was in no mood to entertain a long speech, I made a few short comments and described the legal standard that the defense surely had not met. Al flailed about for a minute or two, again arguing that no murders had been shown.

Judge Cooper wasn't buying it, and said, "Having already researched this issue on a previous occasion, the defendant's motion for a directed verdict is denied." Court was recessed until 9:00 a.m. the next day, February 5, and the judge added, "Mr. Binder, be prepared to go forward at that time."

WITNESSES FOR THE DEFENSE

We hurried back to our offices to prepare for the attacks we expected the defense to make. The defense team was not required to tell us who they would call as witnesses. It was now their show, and they would try to nibble away at our case, to undercut everything we had presented. And we would try to limit that effort.

As we resumed court on Friday, February 5, 1982, our boss, Lewis Slaton, stood and invoked the "rule of sequestration." This rule requires that witnesses remain outside the courtroom so they don't tailor their testimony to fit what others have testified.

Mary Welcome rose to remind us that we had agreed to let Homer and Faye Williams remain in the courtroom if we were allowed to have our investigators in the courtroom, in addition to the parents of the victims. Slaton started to argue with Welcome, but I reminded him that we had agreed to let Homer and Faye Williams stay in the courtroom. I let the judge know we didn't mind both parents' being in the courtroom, except when they were testifying: "We don't want one in and the other listening." At that point, Judge Cooper cleared the courtroom of any other witnesses who were there to testify for the defense.

"Call your first witness," Cooper announced. Mary Welcome called Leonard Harbison, a deacon at True Light Baptist Church. Harbison said he didn't know Nellie Trammel, the woman who had seen victim Larry Rogers in a station wagon with Wayne Williams. Ms. Trammel had mentioned that she attended that church. Jack cross-examined Mr. Harbison, who admitted that he didn't know everyone who came to church by name and that he had no idea what Nellie Trammel looked like. Defense witness Pastor J. H. Jordan said he knew Nellie Trammel, adding that she could have visited his church but she just wasn't a regular member.

Jim Kitchens called to the stand Kenneth Lawson, a former Atlanta police recruit. Lawson said he knew Robert Campbell and Freddie Jacobs, the recruits who had been at the James Jackson Parkway Bridge on the night Wayne Williams was stopped. Lawson accused Jacobs of complaining about seeing ghosts and being afraid of the dark, and he accused Campbell of drinking on the job. He claimed Campbell and Jacobs were actually asleep in a tent on the same side of the river the night of the bridge incident.

Lawson also tried to discredit Nellie Trammel, who had seen Williams in a car with victim Larry Rogers. Lawson said she hung out at the Task Force office, knitting, and claimed to be a psychic who had visions. Although Lawson had resigned from the recruit program with the Atlanta Police, Jim Kitchens made Lawson out to be an experienced and decorated police officer, a veteran of many police departments.

Gordon Miller cross-examined Lawson, who had not even been working on the night of the bridge incident. Lawson had been told he was going to be fired or he could resign, and one of the reasons he was going to be fired was for "being untruthful." In regard to Nellie Trammel, she was not even identified as a witness until two weeks after Lawson had resigned—there was no way he could have seen her knitting at the Task Force office.

Dr. Dan Stowens, the next defense witness, was a physician and pathologist who specialized in pediatrics and had published a textbook on pediatric pathology. He boasted that he had performed, reviewed, or consulted on over ninety thousand autopsies during his forty years of practice. Al Binder presented Stowens as an expert. Gordon Miller took the opportunity to ask a few questions about Stowens' qualifications. Stowens said he had personally done over four thousand of the autopsies, most recently having done an autopsy in which stabbing was involved, just two weeks earlier. And, he said, he had done an autopsy on a strangulation case a few years earlier. He claimed to have done forty to fifty autopsies in 1981, and about the same number in 1980 and in 1979. Judge Cooper permitted Stowens to testify as an expert in pathology, the study of the causes and effects of disease and injury.

Stowens had reviewed the autopsies of Nathaniel Cater and Jimmy Ray Payne, and he thought Payne may have drowned. As for Cater, he likewise saw no indication of any criminal activity, and he opined that Cater had been in the water for more than a week. This directly conflicted with other known evidence. Stowens didn't think that either Cater or Payne were murdered. As for the other victims, he disagreed with the results of the autopsy of JoJo Bell, and said that Charles Stephens could have died from kidney problems. In regard to fiber evidence, Stowens said that anything on a body would be washed away after a few days.

Stowens was sixty-three years old and distinguished-looking, and he appeared to speak with authority. He was suggesting that Nathaniel Cater, Jimmy Ray Payne, and JoJo Bell had just fallen in the river naked, or in their underwear, and died. And that Charles Stephens had deliberately laid himself out on the shoulder of a road overnight while he died of kidney failure.

Before we left the courtroom for the weekend, Judge Cooper asked if anyone objected to members of the jury being allowed visits from their spouses. Binder had no objection, and Wayne Williams, for the record, agreed. So did Lewis Slaton. Cooper gave instructions to the jury, which was frustrated with being locked up together for more than a month. Whatever they did, Judge Cooper said, they were not to discuss the case with anyone. We recessed for the weekend, with Dr. Stowens set to return on

Monday morning.

Back at the office, I called Utica, New York, and spoke with people in the district attorney's office familiar with Dan Stowens. Stowens had botched cases there and was no longer permitted to perform autopsies in the Utica area. He was a hospital doctor, which meant that he just looked at reports from other physicians. "Just ask him about the Migliaccio case!" they said.

The next morning, Saturday, February 6, we met in our war room at the courthouse and discussed Stowens' testimony. Lewis Slaton offered to cross-examine him. We discussed it and concluded that Jack Mallard would be our best examiner. Slaton agreed.

Gordon Miller and I began working on questions to ask Stowens based on what we had learned from police, prosecutors, and reporters in Oneida County, New York. Gordon and I also got help from medical examiners Saleh Zaki, John Feegel, and Randy Hanslick from the Fulton County Medical Examiner's Office.

As we worked that Saturday, calls came in about defense witness Kenneth Lawson, who had disparaged our witnesses Robert Campbell, Freddie Jacobs, and Nellie Trammel. The chief of police in Texas City, Texas, had nothing good to say about Lawson, who had omitted a few important things about his background. Lawson was not even living where he claimed, and his sister-in-law called around noon to give us a laundry list of information that could materially weaken his credibility.

On Sunday, February 7, I spent the day at the office going through boxes of evidence taken from the Williams home, on the chance that we had overlooked something. Williams' lawyers had continually sought to look through the evidence. They were still looking for something, and I didn't know what it was or whether we even had it.

Chapter 15

VISIT TO THE BRIDGE

The Trial—Week Six

𝔄 s we started yet another week, Dr. Stowens returned to the witness stand, boasting that he had served as a coroner in Louisville, Kentucky, and in Oneida County, New York. He lectured the jury on how autopsies are conducted and suggested that Nathaniel Cater's body should have floated when dropped in the river.

Jack Mallard got up to cross-examine Dr. Stowens. Al Binder objected, claiming that only Gordon Miller could cross-examine because Gordon had asked the questions regarding Stowens' qualifications. After a fifteen-minute recess, Judge Cooper overruled the objection.

Stowens acknowledged that he was actually an anatomical pathologist, one who deals with the study of tissues and organs removed during an examination—he was not a forensic pathologist. He only looked at written reports of autopsies performed by someone else, and he usually dealt only with cases involving diseases. Jack then asked Stowens how many homicide cases he had performed autopsies on in the previous year, 1981.

"I think there was only one," he said.

Jack continued, "Were there any in 1980?"

"I don't think so," Stowens said.

"I'm going to put down zero. How many in 1979?"

Stowens replied, "We don't have very much homicide in Oneida County."

Jack replied, "Would I put zero on that, too?"

"It's either zero or one," said Stowens.

"Did you do any homicides cases in '78?" Jack asked.

"I remember a ligature strangulation," said Stowens.

"Maybe one? Do you think that's right?" Jack asked. "How about in '77?"

"I can't remember," said Stowens.

"Zero?" Jack asked.

"Probably," was the response.

Jack asked, "How many criminal asphyxia cases have you handled in the last five years?"

"One ligature strangulation," was Stowens' response.

Stowens acknowledged that as a hospital pathologist he dealt only with "diseases and things that go on in hospitals," and he conceded that as a pediatric pathologist he dealt mainly with childhood diseases, and nothing more. Jack asked if Stowens had ever served as a medical examiner. He had been an assistant, he said, in Louisville, Kentucky.

Stowens admitted that in the one autopsy he had attended in New York City two years earlier, he was one of twenty or thirty pathologists in the room, and it was part of a seminar he attended. In other words, he just watched.

Stowens confessed to talking to the press after being warned by Mary Welcome and Al Binder about Judge Cooper's gag order. He told reporters that he was an experienced forensic pathologist and was looking for another reasonable cause of death of the victims, such as meningitis or pneumonia.

He admitted that he never handled a drowning case, and he knew nothing about fiber evidence or how long fibers might stay on a body.

Jack read from medical texts provided to us by our Fulton

County medical examiners. In regard to asphyxial deaths, just about everything Stowens had said conflicted with the experts. Stowens became irritated, shifting a lot in his seat and starting to sweat. He shot back at Jack, saying, "I am only a pathologist; I use the autopsy results and nothing else."

Cooper allowed Stowens a break and called a fifteen-minute recess.

We resumed at 1:15 p.m. Jack confronted Stowens with the fact that his boss in Louisville said Stowens wanted to work in the medical examiner's office so that he could do research on Sudden Infant Death Syndrome. Stowens was flustered and clearly uncomfortable. He claimed that he had done a few autopsies, but he didn't remember how many, and he admitted that all his books and writings were about childhood diseases, not about homicides.

Jack grilled Stowens about his opinion that Cater had been dead for over a week when he was pulled from the river on May 24, 1981. Jack asked if his opinion would change if he knew that Cater had visited a blood bank three days earlier, on May 21, was seen by the manager of his hotel on May 21, and was seen holding hands with Wayne Williams on May 21. Despite the evidence that Cater was alive on May 21 and pulled from the river on the twenty-fourth, Stowens said, "My opinion is still that the body had been dead seven days."

Jack showed Stowens a photograph of Charles Stephens' body laid out, partially clothed, along a roadside in East Point, Georgia. "Is this the one you said could have died from kidney failure?" he asked. It was. Stowens had never seen any pictures of Stephens and had restricted himself to the autopsy report alone.

Stowens admitted he had not been to a crime scene in twenty-five years and that another doctor, Charles Brady, actually performs all the criminal autopsies in Utica, New York. "How many autopsies have you done in murder cases in the last ten years up there?" Jack inquired. "Was it one?"

Stowens lost it, saying, "I'm sixty-three years old. I gave forty years in pathology . . . I paid my dues!" Stowens was near tears.

By this time, Al Binder was jumping from his seat to try to slow down Jack's cross-examination.

Stowens now admitted that he didn't really do pathology work anymore. "I have two pathologists . . . so that at my age I don't have to do this kind of manual work. Everything that comes out of my laboratory I review. I look at, I check."

Now Jack got to the best part. Jack said, "If the district attorney and his assistants said you had only handled one criminal autopsy in Utica since 1968, would they be correct?"

"It depends," he responded.

Judge Cooper showed mercy and took another fifteen-minute recess. When we returned, Jack asked, "Does the name Migliaccio mean anything to you?" (This was the case the district attorney from Utica had told us about.)

"Yes," Stowens responded.

"You did an autopsy on Mrs. Pikey?" Jack asked.

"Yes," he quietly responded.

"And Migliaccio was the accused, wasn't he?" Jack continued.

"Yes."

"And since that autopsy in 1975, have you done any autopsies in any murder cases in that county?"

"None," Stowens answered.

Binder quickly got Dr. Stowens off the stand.

Periodically during the trial, Wayne Williams would get restroom breaks or, for other reasons, have to leave the courtroom. Deputy sheriffs would take him out a door to the left of the judge's bench, away from witnesses, reporters, and the public. On each exit from the courtroom, Williams would pass directly in front of our counsel table, just a few feet from where we sat. Williams often expressed his displeasure at our work, muttering things like "You bastards!" or "You sons of bitches!" It was nice to know we were appreciated. At one point late in the trial, Al Binder overheard one such comment. He stepped closer to our table and whispered, "Now you know what I have to put up with!"

The defense resumed. Binder, for the second time, attempted to call former DeKalb Detective J. B. Wilhoyt as a witness. He hoped

Wilhoyt could tell the jury that Dr. Zaki had lied on the witness stand in describing the cause of Jimmy Ray Payne's death. Jack objected. Judge Cooper asked my position on the issue. I pointed out that Dr. Zaki had at least partially admitted whatever Wilhoyt would bring out and that Dr. Zaki had been extensively cross-examined about what he said to Wilhoyt. Wilhoyt, if allowed to testify, wouldn't contradict anything. Cooper asked Al Binder to call another witness while he had his law clerk research the issue.

Al Binder called Lois Evans, victim Alfred Evans' mother. Although she was a victim's mother, we had not called her as a witness since she denied that her son Alfred was dead. As Binder questioned her, she said she didn't know whether Alfred was dead or alive. She had looked at a body in the medical examiner's office but couldn't tell if it was her son. She did, however, identify a photograph of her son taken not long before his death.

The next witness was Donald Wright, who, like Kenneth Lawson, had briefly been a police recruit, answering phones at the Task Force. He said Freddie Jacobs talked about ghosts. He had seen Nellie Trammel at the Task Force office, where she would come in and knit and have long conversations with one of the officers there. Wright had worked at the Task Force for just a few months, from January to April of 1981.

Lewis Slaton cross-examined Wright, who had resigned on April 12, 1981, two weeks *before* the first bridge detail and long before Jacobs had ever served on such a detail. Slaton showed Wright a group of photographs, and Wright identified photo number two as Nellie Trammel. Slaton asked Wright if he would be surprised to know that the woman whose photo he chose was *not* Nellie Trammel, but the mother of one of the Task Force officers who often waited at the Task Force for her daughter.

Judge Cooper had now decided to allow former Detective J. B. Wilhoyt back on the witness stand to be questioned about what Dr. Zaki told him. This made me nervous. I wondered if Wilhoyt might have some vendetta against Zaki or his former employer. To my great relief, Wilhoyt confirmed exactly what Zaki had said, that Jimmy Ray Payne had died from asphyxia, mechanism unknown, and there was no trauma to the body that would rule out drowning. Zaki had already testified that under normal circumstances, he would not have ruled out drowning, but that in his opinion, the death was a homicide. The circumstances surrounding Payne's disappearance and death and the evidence found on his body made that apparent. Nothing Wilhoyt said was inconsistent with what Zaki had testified earlier.

On Tuesday, February 9, Jim Kitchens presented more defense witnesses. Michael Bucki was a freelance reporter who claimed to know how to make sound recordings, having worked in the radio industry. He and some defense investigators had recorded sounds of the expansion joint on the James Jackson Parkway Bridge by putting a tape recorder along the riverbank and driving a car over the bridge at different speeds. Bucki admitted that the car he used was not similar to Wayne Williams' station wagon and that it was freezing cold when they conducted the test. He had no idea if it duplicated what Robert Campbell might have heard from under the bridge.

Before Kitchens could call any further witnesses about sound tests, I approached the bench and objected to any testimony relating to experiments. The witness had already admitted that the conditions were unlike the conditions on May 22, 1981, and none of the people conducting the test were experts of any kind. Al Binder joined our group at the bench, complaining that we had been allowed to put in evidence from experiments. Judge Cooper said there would be a hearing outside the presence of the jury before any test results could be considered.

Binder and Kitchens took turns arguing in favor of admitting the tape recording. I pointed out that the issue was not the recording, it was its reliability as an experiment. The tape was made under different conditions as to temperature and size of the vehicle, the speedometer on the vehicle used had never been calibrated, and the only indications of speed were whatever the driver announced during his experiment. This was hardly a scientific test. In regard to the tape, the volume on the tape, if it were played, depended on simply turning the knob on the tape recorder. Playing it at high volume would make the expansion joint seem easier to hear, and playing it at low volume would make it harder to hear. This would prove nothing.

The only real issue was whether Robert Campbell could hear the sound of the expansion joint at the time of the stakeout on the bridge. Unless one had knowledge of Campbell's hearing ability, no experiment would have any meaning. Without having a baseline of Campbell's hearing level and a valid objective comparison, the proposed experiment was worthless.

Cooper had heard enough. We were beginning to repeat ourselves, each time a little louder. Cooper took a brief recess. When he returned, he announced that the experiment was substantially different from the event in question and that it would be misleading for the jury to hear it.

The defense now moved to another experiment, which Cooper permitted, though it was no better than the last. David Rufus Dingle was a hydrologist who had, for a time, assisted Benjamin Kittle, our expert from the Army Corps of Engineers, in a study of river currents and their effects on a dead body.

Dingle was concerned that there was a supplemental report completed after he submitted his data. He disagreed with that supplemental report, issued in December of 1981, because it had not considered the I-285 bridge as a possible point from which Cater and Payne could have been dropped into the river. The report disregarded the I-285 bridge simply because eyewitnesses had seen the two bodies floating in the river at a point *before* they reached the I-285 bridge. Despite the impossibility that the bodies had been dropped from that bridge, Dingle still wanted the bridge to be considered as an entry point for the bodies.

When the Corps of Engineers rejected his offers, he offered to help the defense. On his own, he conducted tests with a floating mannequin, with a submerged mannequin, and with oranges, a test unlike anything ever done to observe river currents. He said he was not concerned with the movements of an actual decomposing body dropped in a river or with any actual sightings of the bodies of Nathaniel Cater or Jimmy Ray Payne. His dummies either floated on the surface, like a balloon, or they dropped to the river bottom like a rock. The ones that went to the bottom just lay there. His floating mannequin was a stiff blow-up dummy that floated on its back with arms at its side. Some of the dummies and some of the oranges made it to where Cater and Payne had been found; some did not. None were actually dropped from the bridge at the spot where Wayne Williams' car had stopped. Instead, Dingle released his dummies from alongside a boat. Dingle even had a slide show. The jury did not seem overly impressed. Like me, they were probably trying to figure out what the point of all this might be since Cater and Payne had been seen floating down the river, and there was no doubt about where their bodies had been recovered.

Dingle was unaware that a later study of the Chattahoochee River, a United States Geological Survey, showed a current at Cross-section "K" in the river, just past the I-285 bridge. This cross-current would pull objects to the left, precisely where Cater and Payne's bodies were seen moving from the Cobb County side of the river toward the left side of the river, the Fulton County side. The report concluded that "this is consistent with the fact that Cater's body was discovered on the left bank."

It was late afternoon, and the flow of the trial was interrupted. Binder and Welcome had issued subpoenas for former United States Attorney Dorothy Kirkley and the FBI's special agent in charge of the Atlanta office, John Glover. A lawyer from the United States Attorney's Criminal Division filed motions to quash the subpoenas and was in court ready to explain why the subpoenas were defective. A lawyer from the Georgia Attorney General's Office also stood before the judge, as Binder and Welcome had issued subpoenas for Governor George Busbee, Attorney General Arthur Bolton, GBI Director Phil Peters, and Governor Busbee's executive counsel, Charlie Tidwell. None of these state officials had any information relevant to the prosecution of Wayne Williams. Binder argued that the governor had interjected himself in the prosecution in a meeting with Lewis Slaton in June of 1981. Subpoenas had also been issued for Mayor Maynard Jackson and an Atlanta Police sketch artist, Marla Lawson. Judge Cooper said he would rule on the matters the next morning.

Mary Welcome announced that she had another motion, to have the court arrange to take the jury out to see the James Jackson Parkway Bridge. I explained the logistical problems involved in taking the jury on this kind of "field trip," although I conceded that it was entirely within the discretion of the judge. It was unnecessary for the jury to see the actual bridge since we had recreated the bridge with a large-scale model which sat before the jury. Mary Welcome clarified that all she was asking was for the jury to go see the bridge, and nothing more. Like other motions the judge had just heard, he said he would let us know in the morning how he would rule.

Finally, we resumed testimony from David Rufus Dingle. It dragged on, finally concluding before lunchtime.

When court resumed after a lunch break, Jerry Hightower, from the National Park Service, testified that there were a lot of beavers in the Chattahoochee River and that they flap their tails and make a splashing noise. Lewis Slaton rose and said, "If they are making the point that there are beavers out there, we'll stipulate it." Hightower attempted to show a slide show with photos along the river, but his slide projector wouldn't work. Jim Kitchens tried to get Hightower to offer an opinion on how long it takes for a dead body to surface after being dropped in a river, but we objected, given that Hightower knew nothing about hydrology or the decomposition rate of human bodies.

Mary Welcome questioned Mike Gurley, a diver with the Fulton County Fire Department, who had searched for a body under the James Jackson Parkway Bridge on Saturday morning, May 23, 1981. He started upstream from the bridge and went thirty-five to forty feet past the bridge and didn't find anything. Gurley admitted that he thought a body had been dropped from the bridge that *Saturday* morning, at 3:00 a.m., rather than Friday morning, and he didn't know that thirty-one hours had already elapsed before he and his crew got to the search site. He also acknowledged that they were just looking "under the bridge" and had no idea where a body was supposed to have been dropped.

Mary Welcome then called a helicopter pilot as a witness who had flown over the area at the same time the dive team was looking under the bridge. Robert Ingram, an Atlanta Police helicopter pilot, had seen no bodies or other objects in the river. However, he looked only in the area right around the bridge, and he could see only the very center of the river. Overhanging trees blocked his vision on either side of the river. Lewis Slaton said, "No questions!"

Wayne Williams' optometrist testified that Wayne had poor eyesight—he is nearsighted. With glasses, he has 20/20 vision. Slaton again said, "No questions!"

Al Binder called Keith Andrews, the husband and co-owner of Atlanta Studios. Andrews confirmed that Williams had been in the studio in the late afternoon of Saturday, January 3, 1981. Lubie Geter had been reported missing that same day and had been seen with Williams by Ruth Warren and Daryl Davis. Binder was trying to show that Williams had an alibi if he was at Atlanta Studios when Geter was picked up. Unfortunately for Williams, all the witnesses remembered that the day they saw Williams and Geter together was on Friday, January 2, 1981, the day *before* Geter was reported missing.

Al Binder asked Keith Andrews if he had ever seen scratches on Wayne Williams' face, and he said no. I doubted that Binder would ask about scratches on Wayne's arms, but after a few other questions, Binder took a chance and asked if Andrews had ever seen scratches on Wayne Williams' hands or arms. Andrews remembered the scratches and remembered that they were on Williams' forearms, "either one or mostly both." Our evidence had been reinforced, and Slaton again said, "No questions!"

Slaton at this point was wisely minimizing the impact of defense testimony. The testimony hadn't really hurt our case, and there was no reason to keep going over it. And there was the hope that the jury would conclude that the evidence was of no importance if we didn't even ask a question about it.

The last witness of the day was Paul Crawley, a reporter from Channel 11 News, WXIA-TV, the NBC affiliate. Crawley had talked to Margaret Carter in August of 1981 about her sighting of Wayne Williams in a park with Nathaniel Cater. Crawley said Margaret Carter was confused as to the exact date when she saw Cater and Williams together, but she was certain she had seen them together before Cater's death. We weren't sure why the defense put Crawley on the stand.

Cliff Bailey approached me as we left court and told me that they wouldn't need to keep looking in the boxes of evidence—they had found a photograph they had been searching for. I wondered just what photograph they had found and what it would mean to our case.

On Thursday morning, February 11, court convened early, and Judge Cooper asked if the exhibits that David Rufus Dingle had used were going to be offered in evidence by the defense. Mary Welcome said they were not offering the blow-up dummies that had floated down the river, but they did want to offer the report that Dingle had prepared. Jack told the judge we would like to review it before he made a decision.

Edward Mays, the half-brother of victim JoJo Bell, was the first defense witness that day. He and JoJo had the same mother, Doris Mays Bell. Mays had gone looking for JoJo, and he talked to Lugene Laster, who had testified earlier in the trial. Laster had seen JoJo leave the outdoor basketball court where they were playing ball. Jim Kitchens now wanted to impeach the testimony of Lugene Laster by showing that Laster never mentioned Wayne Williams or a station wagon when he was questioned by police. To "impeach" a witness is to contradict a statement made by the witness, thus reducing the credibility of that witness. Jack stood to explain why the evidence was not admissible. Al Binder joined Kitchens in the argument as Jack explained that to impeach a witness you had to confront the witness with the statement he was supposed to have made. The witness could not be impeached on a statement he had never been asked about. Cooper took a brief recess to look at the authority presented and returned moments later, saying, "No proper foundation has been laid for this testimony. If you want to use that testimony, you will have to recall Mr. Laster." That was not something the defense wanted to do.

Judge Cooper then announced to all assembled in the court-room that he would be allowing the jury to visit the James Jackson Parkway Bridge— we would be taking a field trip.

The jury was invited back into the courtroom, and Jim Kitchens resumed his questioning of Edward Mays. Mays said he had never seen Wayne Williams around his half brother, JoJo Bell. Jack had no questions, and the witness quietly stepped down from the witness stand.

Binder now started calling Wayne Williams' friends to the wit-ness stand, and I was perplexed by much of what followed. Based on their testimony, it seemed that Williams was defending him-self against the suggestion that he was gay as much as he was defending against a charge of murder. We really didn't care if he was gay.

Howard Peoples, thirty years old, said Wayne had helped him with his singing career and had never made any sexual advances; he thought Wayne was a nice fellow. Jack announced, "I don't believe there're any questions of this witness."

Carolyn Bailey had known Wayne Williams for thirteen years, and he helped her with her singing. She thought Wayne seemed knowledgeable, he didn't smoke or drink, always wore glasses, and she had never known him to brag or exaggerate. Williams sometimes borrowed her burgundy Chevy Camero with a black vinyl top. Bailey admitted that Williams had no job and lived off his parents. Though she now claimed he had dated her sister, Gwen Hardin, she acknowledged that she had told the police ear-lier that Williams never dated anyone.

Thirty-year-old Kenneth Wright ran a recording studio where Williams was a regular customer. Wright didn't think Williams was homosexual because he would make crude comments about women. Williams, he said, used the N-word but the term, he thought, could be used in an endearing way among Blacks. From the bench, Cooper admonished Kitchens and Binder about having witnesses refrain from using the N-word.

Kitchens tried to get the witness to talk about what Jack and I had discussed with him when we interviewed him. Jack objected. Kitchens seemed to back off. After talking with Al Binder, Kitchens renewed his efforts to have this witness share what we discussed with him. Mary Welcome now joined the fray. I rose to remind Judge Cooper that "we have not testified, so we can't be impeached." Kitchens was trying to make it look like we only wanted witnesses who would say something bad about Williams, and while that may have been generally true, it was not relevant. While the judge took a short recess, Kitchens decided against going forward with that line of questioning, and Kenneth Wright stepped off the witness stand.

Now came a witness we had long wanted to hear from: Willie Hunter. Witness after witness had described this thin young Black man who often was in the company of Wayne Williams.

Thirty-two-year-old Willie Hunter bragged that he was a leader in the entertainment business and was on a music advisory committee set up by the Georgia State Senate—as if that was a validation of his greatness. Having long worked with the Georgia General Assembly, I knew that being on an advisory committee was only slightly more prestigious than being a subscriber to *National Geographic* magazine. Hunter also professed that "In my lifetime, I have never exaggerated!"

Hunter said he was trying to help the inexperienced Williams, who was a "business acquaintance" and looked up to Hunter. Hunter was impressed that Williams had operated a small radio station and had interviewed him for a program.

Hunter denied that he had been referred to as a psychiatrist by Williams, but "he may have mentioned that I did some counseling and some advising." As Hunter testified, one thing became clear: Willie Hunter was trying to distance himself from Wayne Williams. He denied attending auditions with Williams and said he had known him for only a short time. He said he was unfamiliar with Williams' business dealings and denied ever being a coproducer with him. As I glanced over at Williams, he appeared rattled at the way Willie Hunter was denying any associations with him. Binder said, "My client has told me to ask you, were you on some type of committee that was helping him set up these auditions?" Hunter denied that he was ever on any committee. Binder backed off, saying, "I appreciate you talking with me today."

Jack Mallard questioned Hunter, who said he was unfamiliar with Gwen Hardin, whom Carolyn Bailey had said was dating Wayne. Hunter claimed Williams didn't exaggerate but was just "overly optimistic." When shown Williams' inflated résumé, Hunter still said he believed whatever Wayne said. He conceded that Williams' radio station broadcast for a distance of just a few blocks and that it was a tiny operation out of a utility room in the family home. Hunter admitted that he had been in frequent contact with Williams during the first half of 1981, right before Wayne was arrested, and that he and Williams had talked on the phone numerous times since Williams had been in the Fulton County Jail.

Judge Cooper let the jury go for the day and turned his attention to the subpoenas for Mayor Maynard Jackson and police sketch artist Marla Lawson. A lawyer from the City of Atlanta Law Department challenged the relevancy of anything Maynard Jackson might know. The mayor knew nothing about the guilt or innocence of Wayne Williams. In regard to sketch artist Marla Lawson, Binder had subpoenaed "all composite drawings" made during the missing and murdered children's case. This was overly broad, city lawyers argued.

Binder was indignant and said all he wanted were composites showing that other people had been suspects, and Wayne Williams was not among them. Cooper reminded Binder that he had already been given every composite drawing related to the cases being considered during the trial—he already had what he was asking for. Cooper said he would rule later on the matter, and we recessed for the day.

I began Friday, February 12, with a brief discussion with Judge

Cooper's law clerk regarding our visit to the James Jackson Parkway Bridge. My concern was to avoid any legal problems or logistical difficulties. I suggested that we have the entire area secured and make sure that no one but jurors went on the bridge. I assured the clerk that I would be there on behalf of the prosecution team.

In court, Al Binder announced his next witness, a mysterious man named Maurice Rogoff. Rogoff was an exotic character with an eye patch and a face lined with age and experience. He was a doctor for the Israeli Army and spoke with an accent unfamiliar, I was sure, to most of the jury. He had degrees in medicine and surgery from the University of Cape Town, was licensed in forensic pathology in Israel, and had studied in London and in Kenya, where he had been former president Jomo Kenyatta's personal physician.

Rogoff was obviously there to fill the gap left by Dr. Dan Stowens' poor showing. Unlike Stowens, Rogoff had performed autopsies on drowning victims and victims of asphyxia. He had also looked at photographs of the victims in our case, in addition to reviewing autopsies.

Jurors seemed to be having trouble understanding Dr. Rogoff's accent, which appeared to be Russian or eastern European. Judge Cooper asked the jury about it, with one juror saying he didn't get the witness' name. Al Binder spelled it out for the jury, and Rogoff said, "I apologize if I go too fast or my accent is too bad."

Al Binder now tried to show, through Dr. Rogoff, that blood bank records where Nathaniel Cater gave blood were somehow fabricated to indicate that he had been there on May 21, 1981. Al claimed he had been there only on May 19, 1981, three days before the bridge incident and five days before his body was found in the river. We all approached the bench, and Binder and I ended up in an animated argument. Mary Welcome tried to jump into the conversation, but Cooper intervened, saying, "Let's recess. You get together calmly!" The long trial was wearing on all of us. Not only was it stressful, but being locked in uninterrupted legal combat for extended periods made it difficult to maintain civility.

After Jack and I talked with Binder and showed him that Cater really was at the blood bank on May 21, 1981, he withdrew his allegations of forged blood bank records. Maybe that would put to rest any doubts raised by Dr. Stowens' testimony four days earlier about how long Nathaniel Cater had been in the river. After the recess, Judge Cooper told Rogoff he could talk about his findings, but not about any forged blood bank records.

Rogoff suggested that Nathaniel Cater "might" have died from an enlarged heart, and he thought Cater's body should not have surfaced in the river for four or five days. Although he conceded that there were hemorrhages in the tissue of Cater's neck, he still said he couldn't exclude drowning as the cause of death. He would provide no conclusion as to what actually happened to Cater or to Payne.

Rogoff's testimony had taken all morning, and during the lunch recess, we had an opportunity to check up on some of what Rogoff said and a brief period to try to counter his testimony. Rogoff seemed credible, and we certainly didn't want the jury to begin thinking that there really were no murders here—just some random people popping up in rivers naked.

Our lunch break research was fruitful, as Rogoff was simply wrong on much of what he had said, and just wrong enough that we might be able to undermine his conclusions. Jack pointed out how little Rogoff knew about the murders. Like Stowens, he had based almost everything he said on the written autopsy reports. He had seen only two photographs of Cater and Payne just hours earlier in the courtroom. He had not talked to any of the investigators, nor had he met with any of the medical examiners.

Rogoff admitted that many of the tests for drowning he had discussed had no validity if a body had been in the river for more than twenty-four hours, and he acknowledged that hemorrhaging around the neck could not occur after death, since the heart would no longer be pumping blood. The ligature marks on Cater's neck were the result of strangulation and could not have been caused by floating in the Chattahoochee River.

Rogoff had also assumed the wrong temperatures for the

Chattahoochee River in making his calculations. The water was much warmer when Cater's body went into the river, which would cause his body to rise much faster than Rogoff asserted. He admitted that the blood bank records showed Nathaniel Cater had tried to give blood on May 21, 1981, the afternoon before his murder and a little more than three days before his body was pulled from the river.

Binder was jumping up frequently with objections to interrupt the flow of Jack's cross-examination, as Rogoff was looking fallible, and his lack of knowledge about the case was becoming evident. He was an impressive witness, but he was unable to back up what he said.

The court took a short recess, and the judge invited us into his chambers, along with Wayne Williams. Binder said Williams was waiving his presence at the jury visit to the bridge. Williams acknowledged Binder's statement and agreed that he was waiving his presence.

Binder then changed the subject, possibly out of fear that we could do yet more damage to the testimony of Dr. Rogoff, who was still on the stand. "Your honor, the prosecutor says he has no further questions. May we ask that this witness be excused, period?" I responded that we had no further questions of Dr. Rogoff. We were happy to see him go.

The judge returned to the bench, and we resumed hearing defense witnesses. Nathaniel Cater's brother, Anthony Cater, answered questions from Mary Welcome. According to the brother, Nathaniel was drunk or on drugs most of the time, and Anthony had last seen him on the Saturday before he disappeared. When he talked to Nathaniel a few days later, Nathaniel said he would see Anthony on Wednesday, his birthday, or on Friday. He never saw his brother Nathaniel again. We had no questions for cross-examination.

John Henley, Cater's roommate from the Falcon Hotel, testified that he had never seen Cater holding hands with any men.

On cross-examination, Henley told Jack he had last seen Cater on Thursday, May 21, 1981. Jack asked if Cater had a nickname, which he did: they called him Silky. And Henley knew Robert I. Henry, the man who had seen Silky holding hands with Wayne Williams.

Now Mary Welcome responded with a few more questions. She asked about Robert I. Henry: "Could you tell us whether or not he's reliable or unreliable?"

She expected a different answer and probably didn't like the answer John Henley gave. "I guess reliable," he said. Mary suggested Henley was lying and told the judge she wanted to impeach her witness. Jack objected, and Judge Cooper reminded her that she could not call a witness and then try to show that her own witness was lying.

The defense continued with a string of witnesses on relatively inconsequential matters, defending Wayne Williams against a perceived "accusation" of homosexuality, in addition to trying to chip away at our case. I began wondering whether Williams was going to testify. Only rarely can a defendant help his own case by testifying, but juries expect to hear from a person accused of a crime. A criminal defendant doesn't usually "win" by testifying. He can then be cross-examined, and after that, most people are lucky to get a "draw" and survive without serious damage to their defense.

Back in the courtroom, we resumed testimony as Gwen Hardin took the stand. She had been described by her sister Carolyn Bailey as having "dated" Wayne Williams. Binder led her through what appeared to be a well-rehearsed but painfully awkward presentation. She had known Wayne for eleven years and had worked with him on his radio station. Her answers to questions were short, staccato yes or no responses. Al asked if she had ever been to "a picture show" alone with Wayne Williams.

"Yes," she said.

Then Al asked a series of questions to which she robotically responded each time, "Yes, he did."

Al asked, "Did he ever kiss you?" "Did he have affection for you?" Then he got to the final question: "Have you ever been intimate with him, have you had sex with him?"

She responded with the same flat affect that she had had with other questions, saying, "Yes, I did." Al had no more questions.

Jack had just one question for Gwen Hardin. Did she remember telling the FBI that Wayne Williams had no girlfriend? She remembered talking to the FBI and acknowledged that she had told them he had no girlfriend. I glanced over at the jury, and two or three jurors were shaking their heads.

By this time, it was nearing 4:30 on a Friday afternoon, and Judge Cooper told the jury it was too late to call any more witnesses. Tomorrow, they were told, they would visit the James Jackson Parkway Bridge. We had all reviewed and approved precisely what the judge would tell the jury about the bridge visit. Cooper explained that they would simply be able to see what the bridge looked like and nothing more. They could speak to no one, and no one would speak to them.

As court recessed, we met with Cooper in his chambers, where Binder announced that he was considering calling a psychologist who would testify that, in his expert opinion, Wayne Williams was not the kind of person who would be a serial killer. Al was obviously unaware that a new FBI unit had been studying serial killers for years and had provided the Task Force with a profile of Atlanta's killer. Before Williams was even a suspect, the FBI's Behavioral Science Unit had suggested that the killer would be someone just like Wayne, a frustrated only child who had failed at most endeavors and who was relatively bright and articulate, but a low achiever. He would have a history of frequent changes in employment or self-employment, and he would closely follow the murders, show up at crime scenes, or attend funerals, and change his modus operandi to suit his needs. He might also be a police buff, and although he might project superiority and confidence, he would have personal feelings of inadequacy. The FBI profile was wrong in one respect, as it suggested that the killer would be slightly older, and Wayne Williams was just twenty-three.

John Douglas was the coordinator of the Criminal Psychological Profiling Program in the Behavioral Science Unit and had occupied a seat directly behind me on a long bench that backed up to the railing separating the court from the spectators' area. Douglas had been quietly observing Wayne Williams as the trial wound down. No one particularly noticed him, seated as he was with some of our investigators and staff. John and his team had prepared an eight-page paper on serial killers for us, with suggestions on how to proceed if Williams took the witness stand.

After Al Binder made his announcement, I made one of my own: "Judge, if Al brings in a psychologist to say Wayne Williams doesn't fit the profile of a serial killer, I will bring in a witness who has studied serial killers for years to say Wayne Williams fits the profile of a classic serial killer."

Al thought I was bluffing, saying, "Who is this so-called expert on serial killers?"

I replied, "His name is John Douglas, and he is with the FBI's Behavioral Science Unit. His unit has studied hosts of serial killers, and he had been studying Wayne Williams for some time. He has been sitting right behind me. Would you like to meet him?"

Al's response was immediate: "Oh, shit!"

I explained that John was sitting outside in the courtroom and offered to introduce him to Al. Judge Cooper excused us from his chambers, and I took the pair downstairs to the vacant Grand Jury room. I left them together to have a chat. After that chat, the defense apparently abandoned the idea of presenting a psychologist to testify.

On Saturday morning, Mary Welcome offered to pick me up at the courthouse, and we rode to the bridge together, exchanging small talk. We arrived a little after 8:00 a.m. on that overcast and chilly morning. Access to the bridge was closed to the public, but we were permitted to park near the end of the bridge, on the Fulton County side, in a position to watch as the busload of jurors arrived. We were near the spot where Freddie Jacobs crouched in the bushes and watched Wayne Williams make a U-turn and head back across the bridge.

The bus arrived with jurors, Judge Cooper, and court reporter Susan Northington, and at 8:30 a.m., Cooper repeated his instructions to the jurors and let them file off the bus and onto the bridge. Patrol cars blocked access to the bridge from both ends, and news crews lined up on both sides of the river, perched on the tops of vans and anything else they could climb on. Media representatives, court staff, law clerks, and numerous deputies and police officers milled about, with nothing in particular to do, as hordes of gawkers took up positions along the river on both sides, peeking from trees and any perch that would give them a view. Multiple news helicopters hovered directly above the bridge, their noises making conversation difficult.

I asked Judge Cooper, who was now standing with us at the end of the bridge, to make sure no one but the jury went onto the bridge. Two bailiffs had wandered onto the bridge with the jury, and Cooper quickly got them to scurry back to where we stood. Cooper cautioned jurors not to converse or to point at anything.

The jurors wandered on the bridge, some looking down over the low railing at the river and some walking partway out on the bridge and then back toward the warm bus that awaited them. Others were looking at the metal expansion joint and the area where a body had been dropped. Some glanced at the narrow sidewalk.

After a short time, jurors started back toward our end of the bridge. Some wanted to see where Officer Carl Holden had been hiding in his unmarked police car near the abandoned liquor store. Cooper directed all the court personnel and law enforcement officers out of the way to clear a path for the jurors. Some jurors went behind the liquor store for a view and checked out the old pay phone on the side of the abandoned store. After looking at everything they wanted to see, jurors were now milling around aimlessly. It was time for the jury to return to the bus.

The judge corralled the group and escorted them back to the bus, which backed up, turned around in the same parking lot where Wayne Williams had made a U-turn on May 22, 1981, and headed to the hotel, where they would continue their sequestration. The court reporter noted that the proceedings on the bridge concluded at 9:17 a.m.

Mary Welcome dropped me back at the office, where Jack, Gordon, Wally, and I went over information about witnesses we expected the defense to call during the coming week. There was now a rhythm to our activities, and each of us knew his job. The jitters of the first few days of trial were long gone, and it was a matter of grinding on in what seemed like an endless trial. We repeated the process in abbreviated fashion the next day, Valentine's Day, and we all spent a little extra time at home. The trial was an all-consuming obsession, and after being immersed in the process for nearly seven weeks, it was all I could think about.

Chapter 16

THE DEFENSE GRINDS ON

The Trial—Week Seven

On Monday, February 15, another week began, and Israel Green, a member of the Techwood Homes "Bat Patrol," took the stand for the defense. The Bat Patrol was the vigilante group organized during the murders to protect residents of the Techwood Homes housing project. Green was called for one purpose, to say that he didn't see Wayne Williams at the press conference announcing the formation of the group. Nellie Trammel, a witness the defense particularly feared, had testified that she saw Williams get out of a station wagon with a camera on the day of the Bat Patrol news conference. Green said he had no idea what might've gone on outside the room where they held the press conference. Jack asked Green if he was "aware that while Wayne Williams was under surveillance . . . he came over there to the Techwood Homes area?"

Green said he didn't remember, adding, "I decline to answer any more questions under the Fifth Amendment!" I wasn't sure what to make of his invocation of the Fifth Amendment, and I suspect the jury wondered too.

Jimmy Ray Payne's twenty-four-year-old sister, Evelyn, was

called to the stand as Jim Kitchens attempted to get her to say she had been threatened by a former boyfriend and therefore thought maybe the former boyfriend had killed her brother. Jack objected. A threat against *her* was irrelevant. Judge Cooper pressed Kitchens on any possible reason to allow the testimony. Kitchens had none.

Faith Swift, a twenty-three-year-old friend of Williams, had known him for three years and said he was a flirt. He didn't like gay people and called them "twinkies," she said. Jack elicited that Swift had met Williams at the Omni and had seen him there two or three times. Swift admitted that she and Carla Bailey had spent time at the Williams home and that they had even been there "last night," the very evening before she testified. She refused to answer when Jack pressed her about what cars she had seen Williams driving.

Clara Howard was the mother of Jimmy Howard, a teenage acquaintance of Williams. Mary Welcome asked Ms. Howard how she felt about Wayne Williams. Jack objected to questions about feelings. Welcome persisted, Cooper intervened, and she finally abandoned that line of questioning.

Jim Kitchens called Ms. Howard's seventeen-year-old son, Jimmy Howard, to the stand. Williams had auditioned him, picking him up in a Ford Fairmont rental car. Jimmy said he later saw Wayne in a white station wagon. He didn't think Williams was a homosexual.

Al Binder now questioned Carla Bailey, another of Williams' friends. She berated Kent Hindsman, who had earlier testified for the State. She denied that JoJo Bell had been in Wayne Williams' car with her and Hindsman. She had never seen scratches on Wayne Williams' face or hands, she said. Like previous defense witnesses, she said Wayne didn't like gay people and called them "twinkies."

After a lunch break, we cross-examined Carla Bailey, who admitted she had just spent the previous evening with Homer and Faye Williams. She claimed to hang out with Williams almost daily, yet she said she had seen Willie Hunter only once, and she had never been in any of Wayne's police-type cars. She was unco-operative on cross-examination and refused to answer some ques-tions. She also disavowed the detailed statement she had earlier made to the FBI.

Fourteen-year-old Stewart Flemister had been interviewed by Wayne Williams when he was just twelve years old. Williams made some demo tapes, and Stewart remembered being picked up in a tan Ford Fairmont, a rental car, and a burgundy Ford LTD. We had no questions of Flemister.

Stewart's mother, Shirley Flemister, said that she was not afraid of Wayne Williams and that she had never heard him say bad things about Black people. She described a time when Wayne brought a poor, depressed fifteen-year-old over to her house, and Williams told him he had much to live for. Neither Ms. Flemister nor her son had seen Williams since early 1980, some two years earlier.

Fire Department Investigator Joe Haynie was called by the defense to testify that years earlier, Williams had offered the department photos he had taken at fires. Some of the photos may have been from arson cases, but the fire department had never bought any pictures from Williams. Haynie had not seen Williams since 1978, four years earlier. Mary Welcome asked Haynie if Williams had done anything to indicate that he was homosexual. Haynie seemed perplexed by the question, and so did the jury.

Lula Burns' son was auditioned by Williams, and she said she never had problems with him when he visited them in Techwood Homes. She had seen Williams in a blue Plymouth, a burgundy LTD, a small green car, and a white station wagon. In 1979, she let her son Broderick Burns go to Los Angeles for a one-day trip with Williams, who was supposed to be taking a demo tape to someone.

Broderick, seventeen, said he was in Wayne Williams' Gemini group—but he didn't seem to know the names of any other mem-bers. He didn't know Jimmy Howard, a member of the group who had testified a few hours earlier. Broderick said they practiced sometimes at Williams' house and sometimes they just watched

TV. Broderick went on an overnight trip to California with Williams, who told him he was delivering a cassette tape to someone he knew. The trip was uneventful.

I was getting bored with the defense witnesses, and I expect the jury was too. The string of witnesses continued, as an entertainment attorney testified that fewer than 3 percent of entertainers actually make money. I guess he was there to explain Williams' failure as a music promoter. The lawyer had never met Wayne Williams.

When Williams' uncle, Ralph Barnhart, was called to the stand, Wayne Williams suddenly became ill, requiring medical attention. He was rushed to a restroom, and after about thirty minutes, Cooper recessed the trial for the day. Williams seemed frustrated.

Tuesday morning, February 16, began with a conference in Judge Cooper's chambers. Binder and Welcome wanted a new fiber expert to have access to the fiber evidence at the crime lab. I reminded the judge that for over three months they had complained about needing more access for their fiber expert, Charles Morton. Cooper had given Morton additional time to go to the lab, even as the trial moved on. Now, twelve days after we rested our case, the defense wanted to start over with a new expert.

I argued that it was too late for a do-over. Cooper wanted to know what happened to Charles Morton, and Al danced around the issue, saying that he was in contact with Morton but was unsure if he would be able to come back from California. I was pretty sure what that meant—Morton had looked at the evidence and was unlikely to disagree with our three experts. Morton was a respected expert. An objective analysis of the evidence was unlikely to help Wayne Williams. We suspected that Morton had been dismissed by the defense and sent home.

Binder said his new expert would only need one day in the lab, as he was not going into detail on cases like Morton did, and there would be no delay to the trial. Gordon Miller now chimed in, saying that the new expert was not a fiber analyst, he was a college professor from Kansas and had never been a witness in a criminal case, and he might not even qualify as an expert in fiber comparison. Cooper wanted to think about what he had heard.

We returned to the courtroom, and Williams' uncle, Ralph Barnhart, was again called to the stand. We had already stipulated, at the beginning of the trial, that Barnhart had loaned the Williams family his white 1970 Chevy station wagon on October 20, 1980. Ralph Barnhart had nothing to add. Jurors seemed really bored. Like me, they probably wanted to hear some substantive testimony, perhaps from Williams or his parents.

Jim Kitchens called a witness named Joseph Bell, implying that witnesses may have been confused about which Joseph Bell they saw with Williams. Victim JoJo Bell had been pulled from the South River dead of asphyxia. This Joseph Bell had been interviewed by Wayne Williams in 1980 but had never been to the Williams home, never been in Williams' car, and he didn't go by the nickname "JoJo." On cross-examination, this Joseph Bell said that a man named Willie Hunter had been with Williams when they met, and that Williams claimed to have hypnotized Bell. Bell had last seen Williams in the summer of 1980, almost a year before the disappearance and murder of victim JoJo Bell.

Charlotte Stephens cooked hot dogs at a Sambo's restaurant in DeKalb County and saw Terry Pue in the restaurant after she had seen his picture on a flyer. He was sitting with a man other than Wayne Williams. Jack Mallard brought out that this was well before Pue was found dead. In addition, Pue had been seen alive in the days after his visit to the Sambo's restaurant.

Wayne Williams' seventh-grade social science teacher, Archie Wilson, said Williams was a good student. Jack objected as to the relevance of this testimony. Welcome and Binder said they just wanted to show that Williams had had a radio station when he was a kid. Cooper permitted Mary to continue, but Wilson really didn't know much of anything about Wayne Williams.

The judge, sensing a lull, recessed and had the jury escorted out. Cooper then announced his rulings on the various subpoenas for the governor, the United States attorney, the mayor, and other officials. He granted all the motions to quash the subpoenas, except the one for Marla Lawson, the sketch artist. She would be required to produce her drawings, but only the ones regarding the twelve victims.

Al Binder called Terry McMullen, a photographer at the crime scene where Terry Pue's body was found. McMullen said he had given his card to a deputy and a state trooper at the scene. This conflicted with the testimony of a Rockdale County deputy at the Pue crime scene, who said he saw Williams at the scene with a camera. McMullen took pictures at the Pue crime scene and at Lubie Geter's funeral, and he had not seen Wayne Williams at either place. McMullen, who bore no resemblance to Wayne Williams, admitted that he got to the scene between 11 a.m. and noon and that the body of Pue had been discovered at 7:30 that morning.

Al Binder now wanted to call sketch artist Marla Lawson to talk about her drawings, but she was not present in court. Binder accused me of telling the witness not to come to court. I had not spoken to her. Court recessed until 1 p.m. so that Al Binder could come up with some other witnesses.

After lunch, Al complained that Gordon Miller was blocking Jim Kitchens and Randall Bresee, the new defense fiber witness, from looking through the fiber evidence that had already been admitted in evidence. Gordon had earlier told deputies not to let spectators touch any evidence. Al and Gordon argued and raised their voices until Cooper said, "Let's not bicker about that. I'm sure Gordon has no problems with allowing the man to see it so long as he doesn't touch it."

With the jury out of the room, Cooper told us that the jury was getting restless. We would begin having testimony on Saturdays, to speed things up. The jury, he said, "was becoming very bored with all this." To speed things up, Judge Cooper said he would allow the new defense fiber witness, Randall Bresee, to have one-day access to the crime lab.

Given the concerns he had just expressed, Judge Cooper wanted to get moving again with testimony. Mary Welcome called another relatively unimportant witness: Aisha Nanji. She taught "news writing" part-time and had a public relations firm. Jack questioned the relevance of Ms. Nanji. Welcome said she knew Williams and had met him at a press party. Judge Cooper was becoming impatient with irrelevant evidence. Mary then elicited from Ms. Nanji that, in her opinion, Sharon Blakely had a reputation for dishonesty and unfair dealing. We had no questions for the witness.

Mike Lawrence, who worked at WSB-TV, the local ABC affiliate, testified that Williams seemed eager to learn and had helped folks get into the music business. He was impressed that Williams had operated his radio station out of a utility room, though it was very small and did not require an FCC license. Lawrence knew Williams to be what he called a "night person," and he thought Williams had gotten paid for photos of fires and been dispatched by the police department to fire scenes. Lawrence had loaned Williams money to buy one of his Plymouth police-type vehicles.

Fulton County Commissioner A. Reginald Eaves served as commissioner of public safety years earlier and had stirred up considerable controversy in that role. Homer Williams had asked Eaves if his son, Wayne, could take some pictures for the arson squad and Eaves had referred him to someone in the fire bureau. Eaves knew nothing else about the case, but he assumed that Wayne must have taken some pictures.

Lester Butts, the principal of Douglass High School, took the stand to say that Wayne Williams' parents wanted him to attend Douglass, where Mrs. Williams had worked. Butts thought Wayne was a good student. Jack pointed out that this was simply "character evidence" and not evidence relating to the charges against Wayne Williams.

Finally, the defense was calling a witness who might have something relevant to the case. Binder called our police sketch artist, Marla Lawson. Marla was an identification technician and made composite drawings. She identified various of her drawings that had been based on descriptions from witnesses and psychics. Only the drawing based on Ruth Warren's description looked like

Wayne Williams. Warren was the witness who had seen Lubie Geter get in a car with Williams on the Friday before he was reported missing. Ms. Lawson said most of the other drawings were from psychics who had visions of what they thought the killer would look like.

Radio announcer Doug Candis remembered Williams' radio station, and although the station only broadcast about a block or block and a half from the Williams' home, he was impressed that such a young person would be involved in the venture. Candis also knew Williams as a news stringer, one who would be out filming news events after midnight.

After lunch, James Comento, a paramedic, testified that he knew Williams and would see him at accident scenes. Williams had emergency equipment in his cars, including a siren. He didn't think Williams was homosexual.

Wednesday, February 17, started with a conference in chambers, where we argued about whether the pile of Marla Lawson's composite sketches should be admitted in evidence. I went through the stack of sketches for the judge and pointed out that most of them were sketches of people tied to cases unrelated to the trial of Wayne Williams.

Back in the courtroom, Jim Kitchens called twenty-three-year-old Keith Knox, a former next-door neighbor to the Williamses. Knox was twelve years old when he, Wayne, and one other young man set up the little radio station in Wayne's house. He remembered Wayne's having the Plymouth Fury, a burgundy American Motors Matador, and a green Maverick. Knox didn't think Wayne was homosexual, nor had he ever heard him say derogatory things about poor Blacks.

Knox remembered the electrified fence around the backyard of the Williamses' house and could not recall Wayne ever dating any girls. Williams had taken him to Willie Hunter's apartment, and he added that Hunter was quite effeminate and made Knox very uncomfortable. Hunter and Williams talked about going "swashbuckling," and Knox wasn't quite sure what that meant. Right after the bridge incident, Knox was visiting Williams' house, and

Wayne was "cleaning out" items in his office in the back of the house and loading things into boxes.

Josephine Derrico was the mother of Stanley Derrico, one of Williams' Gemini group members. Williams was never violent around her, she said, and he didn't seem to be a homosexual. Her son Stanley testified next, saying that he knew JoJo Bell but hadn't seen him with Williams. Derrico was with Williams' group for six months, found the group to be poorly organized, and finally quit.

Judge Cooper suggested that Mary Welcome stop parading redundant witnesses to the witness stand. Nonetheless, the parade of inconsequential witnesses continued.

Jim Kitchens presented the next one, Sharon Phillips, a singing teacher at Martin Luther King, Jr. Middle School, who thought Williams seemed professional. Corrine Brown said Wayne Williams helped out at a talent show, and Homer Williams came and took pictures. Pamela Sanders was a singer who worked some with Williams, and she suggested that people calling for interviews often left wrong numbers.

Darlene Cann, a college student, wanted to develop high school talent, and Willie Hunter was her advisor. She berated the State's witness James Thompson, who had traveled from South Carolina for the trial. Williams, she said, didn't want to mess with James Thompson because he thought Thompson might be homosexual.

Antwon Holland, another member of the Gemini group, did nothing but bad-mouth a few of our witnesses. On cross-examination, he acknowledged that Williams used a string of different cars, including a light-colored Ford Fairmont. He had met Willie Hunter and "had his doubts" about him.

Donald Lee Simpson testified that Williams helped him get started in the music business.

Helen Greer booked entertainers and said she had helped Williams get started in the music business.

Al Binder asked Judge Cooper if we could recess early so that he could meet with his remaining witnesses. Al said he had many more witnesses like the ones he had been presenting for the past two days, and he would agree not to call them if we could quit early for the day. Cooper jumped at the offer, and we were in recess until the next morning.

As court began on the morning of February 18, Judge Cooper let us know that he was allowing David Rufus Dingle's exhibits in evidence, except for Dingle's report on river currents, which we had objected to. Dingle was the man who had floated oranges and inflatable dummies down the Chattahoochee River.

Now we were finally going to hear from much-anticipated witnesses. Randall Bresee was a professor at Kansas State University who taught graduate courses in textile fibers and chemical analysis of textiles, and he was being put forth as an expert on fiber. Gordon Miller examined him as to his qualifications and expertise. Bresee had never testified before and had done fiber comparisons only once. When Bresee said his PhD had been awarded by Florida State's College of Home Economics, Gordon Miller could not resist making a comment: "I'm not going to ask you any questions about baking pies right now."

Binder was indignant, and rose from his seat to ask Judge Cooper to make Gordon refrain from making such comments; Cooper accommodated his request. Gordon then sparred with Bresee, whom Binder insisted on calling "Doctor Bresee." The jury seemed totally bored and probably had no idea what Gordon and Bresee were talking about. Neither did anyone else in the courtroom. It was obvious that Bresee knew a lot about fiber, but not so much about fiber comparison. And he admitted he had never used a microspectrophotometer, the scientific instrument that measured the precise color of a fiber. Gordon objected to Bresee's being declared an expert, based on his lack of fiber comparison experience. Cooper noted that his inexperience went only to the weight of his evidence, and it would be up to the jury to determine how much weight they would give to his testimony. He was qualified as an expert.

Binder now tried to get Bresee to testify about the results of a study done by the Law Enforcement Assistance Administration on the proficiency of crime laboratories around the country. Gordon objected, and I joined him, explaining that it would be like me testifying about the truth of some article I had read criticizing someone I didn't even know. Judge Cooper was skeptical of Binder's offer of the evidence. It did not relate to any fibers he examined.

Jim Kitchens joined the fray, and I announced that I had a case on the subject.

Binder shot back, "You've always got a case. You always say you've got a case right on it!" He was right—that was my job. I read from a Georgia Court of Appeals case called *Porterfield v. State*. "Testimony about information that one has acquired from books and records kept by someone else is inadmissible." Judge Cooper took a brief recess, returned, and agreed with Gordon and me.

That issue having been resolved, Bresee now testified how he bought a pillowcase at K-Mart and dipped it in the Chattahoochee River for thirty minutes. He then examined it and found that it had fibers on it, although none looked like the Wellman fiber. He thought fiber samples from the carpet in Mary Welcome's office looked like the Wellman fiber, although he only used a pocket magnifying glass to make his comparisons. Bresee had never heard of the Wellman 181b, Nylon 6,6 fiber.

He criticized the techniques used by our experts, Deadman, Peterson, and Gaudette, although he wasn't sure which techniques they had used. He assumed, incorrectly, that they had done no elimination of fibers from other environments, and he admitted that multiple fiber associations may be proof of contact.

The next witness was Homer Williams, Wayne's father. Attorney Lynn Whatley now stepped forward, saying that he represented Homer and Faye Williams, and he wanted to be able to object to questions. Gordon suggested that he pass his objections on to Al Binder since Whatley was not an attorney involved in the case. Jim Kitchens noted that Faye Williams was leaving the courtroom as we had agreed upon earlier. We knew that Wayne's parents would try to make their testimony consistent, and that Faye would not want to be contradicting something Homer said and vice versa.

Homer Williams was a sixty-eight-year-old former school-teacher who became a father late in life. He was considerably taller and a bit thinner than his son, Wayne. As a witness, Homer tried to shoot down just about everything he could regarding the State's case against his son, starting with the fiber evidence. He claimed that he had just replaced carpet squares in a rear room of the house on May 25, 1981, right after Wayne was stopped on the bridge and right *before* the June 3, 1981, search of his home. *Convenient timing,* I thought.

He claimed he had purchased the wall-to-wall green carpeting in 1968, years before the Wellman Company had made their infamous trilobal fiber. He had a copy of a newspaper ad from 1968 and suggested that the ad proved the date of purchase. He had a photographic slide from 1970, which he said showed the carpet. It didn't look much like the carpet—it was brown and quite different from the green carpet that had yielded the Wellman English Olive fibers found on various victims.

Homer Williams had been in court from the beginning of the trial, and he knew that our fiber experts had said that certain fibers found on Charles Stephens' body on October 10, 1980, could have come from the trunk liner of his Ford LTD. Homer was about to prove us wrong. He had bought that red Ford LTD in 1979, but he said it was a lemon and broke down on August 6, 1980. The family never used it again and didn't have that red Ford on October 10, 1980.

What Homer Williams did next I couldn't believe. He explained how he had rented, from B & M Equipment Company, a series of three different cars during the period from August 6, 1980, until they borrowed the white Chevrolet station wagon on October 21, 1980. Homer Williams identified rental agreements for the cars, labeled as Defense exhibits 108 through 111. I looked at the rental agreements. The cars were all Ford automobiles, all Fairmonts, which would have trunk fibers similar to those found in the red Ford LTD. Homer Williams had done us a favor, inadvertently explaining how Ford trunk fibers could be found on victim Charles Stephens when the Williams family no longer owned the red Ford. They had another similar Ford. Kitchens asked Homer if Wayne had access to these cars, and the answer was yes, he had, Wayne had driven these cars.

Homer gave his version of the events on the evening of May 21, 1981. Wayne went out about 11:30 p.m. and said he was going to pick up a tape recorder from Gino Jordan. Faye Williams had taken a message from a woman and had written it on a pad. Wayne returned home at 4:30 or 5:00 a.m.

Homer Williams described Wayne's wonderful childhood and how he supported his son in all his activities to the point of going bankrupt over the expenses of Wayne's radio station. Wayne had never been away from home except for one night in 1979, when he went to Los Angeles. His son was not a failure, he insisted. Homer Williams described how his wife had been undergoing radiation treatments in late 1980, saying they switched bedrooms with Wayne for a time. Homer Williams continued to testify for most of the afternoon, until we recessed for the day.

Court resumed on the morning of Friday, February 19, and Kitchens' questions went on for hours. Homer claimed the slap-jack found at the house was his, and he accused the police of planting it in the ceiling to make Wayne look bad. Homer said he was the one who burned all the photographs in the backyard barbecue pit, to protect privacy—as he said, "You don't want to just tear them up." He claimed the *Egyptian Book of the Dead*, which showed positions for laying out bodies, was just an art book he had around the house. He admitted taking photographs at the funerals of victims Terry Pue and Nathaniel Cater.

Jim Kitchens finally asked, "Is there anything you haven't covered?"

"No," replied Homer Williams.

On cross-examination, Homer admitted that Wayne did not wear glasses for his senior yearbook picture nor for any of the pictures of him when he graduated from high school. He denied that he ever fought with Wayne, and he claimed the family was very close. He admitted renting lots of cars from Hub Motors, Hertz, and B & M Equipment, and he acknowledged that the red Ford LTD had been driven 3,600 miles per month during the time the family had the car. He knew nothing about blood on the back seat of the white station wagon. Homer's blood type was A-positive, which did *not* match the blood on the back seat. Although the two bloodstains did not match any member of the Williams family, the stains did match the blood type of victims Billy Barrett and John Porter.

Homer conceded that Wayne was not a race car driver and that he never knew him to fly airplanes, as he had bragged on his résumé. He denied ever telling anyone that Wayne just stopped on the bridge to dump garbage.

Although Homer Williams tried hard to show that his carpet predated the 1970 vintage Wellman fiber, he confessed that the man he thought had sold him his carpet back in 1968 denied selling him the carpet. He remembered that a man named Wayne Gano had installed the carpet. He could not explain why the carpeting from a 1970 photographic slide showed a brown carpet. This was inconsistent with his claim that the green carpeting had been installed in 1968.

It was late on Friday afternoon as court recessed, and for the first time in the trial, we would be attending court the next morning, a Saturday. The jury was climbing the walls with impatience, and Judge Cooper wanted to get the trial over with. Watching the jury, it was obvious when they thought a witness was wasting their time, as they shifted in their seats, looked at notes or their watches, and just seemed generally uncomfortable.

On Saturday, February 20, the defense began by offering another demonstration relating to the noise made by the expansion joint on the bridge. Binder called Mark Oviatt, an acoustical engineer, to the witness stand. The jury was out while we determined whether Oviatt could be considered an expert. He had a degree in physics from Georgia Tech and performed sound studies with a firm of acoustical engineers. He had taken a decibel meter out to the bridge and set it up below the bridge while the Williamses' white station wagon was driven over the expansion joint. The meter would measure the level of sound as the car crossed the bridge at different speeds.

I objected to allowing the experiment into evidence. All the previous cases cited by Binder involved the admissibility of recordings from meetings, press conferences, or witness interviews. The only question in those cases was the *content* of the recordings, what people had said in meetings or interviews. The issue here centered on the *loudness* of an event and how well it could be heard by witness Robert Campbell. I argued that the test, conducted on a machine in February, would tell us nothing about what Campbell had heard from a different position under the bridge on May 22, 1981. In addition, the cold conditions in February would probably increase the gap covered by the expansion joint and make it noisier than in the hot conditions on May 22. This would confuse the jury and was not relevant.

Judge Cooper took a recess and then returned with a decision: "I will allow the defense witness to testify as to the results of his test, but the tape itself will not be played because it could possibly mislead the jury as outlined by Mr. Joe Drolet, Assistant DA. Bring the jury in!"

Oviatt explained how he set up a microphone under the bridge and had the Williamses' car driven over it. He said human ears can normally hear at a volume of four decibels, and at 4.3 miles per hour, the expansion joint made four decibels of sound to the microphone directly under the bridge. It was possible, he said, for a human in the position where the microphone was to hear sounds at speeds above that point. Oviatt admitted, on cross-examination, that varying conditions in foliage and temperature would affect the results of his tests. All the test measured was the sound that a machine could hear when pointed up at the expansion joint. Oviatt had no idea what Robert Campbell's hearing ability was or what the conditions were on May 22, 1981, nor did he know exactly where Campbell was standing or sitting or what direction his ears were facing. Oviatt had positioned his microphone directly under the bridge. Robert Campbell, on May 22, 1981, was in a different place, about forty feet away from the base of the bridge where the microphone was located. The jury heard the testimony, for what it was worth.

The next witness for the defense, Tom Jones, an auto mechanic for the city of Atlanta, had almost nothing important to say. The jury continued to fidget. Jones said he had gone to school with Williams and thought Williams hung around with all kinds of people. Jones acknowledged that he played basketball at the Ben Hill Recreation Center, but contradicting Williams, had never seen a Schlitz team there. We had no questions for the witness.

Binder tried to call Detective A. E. Alderman to elicit testimony suggesting that Jimmy Ray Payne might have been suicidal when he was in juvenile detention. We objected—anything Alderman knew would be hearsay, as he had no personal knowledge of Jimmy Ray Payne's mental condition. The judge sent the jury to lunch, and before we could get started again, Wayne Williams was again feeling sick. Court was adjourned until Monday, February 22, 1982.

After court that Saturday, Jack, Gordon, Wally, and I stayed at the office and continued our preparation for testimony from Wayne's mother and possibly Wayne Williams himself. We gathered every bit of information on the statements each had made, places they had been, things found at their house, and any mention of them in any of our records. The FBI's Bill McGrath and Task Force officers Carlos Banda and Frank McClure helped us gather and sort information and exhibits we could use on cross-examination. We filled folders with fodder for cross-examination.

Lewis Slaton dropped by the third-floor war room, offering to cross-examine Wayne Williams if he testified. After some discussion, we concluded that Jack would be the best man for the job, and Slaton agreed. As the elected district attorney, Slaton wanted to be out front, leading the charge. He would handle part of the closing argument and would always be recognized as the architect of the prosecution.

Chapter 17

MOTHER AND CHILD
ON THE WITNESS STAND

The Trial—Week Eight

C ourt reconvened on Monday, February 22, and Mary Welcome wanted to call a witness named Lou Bryant, to show that someone else had been treated more leniently than Wayne Williams when that other person had been a possible suspect in the case. Again, Judge Cooper sent the jury out. I cited Georgia Supreme Court cases that held that evidence regarding the guilt of someone else was not relevant and not admissible. Cooper asked Welcome if she had any cases to cite in support of her position. She had none, and Lou Bryant quietly left the courtroom.

Now Wayne Williams' mother, Faye, sixty-four, took the stand. Binder began the questioning of the tiny, frail-looking woman. We had agreed that Binder could ask leading questions, and we would not object. Normally, the person who calls a witness can't "lead" the witness, which means suggesting the answer as part of the question. We had granted Binder great leeway in questioning Wayne's mother.

Faye said Wayne was a fun-loving, all-American boy and had never been a problem. As her husband had done, she tried to respond to an array of allegations that had been part of our prosecution. For example, she claimed that the slapjack was in a closet, not hidden above a ceiling panel; that Wayne got scratches when he fell and skinned his left arm; and that the carpet was purchased in 1968, and could not be made from a Wellman fiber produced two years later. She recalled a loan from the North American Acceptance Corporation and even had a loan number. She blamed Homer's confusion about which carpet appeared in photographic slides by saying that Homer had used the wrong filter on his camera; it made their present green carpet look brown, she claimed.

Faye Williams tried to back up Wayne's testimony. Cheryl Johnson had called on Wednesday, May 20, 1981, she said, and she had written down the name and phone number and left the message on a "spinner" for Wayne. She said Wayne told her he talked to Cheryl Johnson on Thursday, May 21, 1981, the afternoon before the bridge incident. She said she wasn't in the room when Wayne talked to FBI agents the next morning when they came by the house. Al Binder finished with his presentation of Mrs. Williams around noon, right before we broke for lunch.

Jack cross-examined Faye Williams, who conceded that Wayne was frequently out late at night and kept irregular hours. Faye Williams had no idea how blood got on the back seat of the white Chevy station wagon, and it didn't match her blood, which was type O. This confirmed, without any doubt, that the recently shed blood on the back seat of the station wagon came from someone other than a member of the Williams family.

Faye Williams admitted that she was under oath when she swore to the Fulton County Grand Jury that Wayne never had contact with Cheryl Johnson and that she, and she alone, had spoken with Johnson. She also admitted telling the Grand Jury there was "no such number" as the number left by Cheryl Johnson "so then he [Wayne] decided he'd try to check out the address." Faye Williams said, "That's the statement I made [to the Grand Jury]."

Faye Williams said that the family had lived in their house since

1950, and that the home had only been carpeted once since they moved there, and that was in December of 1968. Jack showed her a slide of the carpeting in her home and asked if this was the carpeting she had described as being installed in December of 1968. She was emphatic that it was and that it had been there continuously since December of 1968. Jack asked her if she had noticed the date on the slide, January of 1968. She didn't answer but wanted to see the slide. Then she said, "The slide could have been taken in December and processed in January." She didn't seem to understand that January of 1968 was eleven months *before* the time she had sworn the new green carpeting had been installed. She claimed to remember the date because she saw an ad in the *Atlanta Constitution* right around Christmas of 1968.

Jack now showed her an identical ad from the *Atlanta Constitution*, dated December 4, 1971: "Three full rooms, wall-to-wall carpet. A hundred forty-nine dollars." Jack asked if she recalled the carpet being installed by Wayne Gano and a company called Southern Prudential. She became noticeably defensive. Jack asked why she had assumed that a loan paid off to North American Acceptance Corporation in 1972 was a loan for 1968 carpeting. She had no answer except that she and Homer Williams had destroyed all their old records when cleaning out the house. She assumed that the loan paid off in 1972 must have been for carpeting put in four years earlier. She was shown a copy of the deed to secure debt that she and Homer Williams had signed, on December 7, 1971, when they bought the green carpeting now in their home. She did not want to admit that this loan document to Southern Prudential could be for the carpeting, which would be admitting, in effect, that this carpet was in fact a 1971 carpeting composed of the rare Wellman fiber. She dodged the question, saying, "I understand there is some forgery in this." When pressed about the document, she admitted that the signatures were hers and her husband's, and she quietly stepped down from the witness stand.

Judge Cooper announced: "Call your next witness, Mr. Binder." Binder responded, "We'd like to call to the stand the defendant."

This was the moment we had long anticipated, and this was the moment that hundreds of reporters, spectators, and observers from around the world were waiting for. Wayne Williams was about to answer some questions.

It was early afternoon on Monday, February 22, as Wayne Williams rose dramatically from his seat at the counsel table to my right and confidently strode past me to the witness stand. Having sworn to tell the truth, Williams began delivering a well-prepared and choreographed series of answers to questions propounded by Al Binder. Wayne started by saying, "I'm scared!"

He recited the story of his life, from his earliest memories, the story of a loving and happy home with no secrets among family members. Binder calmly led Wayne through his testimony as the jury heard of every childhood school award, no matter how trivial. Wayne mentioned various jobs he had held and his ill-fated radio station, which he spoke of in glowing terms. In his words, he was a "carefree, happy-go-lucky person and nothing ever really bothered me." He bragged and exaggerated as he confidently described events that never happened, such as taking arson pictures and being directly responsible to Reginald Eaves, the commissioner of public safety. Binder asked Wayne to step down from the witness stand, and as Binder and Williams stood facing the jury, just a few feet away, he challenged jurors to touch Williams' hands to see if he had calluses on them (most jurors declined the offer). Binder seemed to be trying to get jurors to form some bond or personal relationship as one might do if shaking hands. Returning to the stand, Wayne spoke of family vacations, jobs, and community activity, painting a beautiful picture of a peaceful, wholesome, and happy home.

Binder told Cooper he would like to bring Sheba, the Williamses' dog, into the courtroom to be displayed for the jury. I couldn't help but smile, and I wondered if we would have an opportunity to cross-examine Sheba. Lewis Slaton, seated to my left, couldn't resist—he objected, saying, "Why do we want the dog?"

Binder responded, "Mr. Slaton, give me just one thing." Slaton gave in, and Cooper admonished everyone in the courtroom to be absolutely quiet as Sheba became the next "witness." Binder slowly walked Sheba, the German shepherd, into the courtroom and in front of the jury. Sheba staggered as Binder pulled her around the courtroom. Binder then said for the record, "The jury has had an opportunity to observe the dog to determine whether or not the dog is frisky." Al was trying to offset the testimony of witness Margaret Carter, who had seen Williams and Nathaniel Cater together in a park. She had said there was a German shepherd dog nearby, and it seemed "frisky."

Williams now skillfully downplayed his predilection for police cars, police radios, and sirens and casually and confidently explained how they were all necessary in his business. He made it sound like he was working for, and being "dispatched" by, the police and fire services and responding to their calls. It sounded so very reasonable, and he didn't even sound defensive.

Wayne suggested that Bobby Tolin hated him because he had complained about Tolin's use of the N-word. Wayne denied ever making derogatory statements about Blacks, poor people, or anyone. He just tried to help people, he said.

Williams praised District Attorney Lewis Slaton, saying he was just doing his job. Williams praised the sheriff, saying the sheriff had treated him well and that the deputies had made "accommodations for me that they didn't ordinarily make, and I appreciate it."

Williams tried to back up his parents in regard to the age of the carpeting. He claimed to vividly remember details about the carpeting, the furniture, the air conditioner, and even the molding holding down the carpeting, and he swore it was there by 1969—when he would have been eleven years old.

As Wayne continued his testimony, he became more comfortable and almost cocky. He boasted that when he held "auditions," he got "about five thousand phone calls." In regard to homosexuals, he was indignant: "There ain't no way I'm no homosexual, huh-uh. No. I have no grudge against them, as long as they keep their hands to theirselves, stay away from me, I'm all right. But don't come near me." He denied ever holding hands with anyone or touching anyone inappropriately.

Wayne bragged about his "news" business and how it took him all around the metro area. He seemed proud that he "averaged at least two hundred miles a day." By saying that, he had just confirmed what we had attempted to prove: that he was out cruising the streets, driving hundreds of miles each day, and most of it, as even his mother confirmed, was at night.

Wayne agreed that Willie Hunter had strange mannerisms, talked a little funny, and that some people thought he was gay. Wayne said, "That stuff is immaterial."

Wayne explained the exaggerations on his résumé as "hype," a form of self-promotion. But contradicting his parents, he claimed he really had flown airplanes on three occasions and had raced cars at a track near Fairburn, Georgia. It was "street stockcar drag racing," he said.

He denied that there was a length of nylon ski rope in the station wagon when he was stopped near the bridge, and he indicated he hadn't seen the slapjack in fifteen years. He had never seen the *Egyptian Book of the Dead*, he said.

Now, late in the afternoon of February 22, we finally got to the good part—the James Jackson Parkway Bridge. Binder led into it, saying there's been "all this hubbub" about the ride on the bridge. "I want to talk to you about the morning of May 22, 1981." Binder now asked the question everyone wanted to ask: "Tell the jury, what in blazes you were doing on the Jackson Parkway Bridge on the night of May 21, or early morning hours of May 22?"

Wayne answered, "To be honest with you, trying to get to the other side of the bridge so I could get home!" Wayne described how it was foggy, saying he was going between twenty and thirty-five miles per hour as he crossed the bridge, with lights on, and never stopped.

It was time to recess for the day. Wayne Williams had done well. He was smooth and confident and could make any lie sound like the truth. He seemed likable and charming and sure of himself. He was in control and seemed to be loving it.

We returned to the office and talked further about how to cross-examine Wayne Williams. I reread the suggestions that FBI profiling expert John Douglas had prepared for us. The next morning, Williams, neatly dressed in a suit, again climbed into the witness chair. Binder was giving him the forum he wanted, asking friendly questions and letting Wayne cut loose with tirades against the police and those who had been witnesses against him.

Now Wayne gave a long and detailed account of how Cheryl Johnson had called him on Thursday afternoon, May 21, 1981, the day after she had left a message with Faye Williams. She wanted an interview the next morning, Friday, May 22, "because we were having auditions that Saturday, the twenty-third." He set up an appointment, he said, for "May 22, before 8:30 in the morning." She was "vague" about her address, but she thought it was Spanish Trace Apartments.

Wayne said he took a nap and was awakened by his father at about 10:00 p.m. He talked on the phone, he said, until about 1:00 or 1:30 a.m., when he remembered that he had to get his tape recorder from Gino Jordan because he needed to use it the next day. He told his parents he was going to a club to get it, and he went to the Sans Souci nightclub, and "there was a gentleman with glasses, a dark-skinned older man at the register." He asked for Gino Jordan; a woman on the phone behind the register said, "He's busy." Wayne claimed he then left. (This was the first time anyone had heard this version of Wayne's visit to the Sans Souci; he seemed to be trying to shape this version of events to match the testimony of witnesses from the Sans Souci. As he had done with previous accounts of these events, Wayne sprinkled his testimony with lots of detail and description, perhaps to make things sound more credible.)

Wayne then proceeded, he said, to South Cobb Drive and Benson Poole Road in Smyrna. He was looking for Apartment C-4. He found some apartments, but they were not Spanish Trace, so he headed south toward the James Jackson Parkway Bridge. He stopped north of the bridge, on the Cobb County side of the river, and used a pay phone at the RaceTrac gas station, north of I-285. He said he then drove over the bridge, and there were two cars just ahead of him, a brown car and a camper truck or El Camino. He claimed he continued a half mile past the bridge to the corner of Bolton Road and James Jackson Parkway, where he used the phone again—this time at the Starvin Marvin store at that intersection. He also picked up some empty boxes and drove back over the bridge and was stopped when he got onto I-285.

Williams explained what happened when he was stopped but neglected to mention the very different stories he had told the police. As he described it in court, the police shined lights in his car, and he gave them permission to look inside. He claimed he said, "This is about these killings, isn't it?" (denying that he had said, "This is about those *boys*, isn't it?") They questioned him, he said, and he noticed a helicopter following him when he left the area. He went back to the Sans Souci, he said, but it was closed, so he went home.

Wayne said he agreed to talk to FBI agents at his home a few hours later, but again, he didn't go into detail about what he told them. Had he done so, it, too, would have conflicted with what he had just told the jury. He claimed police were staking out his house and that he gave the FBI agents the note his mother had written when Cheryl Johnson called on Wednesday.

Wayne said the police followed him every time he left the house and that there were police with binoculars "peeping through the fence" behind his house, and that "they had an airplane and a helicopter circling overhead constantly."

He described being taken to FBI headquarters on June 3, 1981, the same night they searched his house. They grabbed him off the street, he said, and wouldn't let him call a lawyer. When he got home, he felt like some kind of "lynch mob" was searching his house.

Wayne explained that when he held a press conference at his home shortly after he got home, he wanted to explain his "side of the thing." He did not go into any detail about the version of events he had provided at the press conference. It, too, conflicted with what he had just told the jury.

Binder then led Wayne through a series of denials, denying just about everything the jury had heard from a multitude of witnesses.

The court took a fifteen-minute recess. It was midmorning, and

Wayne had been testifying since early afternoon the day before. We had lots of notes by this time, jotting down every time Williams contradicted his previous statements or made statements we knew were untrue.

Wayne was performing well and enjoying himself. Binder asked him about using the term "street gruncheons." Wayne denied using the term, saying he used the terms "street urchin" and "dropshot."

Binder finished with Williams at about 11:15 a.m. on that Tuesday, February 23. Judge Cooper said Jack could cross-examine Williams until about 11:45 a.m., when the jury would take a break for lunch.

Jack began slowly and calmly, asking Wayne Williams relatively innocuous questions. What happened to the yellow blanket that had been under his bed? Where did the name "Gemini" come from? What is "hype"? Did you ever really fly an F-4 jet fighter? What's the difference between hype and a lie?

Jack asked Wayne if he had ever gotten completely wasted and drunk as a result of an argument with his father. Wayne said that never happened. In October of 1980, Wayne had done an interview with *Us* magazine, in which he admitted getting "completely wasted and drunk." When Jack read Wayne's words as quoted in the magazine article, Wayne still denied it. Jack handed the article to Wayne, and Wayne claimed that Jack had read the statement out of context. Jack asked Wayne to read it aloud to the jury. Wayne read it, and it was exactly as Jack had quoted.

When Jack pressed Wayne about his music business, he became defensive. He clearly didn't like cross-examination, and tried, unsuccessfully, to spar with Jack. Still handling himself well, he was growing more uncomfortable. Cooper announced a lunch recess, and we took some time to discuss further questions to put to Wayne Williams.

As court resumed, Al Binder and I went through a pile of exhibits and came to an agreement as to which ones were admissible and which were not. I recited for the court which exhibits Al had withdrawn and which exhibits we had agreed to.

Shortly after 1:15 p.m., Wayne Williams again sat down in the witness chair and prepared to answer Jack Mallard's questions. Jack wondered why Wayne, when questioned by Binder, had left out discussion of one of his business "invoices" for a call on Redwine Road? One of the bodies had been found there. Wayne denied being familiar with it or Niskey Lake Road, where the body of Alfred Evans had been found, but his records, taken in one of the searches, showed that he had taken photos on Niskey Lake Road. He wasn't familiar with Winthrop Road, he claimed, where another victim was found, but again his records showed he had done a job right across the street from where Billy Barrett's body had been found. Wayne explained his ride in an F-4 fighter jet as a demonstration ride with a Black Air Force captain, whom he declined to name. And, he now admitted, he did not actually fly the plane.

Jack asked Wayne if he remembered saying at his bond hearing in July of 1981, just after he was indicted, that he and his parents had about eighty thousand dollars of personal money invested in the Gemini project. At that hearing, Wayne had said they were negotiating contracts and had made presentations to Motown and Capitol Records. Wayne now wanted to qualify what he said at the bond hearing. The court reporter, he claimed, had gotten it wrong. He meant "contacts," not "contracts," and it wasn't really eighty thousand dollars. He had actually just sent something in the mail to record companies, and he acknowledged that he hadn't made any presentations to anyone.

Jack went over Wayne's call from Cheryl Johnson. Wayne now added new details. Unlike all of his previous versions, he now said he had *planned* to go look for Cheryl Johnson (earlier, he had said he just happened to be in the area and thought he would check out the location).

Jack asked Wayne why he had to cross the bridge to make a phone call if he had just passed twenty-five pay phones on South Cobb Drive. Wayne said he just knew the phone at the Starvin Marvin store and was comfortable stopping there. Jack then asked why Wayne went back over the bridge to I-285 if he was on his way home. Wayne said, "It was a quick way to get home." Wayne now acknowledged that he had stopped at the RaceTrac gas station north of I-285 on Cobb Parkway before crossing the bridge. For the first time, Wayne claimed he had called two different phone numbers for Cheryl Johnson. The numbers he called, he said, all started with "434," not the "934" he had previously told the FBI and the police.

Jack now asked a question Wayne couldn't really answer. Jack asked, "If you had just used the phone north of the river, at the RaceTrac station, why did you then go across the bridge?"

Wayne replied, "It was on the way home!" Wayne was beginning to contradict himself, and he started getting feisty. He proclaimed his innocence and said he would have told people if he had really done something. Wayne now claimed he made *three* calls from the Starvin Marvin store. He admitted that he had said to the police, "I know, it's about those boys," but now he said he didn't say that until ten minutes after being stopped.

Jack went over each of Wayne's previous statements and asked him which parts were true and which were not. Wayne disagreed with much of what detectives had previously heard him say. They were all mistaken, he insisted. Wayne had made seven previous statements, and each statement differed from the others.

The cross-examination went on for most of the afternoon. Wayne's irritation was growing, but he kept himself under control. He tried to distance himself from his previous statements, saying that none of the statements were "official statements." He insisted that notes taken by law enforcement officers did not reflect what he had said.

Jack asked Wayne about talking to FBI Agent Rackleff. Jack said nothing about the fact that Rackleff was a polygraph examiner, but Wayne did, repeatedly. Jack asked if what was happening in the courtroom was a challenge for Wayne. "Man, this ain't no challenge, right here!"

Jack read from the transcript of Wayne's press conference. Wayne had said he had errands to run in the area of South Cobb Drive, so since he was in the area, he decided to look for the address of Cheryl Johnson. Wayne at first denied saying that, and Jack asked him to read from the transcript. Wayne read aloud, and it became clear that his current version of events differed from his own press conference. Binder could see Wayne beginning to lose control, and he jumped up, trying to interrupt the flow of Jack's questions. The questions were repetitious, he said. Judge Cooper asked for my interpretation of the law, based on the precedents. I explained that once a witness was impeached, you weren't required to place in evidence a document that impeached the witness, such as the transcript of his press conference, but you could certainly continue questioning the witness about his lies. Cooper permitted cross-examination to continue.

Jack continued to quote from Wayne's press conference, and Wayne dodged and weaved and acted like there was no discrepancy between what he said at his press conference and what he was saying now. Jack pointed out that at his press conference, Wayne indicated that he never talked to Cheryl Johnson. Wayne shot back, "Sir, you are reading that totally out of context!"

Wayne denied ever coming in contact with young men such as Darryl Davis or Andrew Hayes. (Davis was the young man who jumped out of Wayne's car after Wayne tried to fondle him.)

Bodies had been found in the South River and on Waldrop Road, but Wayne claimed that he wasn't familiar with either location. Jack asked about the scratches on Wayne's arms, and Wayne claimed he got some scratches from a grease burn while cooking, and some may have come from a fall when he was running to answer the telephone. "I have very sensitive skin," he said.

Jack said, "Isn't it true that while you were choking them to death, with their last breath, they were scratching your arms and face?"

"No!" he insisted.

Jack now came back to our counsel table and leaned over. "Joe, I'm out of questions. What do you think?"

I urged Jack to keep him on the stand as it was now nearing 5:00 pm. We would have many more questions to ask him in the morning.

Jack managed to come up with more questions until Judge Cooper, noticing the late hour, recessed for the day. "We'll begin promptly tomorrow morning at nine o'clock."

After court recessed, we gathered in our war room on the third floor of the courthouse. Jack was frustrated—he had asked all the right questions, but Wayne Williams had remained calm and composed. He had confidently responded with illogical and ridiculous answers while making them sound plausible. He had crossed the bridge to get home, he said, yet he turned around and went back over the bridge. He had used the telephone north of the bridge and then claimed he crossed the bridge to use a telephone on the south side of the bridge. There was no logical explanation for his decision to cross and recross the bridge. If he crossed the bridge to get home, then why did he turn around? If I-285 was the fastest way home, then why didn't he just get on I-285 after using the phones north of the river? But Williams had delivered answers with confidence and, so far, had survived cross-examination.

We compiled a list of the most ridiculous and illogical statements Williams had made during his testimony. We would challenge him on the same things in the morning to see how he would do. The FBI's eight-page summary had advised: "Keep Williams on the witness stand for as long as possible," and "Focus on lies already made by him."

At 9:00 a.m. on Wednesday, February 24, I looked over at Wayne Williams, and he seemed troubled—he was fidgeting and seemed to lack the cockiness he had shown the day before.

Williams looked tired as he resumed his place in the witness chair. Jack calmly asked him if he remembered what he had told District Attorney Lewis Slaton at the Fulton County Jail about the person he had spoken to on the phone on Thursday, May 21, 1981, the evening before he went out to the bridge? Wayne argued with Jack and challenged him to let the jury see a transcript of the conversation he had with Slaton. Jack reminded him that we had tried to get the statement in evidence, but his lawyers had objected. Judge Cooper told Williams not to argue with Jack, and Williams lashed out at the judge, saying, "Sir, I'm not arguing with him. I'm just responding to what I have said. I have no intention of arguing with Mr. Mallard. He asked a question, and I'm entitled to answer it!"

Judge Cooper responded, "I'll give you a chance to explain it. Answer the question!" Wayne Williams was, for the first time in his testimony, showing frustration.

Jack asked if Williams had ever, during his conversation with Slaton, mentioned that he talked with Cheryl Johnson on May 21, 1981. Williams avoided answering, and Jack calmly asked again and again for him to answer the question. Williams said he couldn't answer yes or no, to which Jack said, "You never told the district attorney that you talked to Cheryl Johnson, did you?"

"I didn't say that!" Wayne responded.

Jack came back quickly, saying, "You also denied to Special Agent Rackleff of the FBI that you ever talked to Cheryl Johnson, did you not?"

"That's a lie!" yelled Wayne.

"So, Agent Rackleff was a liar then?" Jack asked. Williams denied that Rackleff had even testified.

Wayne was losing his composure: "You can say anything you want to try to get them to believe what you want, but I told you how it is!"

"Wait a minute!" Binder yelled as he jumped from his seat and approached the bench. Al claimed Jack was misquoting Wayne's statement to Lewis Slaton, even though Jack had already moved on to something else. Al was obviously playing for time, hoping that Wayne would cool down.

Jack continued with more questions: "You don't remember Rackleff taking the stand and testifying that you denied that you ever talked to Cheryl Johnson?"

Williams had no answer. He sat there, fuming.

Jack returned to the bridge incident and walked Williams through some of his testimony from the day before. Williams admitted that he had stopped at the RaceTrac gas station north of I-285 and made a phone call. And he acknowledged that he wanted to go home by way of I-285. "Yes, I said that!"

Jack followed up: "All right. Now, my question is, if you wanted to take the I-285 and I-20 route home, why not, after using the telephone at the RaceTrac station at 285, why not get on 285 there rather than coming south toward the bridge?"

Williams lost control. He was cornered—there was no logical answer to the question. "Man, look, what in the world has that got to do with killing somebody?!"

Judge Cooper admonished Williams: "Mr. Williams, answer the question!"

Williams stood up, sputtering helplessly: "Sir, I cannot answer the question! I explained to this gentleman all day yesterday, we've been over this question time and time again! Now, I've been through a lot and I'm tired and I'm having to do the best I can to answer this question. He keeps asking the same thing! The question is, did I kill somebody, and I done told this man I haven't!" Williams, no longer cocky, was near tears.

Cooper told Binder to approach the bench, where he said, "You need to confer with your client for a minute. I think you need to."

Al said, "The question is repetitious."

Judge Cooper continued, "Tell him you'll get up and start objecting and such things, but you tell him to answer the question!" The judge gave Binder time to calm Wayne down.

As we all waited, Binder huddled with Williams, who now looked like a child caught in a lie. After a brief recess, Williams, more composed, complained that our witnesses were programmed to lie.

Jack responded by asking if Wayne had been programmed. "All of this testimony on direct by you just came out spontaneously?"

Williams: "What has that got to do with what you're asking me?"

Jack: "I'm asking if you were programmed."

Wayne jumped up in the witness box, pointed at Jack, and with eyes defiantly fixed on him, loudly boasted, "No, you want the real Wayne Williams? You got him right here!"

Wayne, standing, almost yelling, out of control, said, "Nobody saw me throw anything off that bridge; nobody saw me kill anybody!" Jack ignored him and calmly stepped back toward our table.

Jack now turned to face Williams and quietly returned to the topic of Williams' news conference. Williams had admitted that he had been advised of his rights and had voluntarily talked to the FBI. Now he was yelling that the FBI agents were "goons" who had forced him to talk.

Wayne began accusing others of causing his problems. He blamed Mary Welcome for the *Us* magazine article. She made him do the interview, he said, to raise money. Jack reminded him that he loved talking to the media and had even called reporters from the jail.

Williams snapped back and in a whining voice, said, "You're trying your best to make these folks think that I fit a profile, and part of your profile has to do with attention. No. I'm not going to sit up here and aid you in doing that!" Williams sneered and openly showed disgust toward Jack.

Jack suggested that Williams was now on "center stage," where he wanted to be, his "challenge of a lifetime."

Williams shot back, raising his voice in feeble defiance, "You must be a fool!" and asking Jack, "Why don't you answer one of *my* questions for once?"

Jack ignored him, further adding to Williams' frustration. Williams admitted that in the *Us* magazine article he had said, "I would compare the FBI to the keystone cops, and the Atlanta Police to *Car 54, Where Are You?*"

Jack was finished, Wayne was exhausted, and after a short recess, Binder had a few more questions. Wayne told Binder that Jack just wasn't fair, and he childishly whined about the questions Jack asked. He didn't like all the attention, he claimed, and the State's witnesses were all lying.

Jack rose for a few more questions. He asked if Williams had ever changed his story. Having changed his story repeatedly, Williams had no answer and just sat, staring intensely at Mallard. Jack asked if Williams had ever called a young man named Ken Kimbro a dropshot—a derogatory term he used for kids living in housing projects. Wayne sarcastically said that anyone could be a dropshot, "And, to be honest with you, *you* are a dropshot!"

We were now done with Wayne Williams.

Al Binder announced: "The defense rests."

We had kept Wayne on the stand, and he had lost control. He couldn't explain his presence on the bridge. He could never explain why he went across the bridge if he wanted to go home by way of I-285. He no longer sounded confident and believable.

We now had a chance to present evidence to rebut what the defense had presented. We knew that the jury was getting impatient, but we had a few things to clear up.

We called Sergeant Troy Daily to the stand to discredit defense witness Ken Lawson. Lawson had claimed that Robert Campbell was a drunk who slept on bridge duty, that Freddie Jacobs saw ghosts on bridge duty, and that Nellie Trammel was a psychic who hung around the Task Force knitting. Binder objected to Daily's testimony, but during a recess, he agreed to a stipulation to be read to the jury: Ken Lawson had lied on his police application, had been fired by four police agencies, and twice had been reported for domestic violence.

Officer Carlos Banda, who had been assisting us during the trial, explained that Nellie Trammel was not the older Black lady described by witnesses as hanging around the Task Force. That person was Detective J. J. Trimble's mother, who would wait for Detective Trimble and ride home with her each day. Detective Trimble followed Banda on the stand and confirmed the identity of her mother and the fact that Nellie Trammel had never come by the Task Force to offer information.

Gordon now recalled our fiber expert, Larry Peterson, who had examined the carpet on the fourteenth floor of the Bank of the South Building, where Mary Welcome had her office. Randall Bresee, the defense fiber witness, had said Mary Welcome's carpet had fibers that looked like the Wellman fiber. Peterson examined the fiber and said that it was *not* like the Wellman fiber, with the unique cross-section, and it was a different color, made with a different dye. Bresee was wrong.

Larry also explained how he had inspected fibers from the homes of victims and public places like the Omni, looking at more than five hundred different fibers in order to eliminate those locations as sources of the fibers found on victims. Three hundred of those samples had been carpet fibers. No samples from other locations matched the fibers found in the Williams home, nor did any of the fibers recovered by Randall Bresee from the pillowcase he had dipped into the Chattahoochee River.

After a brief afternoon recess, we presented a witness from the blood bank where Nathaniel Cater had sold his blood. Jerry Huth knew Cater and had tested him on May 21, 1981, the day before Wayne Williams was stopped at the bridge. He confirmed that Cater was indeed alive on that date.

The people who installed the green carpet in the Williamses' home came next. Wayne Gano had sold the carpeting to Southern Prudential Company and installed the carpeting for the company. He identified the deed to secure debt signed by Homer and Faye Williams, and he recognized his signature on the deed, dated December 7, 1971. The carpet did *not* predate the production of the unusual Wellman trilobal fiber. Homer and Faye Williams were wrong about the carpet being installed in 1968. It was installed in 1971.

Lou Speert was the owner of Southern Prudential Company, incorporated in 1971 to sell carpeting. He had run the ad for carpeting in the *Atlanta Constitution* on December 4, 1971, and he had Wayne Gano install the carpet in the Williamses' home. Speert recognized his own signature on the deed to secure debt, which was held by North American Acceptance Corporation.

Vince Giovannelli testified about seeing Wayne Williams on a bridge in DeKalb County. Williams had denied ever being on a bridge over the South River in DeKalb County. Giovannelli, a Delta Air Lines employee, saw Williams at the rail of a bridge near Winthrop Road, looking into the South River. Williams glanced up at him as he went by, so Giovannelli got a good look at him. The date was March 3, 1981, the day after JoJo Bell was reported missing. Bell's body was later found in the South River, downstream from the bridge.

Angelo Fuster was Mayor Maynard Jackson's director of

communications and was at the FBI's downtown headquarters on June 3, 1981, the night when Wayne Williams was there being questioned. Fuster talked to Homer Williams, whom he knew, and was told that Wayne said he "stopped to get rid of some trash" on the bridge.

Seventeen-year-old Sheldon Kemp testified about being at the Williams house in the summer of 1979 when Wayne Williams was demanding money from his father, who refused to sign a check. Wayne pushed his father down and slapped his mother aside when she tried to intervene. Wayne held his father on a bed, with both hands around his father's throat, until Faye Williams pulled him off. Homer got a shotgun and threatened to blow Wayne's head off.

Al Binder was beside himself and interrupted, accusing Kemp of being a juvenile delinquent who was trying to shake down the Williams family after Wayne had kicked him out of the singing group.

We recessed for the day, knowing we were near the end of the trial. The marathon was nearly over. We had one more witness to present.

On Thursday morning, February 25, the jury seemed more upbeat and animated as they entered the courtroom, and each person took his or her familiar seat, as they had for the last eight weeks. Jack announced our final witness, Henry James Ingram Sr.

Mr. Ingram, a fiftyish Black man, walked to the witness stand. He had a regular full-time job with a furniture company but worked a second job at a parking lot at the corner of Courtland and Cain Streets in downtown Atlanta. One day in May of 1981 at about five in the afternoon, Ingram saw Homer and Faye Williams drive into his lot in a tan Ford. He knew them and noticed that Faye was sitting in the back seat. After being away for about an hour, Homer and Faye returned, accompanied by two young men. Homer Williams got in the front seat of the car, and Faye Williams got in the back seat, directly behind Homer. They sat waiting in the car as the two younger men were over by a dumpster talking. Faye Williams then got out of the back seat and moved to the passenger seat in the front.

The two young men noticed and rushed toward the car, one of them "snatching" the driver's door open. He grabbed Homer Williams, and the two of them "scuffled all the way from the back of the parking lot" to the area where Mr. Ingram sat in a booth. Homer Williams kept throwing his arms up to ward off blows from the younger man. As the younger man knocked Homer's glasses off, Homer Williams yelled that he was going to call the police. Faye Williams retrieved the glasses as Henry Ingram warned the group that they were on private property and needed to leave. They scuffled more as they were leaving, and then Homer and Faye Williams got in the tan Ford—he in the front, she in the back.

They came by Mr. Ingram's booth, and Homer Williams apologized for what happened. He explained that his son had wanted him to rent an automobile for a friend and he had refused. As the Williamses left the lot, the two young men rushed the car again. Homer Williams had locked his door so the young men couldn't get it open, but they did manage to get Faye Williams out of the car. Mr. Ingram approached again, since they were still blocking the driveway to the parking lot. One of the young men yelled at Homer Williams, "Don't come home tonight!"

Henry James Ingram Sr. pointed at Wayne Williams as the man he had seen scuffling with Homer Williams, knocking his glasses off and yelling at him not to come home that night. The man with him, he said, was a slender Black man, about the same age as Williams.

Al Binder tried to confuse Ingram, suggesting the event happened in June. "Do you think that was the first or second week of June?"

"No," Mr. Ingram responded, "it was in May."

Jack announced that we were finished with our rebuttal evidence, and Judge Cooper asked if the defense had anything more. Binder called a karate instructor who testified that you get calluses on your hands if you do karate a lot and that you would have to block neck arteries for about thirty seconds to make a person pass out. We had no questions.

Faye Williams took the stand once again and contradicted Sheldon Kemp, claiming that she had never seen Wayne strike Homer Williams in her presence. She accused Kemp of demanding a minibike for his efforts after he had been dismissed from Wayne's singing group. Faye remembered no incident in a parking lot as described by Henry Ingram, and she volunteered that "they have not produced evidence that my son is a killer!"

"We rest" were the next words from Al Binder. The evidence was now, at long last, finished.

THE EVIDENCE IS CLOSED

We met to confer with Judge Cooper at the bench. Binder wanted to wait until the next day, Friday, February 26, 1982, for closing arguments. As we huddled in front of the bench, Lewis Slaton said we were ready to go. It was just late morning, and we had all day. We had agreed that arguments would be limited to two hours for each side—we would argue first, the defense would argue, and then we would have a final say. Cooper accommodated Binder's request and excused the jury for the rest of the day.

I reminded the judge that we still had evidence issues to go over, in addition to the court's instructions. Cooper explained to the jury that they would hear arguments in the morning and then be instructed on the law. In the meantime, they were not to discuss the case.

Binder rose to make a motion for a directed verdict, the same motion he had made when we rested our case days earlier. This was a routine motion, rarely granted, in which a lawyer suggests to the court that there just isn't a case and that no jury could possibly find the defendant guilty. Binder again asserted that we had not even proven that there were any murders. I pointed out that there was sufficient evidence for the case to go to the jury. Judge Cooper denied the motion, and we recessed for lunch.

Back in court after lunch, we now went through each of the

hundreds of items of evidence. I offered in evidence the deed to secure debt for the carpeting in the Williams home, State's Exhibit 752, which was admitted without objection. We bickered a bit over various exhibits—the blow-up dummies went into evidence over my objection. We argued over sketches based on visions described by psychics. We kept some of those out. I was tired, and we were all ready for it to be over.

We held a conference in the judge's chambers, where the lawyers on both sides were permitted to suggest which instructions the judge should give the jury. Most of the instructions were "pattern" statements that came from a manual of approved instructions used by every Superior Court. There was little disagreement among us. We were not about to suggest using any untested instructions that might later be used to overturn a verdict.

We could now focus on our closing argument, and we gathered in the war room to talk strategy. We had presented 137 witnesses; the defense had presented 68. There were more than 850 exhibits in the case, from a car seat to a ten-foot model of the James Jackson Parkway Bridge. We began listing what each of us thought were the most important points to bring before the jury.

Wayne Williams was never able to satisfactorily explain his reasons for crossing the bridge and then crossing back to the Cobb County side. There were his many other lies, his disproven fabrications of details, and his contradictory statements. Had he spoken to the phantom Cheryl Johnson or had he not? There was the rope in the back seat, the gloves and the flashlight in the front seat, and his statement, "I'll bet this is about those boys, isn't it?" And there was his car, with lights out, stopped directly above where a splash was heard in the river.

There was the fiber evidence, with rare fibers and combinations of fibers that led three experts to say that victims had to have been in contact with Wayne Williams' environment. And there were the fibers from the cars, fibers that changed with each change in the car he drove.

There was the blood evidence on the back seat of the white station wagon, with fresh blood matching the blood shed by victims

John Porter and William Barrett. There were the unexplained scratches on Wayne Williams' arms, seen by four witnesses. And there were a dozen witnesses who had seen Wayne Williams with boys who later turned up as victims.

As district attorney, Lewis Slaton had already decided that he would argue last, the prime spot in a closing argument. We agreed that Jack should handle part of it, as he had been the primary examiner of witnesses. That should have been enough, but we decided to add Gordon Miller, who had spent so much time working with the Task Force and developing expertise on the fiber evidence. He could explain the fiber evidence. As we set about preparing our argument, I tried to anticipate everything that could possibly come up as the end of the trial approached.

On the morning of February 26, 1982, we gathered in the war room and prepared to make our group entry into the courtroom, as we had done each morning for the past two and a half months. We had waited a long time for this day, and so had the jury.

The jury was escorted to the jury box and exuded a new energy, sensing that their confinement was soon to end. Judge Cooper nodded to Jack Mallard, who began the arguments by acknowledging how tired the jury must be. Jack reminded them that we were tired too and that great preparation went into each day of testimony that had been presented to them. Jack outlined the evidence and rejected the defense suggestion that there were really no murders at all. There was solid expert testimony from five medical examiners on homicide as the cause of death; there was the changing pattern relating to fibers discovered on bodies that had been left in the woods versus those that had been dumped into rivers. Jack discussed Wayne Williams, his failures, and his Jekyll-and-Hyde personality. Sharon Blakely had seen it, and so had the jury on Wayne's final day on the witness stand. Wayne was, at times, the intelligent media-savvy manipulator, loving the publicity and talking to the press at every opportunity. There were his late hours as he cruised the streets, his disguises as a police officer and as a news cameraman, and his habitual lying. Jack explained the concept of reasonable doubt and the power of circumstantial evidence, like fingerprints or fiber evidence, which is often far more compelling than direct evidence from a witness.

When Mary Welcome made her argument before the jury, she labeled our prosecution of Williams a case of convenience and expediency. She attacked the introduction of the ten cases tied to Williams, arguing they were only there to prejudice the jury against him. She ridiculed my reasons for presenting the ten similar cases, and she ridiculed Jack's argument. Wayne Williams, she said, was not a failure—he was a dreamer, like Martin Luther King Jr.

Jim Kitchens now had a turn as he explained that he had been a prosecutor, like us, and he could recognize a weak prosecution. He likened it to the Bible story of the man who had built his house on sand. Our witnesses, he said, had identified Wayne Williams only after seeing him on TV. No fingerprints were found in the Williams house, and no fibers from the victims were found in the house. The carpet in the Williams home was not unusual, he claimed incorrectly, and despite evidence to the contrary, he insisted that it had been installed in the Williamses' house in 1968.

Court recessed for lunch. After lunch, Al Binder presented the final argument for the defense. Al said Wayne Williams was as recognizable as the president of the United States, his picture having been flashed all over the world, and that's why people identified him—they had seen him on TV. Al took the blame for Wayne's behavior on the witness stand, saying he had just been following Al's suggestions.

Al claimed there had never been a Black serial killer and mentioned how happy he was to have Mr. Derum, the former police officer, on the jury, as he would understand a lack of evidence.

Al now turned to a visual display he unveiled on an easel. As he pulled a fabric cover off the easel, the jury saw a large wooden puzzle, about four feet square. He said, in his folksy voice, "It's the best that us poor folks can do." The puzzle portrayed a picture of a bridge, made up of multiple wooden pieces.

Al stepped away from the puzzle and berated the pattern we had presented. There was no pattern, he claimed. And if there had actually been a nylon rope in Wayne Williams' car, the police would have seized it. "Where is that rope?" Al screamed to the jury.

Judge Cooper now asked Binder and Slaton to approach the bench. He wanted everyone to know that another snowstorm was coming and that schools were being closed. Slaton said it was nothing: "Let's just stay here."

Binder agreed, saying, "I ain't got no place to go."

Cooper announced to the people in the courtroom that they could leave if they wished. Few people left the courtroom, and Al Binder continued. Nothing, he said, was found in the Williams house. So, he claimed, we shifted our case to say that the victims had died in the automobiles. The fibers in Mary Welcome's office, he said, were the same as the fibers in the Williams house. He ignored the fact that Larry Peterson had explained how very different Mary Welcome's fibers were from the unusual Wellman green carpet fiber. He attacked each of our witnesses and accused Sharon and Eustis Blakely of betraying Williams, after all he had done for them.

Al now returned to his wooden bridge puzzle. He said we had tried to make the puzzle fit, but it didn't. With a theatrical flourish, he yanked on a string at the bottom of the puzzle. With a clatter, puzzle pieces fell to the floor. The bridge portrayed in the puzzle was supposed to collapse. Unfortunately for Al, not all the pieces fell. The image of the bridge remained intact. The jury could still see the picture.

Al ended by telling jurors that the murders had continued, and the killer was still at large. The killings had stopped, of course, as asphyxia deaths had dramatically dropped after Williams' arrest, and bodies covered with rare fiber combinations were no longer being left along roadsides and dumped in rivers.

Gordon Miller now stepped before the jury, explaining that the reason there were no fibers from Nathaniel Cater found in the station wagon was that Cater was naked when he was dumped in the river. We didn't know what Cater had been wearing, and there were no clothes to examine for fibers from the car. Gordon ticked off a list of inaccuracies in the defense arguments and reminded the jury that Wayne Williams had been driving a Ford automobile when Charles Stephens was murdered. The defense had argued that the Williams family didn't have their red Ford LTD at the time of Stephens' disappearance and death. But Homer Williams had presented rental agreements for other Ford automobiles used during that time period, and all those cars would have the same type of ground-up junk fibers making up the trunk liners.

Gordon explained how the fibers from inside the house would get tracked into the automobiles. If a body had been placed on the floorboard in one of the cars, the body would pick up those fibers from the house. Gordon went over the significance of the testimony from our three fiber experts and talked about the improbability that another person would be associated with the same combination of fibers as those found in Wayne Williams' environment.

Judge Cooper gave the jurors a short recess before Lewis Slaton offered the final word. Slaton began by handing out individual photos to each member of the jury, naming jurors as he handed out photo exhibits and explained what they were. The first photo to Ms. Head, then one to Ms. Rucker, and on and on. He was guiding jurors through the mountain of evidence. Slaton reminded jurors how the fibers found on the bodies changed when the cars changed. Slaton explained that snow covering the ground when you wake up in the morning is circumstantial evidence that it snowed overnight, even if you did not actually see it snow. There was nothing wrong with circumstantial evidence.

Slaton clarified that "we are not trying to prove he's a homosexual." The defense had brought that up.

Slaton explained how Cool Breeze, the drug seller, was actually a good witness. He thought Wayne Williams was a police officer and he watched him very closely and could identify him.

Slaton described how the currents in the Chattahoochee River veered to the left at the I-285 bridge. He then began looking through a pile of exhibits. Suddenly, he turned to me and asked, "Joe, what was that exhibit number on the photo of the river?" I was startled, having never been called upon to carry on a conversation with my co-counsel while he was addressing a jury. I tried not to act surprised, calmly responding with what I thought was the appropriate exhibit number and standing to join Slaton as he found the photo. For the remainder of his argument, I made sure I was listening very carefully.

Slaton finished up, ticking off witnesses who had to have been lying in order for the jury to believe Wayne Williams: Jacobs, Campbell, Holden, Gilliland, Rackleff, Margaret Carter, Darryl Davis, Eric Thompson, H. B. Starr, Mike Leathers, Bobby Tolin, John Laster, Lugene Laster, Kent Hindsman, Robert I. Henry, Nellie Trammel, James Thompson, Charmaine Kendrick, James Barrett, Mary Harris, Andrew Hayes, Billy Pittman, Kathy Andrews, Keith Andrews, Anthony Barber, Dennis Bentley, Sharon Blakely, and "it goes on and on." Slaton mocked Binder's suggestion that Jimmy Ray Payne was out swimming in the chilly waters of the Chattahoochee River in April, and he ridiculed Binder's speculation that Nathaniel Cater had died of an enlarged heart and simply fallen in the river naked.

Slaton talked about Williams' singing group Gemini, but he couldn't remember which of the young men had supposedly given it the name. He turned again to our counsel table and said, "Was it Kemp?"

Jack fielded this one: "Yes, Sheldon Kemp."

Slaton now challenged the jury. "You will have to be responsible for putting Wayne Williams back in the community. It won't be us. It will have to be you." He likened Williams to famous killers like Adolf Hitler and Idi Amin, people who were determined to do away with those they saw as inferior.

THE JURY GETS THE CASE

With closing arguments now over, Judge Cooper wasted no time and immediately began instructing the jury. They should elect one of their number as foreperson. Jurors would decide the facts and apply the law as outlined by the judge. Cooper explained intent, reasonable doubt, the presumption of inno-cence, how to impeach the testimony of a witness, the role of expert witnesses, direct and circumstantial evidence, and the purpose of presenting the ten similar cases to the jury. He ex-plained the definition of murder, alibi evidence, the forms of verdicts to be used, and the need for a unanimous verdict.

Judge Cooper now announced something unusual: "Ladies and gentlemen of the jury, the court has designated the courtroom itself as the place where you shall conduct your deliberations." Because of the number and size of some exhibits, there was not enough space for them in the jury room. Cooper told the jurors that they could take as much time as they wanted in deliberating the case. If they were still deliberating at 8:00 p.m., the judge would have them go back to the hotel. If they had questions, they should just knock on the door to summon the bailiff.

Jurors began asking questions of the judge: "Will we be work-ing tomorrow if we don't finish today?"

"Sure," said Judge Cooper, "as long as it takes for you to make a decision."

"Can we go through all these bags [of evidence]?"

"Sure," he said, "but try to put things back the way you find them."

Cooper had the bailiffs take the jury to the standard-size jury room they had been using throughout the trial. The courtroom was emptied row by row of witnesses, reporters, sketch artists, and spectators. At that point, the courtroom became a giant jury room as the jurors returned to begin the work of deliberating. It was Friday, February 26, 1982, at 4:30 p.m. They deliberated until 7:30 that evening, at which time they had not reached a verdict.

We were no longer allowed in or near the courtroom—it was now the jury's. We waited in our offices wondering if we had left anything out. Though I was relieved that the trial was over, I thought of things we could have done differently and worried about mistakes that might have turned the jury against us. I tried to prepare myself for the disappointment I would feel if Wayne Williams walked out of the courtroom a free man. I went home and tried to sleep, exhausted, but with so many thoughts racing through my head.

With little sleep, I joined the others as we gathered at the office on the morning of Saturday, February 27, 1982. Crowds of reporters, cameramen, and news trucks surrounded the courthouse, as members of the public gawked and milled around, waiting for news. In my seventh-floor office, I tried my best to focus on long-ignored office matters. It was a losing battle. I couldn't distract myself. My office was directly above the Pryor Street entrance to the Fulton County Courthouse, where the noise from the street below and the caravan of news trucks was hard to ignore.

I checked periodically with Michael Smith, Judge Cooper's law clerk, to see if he had heard anything. We sent for takeout food at about 12:30 p.m. and ate in our war room on the third floor, speculating about who would be chosen as the foreperson of the jury. We went through the list of jurors, trying to guess who among them might have become an informal leader during the eight weeks they had been together. Between us, we narrowed it down to four jurors. I guessed Mr. Derum, the middle-aged former police officer. But we had no way of knowing what the dynamics in the jury room had been over the weeks of testimony.

By midafternoon we were worried and wondered what the jury might be doing. Had they already taken votes? Were there people adamant for conviction or adamant for acquittal? We waited. We worried. We were impatient.

At about 4:30 p.m. I called Michael Smith. The jury had reached a verdict on one of the two murder counts. They had decided something but he didn't know what it was. Could the jury have found that Jimmy Ray Payne drowned? Were they deadlocked on one of the cases? Worry engulfed me as I speculated about the possible outcomes.

At 6:40 p.m., Judge Cooper called to let us know the jury, after a little over eleven hours of deliberation, now had verdicts on both counts. I put on my suit coat and made sure my tie was tied properly, and we headed for the courtroom. We waited outside. The jurors were still using the courtroom as a jury room. Through the vertical windows in the courtroom doors, I could see one juror, a young woman, wiping tears from her cheeks.

Judge Cooper had the jury assume their usual seats in the jury box, and we were allowed into the courtroom. At our table, we waited as hundreds of reporters, sketch artists, family members, witnesses, and onlookers slowly filed into the courtroom. Tension and anticipation filled the air. Two deputies quietly escorted Wayne Williams into the courtroom, where he joined Al Binder, Mary Welcome, and Jim Kitchens at the counsel table to our right. It was now 7:10 p.m.

Everyone was now in place as Judge Cooper asked, "Will the foreperson of the jury please stand."

To our surprise, Sandra Laney, a relatively young Black female, rose from among the assembled jurors.

"Has the jury reached a verdict on each of the two counts?" the judge asked.

"We have, your honor," was the response.

"Will you please examine the verdict to make sure that it has been signed and dated?" said Cooper.

Judge Clarence Cooper now asked Lewis Slaton to "receive the verdict." Slaton approached Sandra Laney, and she handed him the document. Cooper asked Slaton to return to the podium and "publish the verdict in open court." Such was the age-old procedure dictated by law and custom.

Slaton walked to the podium, unfolded the document, and read it briefly to himself as everyone in the courtroom held their breath. Then he read aloud: "We the jury find the defendant, Wayne Bertram Williams, guilty on Count 1. We the jury find the defendant, Wayne Bertram Williams, guilty on Count 2."

There were gasps of grief and gasps of relief almost simultaneously throughout the courtroom. We restrained our relief, but it was not easy. We retained our composure and acted as if this were nothing unusual. Mary Welcome wiped tears from her face as Slaton handed the verdict to Al Binder to inspect. All Binder said was, "Yes, sir." He handed the verdict up to Judge Cooper on the bench.

Judge Cooper now called Wayne Williams to the podium and said, "Mr. Williams, will you stand in front of the podium and face the court?

The judge invited Binder, Welcome, and Kitchens to stand at the podium behind Wayne Williams. The judge continued: "I want the defendant's father, Mr. Homer Williams, to come forward and stand with his son." Homer Williams now joined the defense lawyers near the podium.

Judge Cooper asked the lawyers for Wayne Williams if there was "Anything you would like to say before the court imposes sentence?"

"No, thank you, your honor," said Binder.

"Not at this time," said Mary Welcome.

"No, thank you, your honor," said Jim Kitchens.

Judge Cooper now addressed Wayne Williams. "Mr. Williams, do you wish to say anything?"

Homer Williams thought the judge was speaking to him. "Yes, sir," he said, as he stepped forward. "This is very unjust. I don't see how anybody, anywhere, could find my son guilty on anything." He went on: "Anybody who'd been in this court for the last nine weeks can see that nobody has brought any evidence to prove that my son is guilty!"

Cooper thanked him for his comments. He now made it very clear: "Mr. *Wayne Williams*, do you wish to say anything before the court imposes sentence?

Wayne Williams wanted to talk too. He was innocent, he said. He had no malice toward the jury, the prosecutors, or anybody. "I just hope that the person or persons who have committed these crimes can be brought to justice . . . I did not do this . . . and that is from my heart. I, more than anybody, want to see this terror ended, but I did not do it."

Cooper now read his sentence: "The Court hereby sentences the defendant, Mr. Wayne Bertram Williams, to the custody of the State Board of Corrections where he is to serve two life sentences, and they are to run consecutive."

Wayne Williams was now escorted from the courtroom by two

deputies. Homer Williams, standing near our table, approached Lewis Slaton, pointed his finger, and said, "You are a lowdown rat!" He then called us all "sons of bitches" and stormed back to the spectators' area. The judge asked everyone to remain where they were while he went back to the jury room to thank the jurors for their service. We now had a chance to congratulate each other and heave a sigh of relief. I couldn't feel anything. Was it really over?

Cooper returned to the bench and wanted to bring Wayne Williams back into court so that he could advise him of his right to appeal. Binder said that was unnecessary: "We know of that right. We will tell him of that right." We shook hands with Williams' lawyers.

The trial was over.

I felt numb, unable to exhale and appreciate the moment. Downstairs in the large lobby of the Fulton County Courthouse, crowds of milling reporters, cameramen, witnesses, mothers of victims, and curious onlookers packed the marble-walled entrance hall. Slaton said, "It's time to go meet the press." The gag order was over, and we could speak freely. With some apprehension we took the elevator to the lobby level, and as the doors of the elevator creaked open, we were engulfed in the din of hundreds of people talking, being interviewed, and celebrating or commiserating about the verdict.

I saw Camille Bell, mother of victim Yusef Bell, holding forth on how unjust the verdict was. She had worked as an investigator for the defense and didn't think Williams could be the killer. Witnesses and police officials were being interviewed. Lights from a number of camera crews flashed like lightning around the cavernous room. There was a large bank of microphones waiting to hear what we had to say.

Lewis Slaton was our boss, the elected district attorney, and he was now in full "politician" mode. We were his assistants and would follow his lead. He spoke of our team effort and thanked everyone imaginable for the great job they had done: Judge Cooper, the jury, the police agencies, the FBI. Slaton mentioned that I would be handling the appeal. Now each of us was invited to say something. When my turn came, everyone wanted to know if the case would survive on appeal. I expressed optimism that we could hold the case on appeal. We were on sound legal ground, I promised. Reporters asked about specifics, such as our decision to offer in evidence the ten pattern cases. I explained that such was permitted under the law. Our comments were carried live on television sets across Atlanta and beyond.

Jack, Gordon, Wally, and I decided to go somewhere special and enjoy a nice dinner. We gathered our wives and joined some of the FBI and police officials who had already headed to Dailey's, a downtown restaurant, for our first chance to relax in over nine months. Unwinding was not easy—I felt totally spent, like one who had just survived a harrowing experience. Returning to normal would take a while.

I tried to sleep late the next morning, a Sunday. I couldn't do it, as my mind was still in high gear, as if anticipating another day of trial.

I awoke to Sunday newspapers blaring the headline: "Williams Guilty!"

Chapter 18

ANOTHER PHASE BEGINS

n Monday morning, March 1, 1982, I joined Lewis Slaton as we traveled to the Task Force office on West Peachtree Street for a press conference. Lee Brown, Atlanta's commissioner of public safety, was going to make an announcement. Slaton and I met briefly with Brown, leaders of the Georgia Bureau of Investigation, and other police officials. We discussed how many cases were likely linked to Williams. I showed the group my chart of the cases.

In addition to the twelve cases we had presented at trial, there were eleven other cases linked either by fiber evidence, by eyewitnesses, or by their strong similarities to the cases of Cater and Payne. Lee Brown announced to the crowd of reporters that the Task Force, as it had existed, was being disbanded, and that twenty-three of the murders could be attributed to Wayne Williams. Days later, Brown backtracked slightly, explaining that the unsolved cases would continue to be investigated by a smaller version of the Task Force, composed of the Atlanta officers who had been among the 102 local police officers working the case.

That evening the *Atlanta Journal* quoted one juror as saying, "We tried every way possible to send him home, but the evidence was so overwhelming, we had no choice but to convict."

As I returned to life in my seventh-floor office in the Fulton County Courthouse, I had an overwhelming feeling of letdown. It was now just a normal week, as I shifted my focus to less noteworthy murders, robberies, and rapes. I boxed up notes, photos, and documents from the trial and tried to organize it for what I knew would be coming—the appeal. I began to reenter the world I had left the previous May. So much of what I had to catch up on now seemed mundane. The transition was depressing.

On March 4, 1982, the *Atlanta Constitution* reported that Wayne Williams, during the height of the murders, had applied for a job working as a medical photographer at the county morgue. That same day, the *Atlanta Journal* carried a front-page story about the psychologist Al Binder had considered calling as a witness for the defense. The psychologist was now reporting to the press that Wayne Williams was "a compulsive liar with a need for power and attention and emotionally capable of killing!" He had interviewed Williams three times and claimed that Williams had tried to run the defense team, loving the attention and the power that it, and the trial, brought. And, he noted, Williams blamed everyone but himself for his own behavior.

Weeks later, Larry Peterson called to tell me that Patrick Roger's clothing, originally submitted as an "unidentified" case designation, had now been examined. Rogers had been victim number seventeen on the list of missing and murdered children, and his body, fully clothed, had been pulled from the Cobb County side of the Chattahoochee River in December of 1980. Rogers, despite being in the river for weeks, still had Wellman 181b, Nylon 6,6 fibers on his clothing, in addition to the unusual violet acetate fibers from Wayne Williams' bedspread, and dog hairs matching Sheba, the Williamses' dog. Patrick Rogers became the twenty-fourth case cleared by the conviction of Wayne Williams.

The Georgia General Assembly was in the final weeks of its session, and over the following days, I attended committee meetings in an effort to catch up on what had been happening while I was living in another world. I went to the Senate Judiciary Committee meeting on Wednesday and met with a coalition of law enforcement lobbyists on Thursday. My old life was returning, but it still felt foreign.

Al Binder and Jim Kitchens returned to Mississippi. Lynn Whatley, who sat in on much of the trial, volunteered to take over the role of representing Williams. Whatley had represented Homer and Faye Williams. Binder remained as lead counsel, but Whatley filed most of the documents, with his name and Binder's appearing as counsel for Williams. Mary Welcome was no longer involved, and within a year she moved back to her hometown of Baltimore. Harold Spence, Cliff Bailey, Gail Anderson, and Ken McLeod withdrew from the case. Our team was scattering as well. Jack Mallard returned to his regular courtroom duties and would retire from the Fulton County District Attorney's Office a few months later to begin a career in another district attorney's office, in Cobb County, Georgia. Gordon Miller left as well, to take a job in drug prosecution with the United States Attorney's Office. Wally Speed resumed his regular courtroom responsibilities. The team was no more, and my role as an appellate lawyer was just beginning.

Al Binder and Lynn Whatley filed a motion for new trial two weeks after the trial. Whatley also filed a motion asking that Williams be declared indigent and that counsel be provided for him. All Williams' lawyers seemed to be bailing out. Whatley filed a pile of motions, asking for evidence to be returned and asking our office to turn over a host of records to the defense. Meanwhile, court reporter Susan Northington began the daunting task of producing the sixteen-volume transcript of the trial.

As March ripened into a long and beautiful spring, my life was consumed with the scores of appeals and other matters long neglected. Legislative work resumed, and administrative duties, including personnel matters, began dominating my time. Even so, there were constant reminders of the trial. Letters about the case continued to come in, as did occasional requests to speak to civic groups.

My life changed considerably in late May, with the birth of my first child, a beautiful daughter named Elizabeth. The joy of fatherhood now occupied my daily life.

Occasionally, news articles would catch my attention. On July 2, 1982, four months after the trial, an article in the *Atlanta Constitution* was headlined "Slayings Probe Is Hit Again." Two of the mothers of murder victims were "decrying official decisions to blame convicted murderer Wayne B. Williams for most of the deaths." Camille Bell, mother of victim Yusef Bell, and Annie Rogers, mother of victim Patrick Rogers, had joined with members of the Revolutionary Communist Youth Brigade in a news conference outside the Fulton County State Court building. Ms. Bell, who had organized mothers two years earlier, was quoted as saying that Wayne Williams was not "the answer to all twenty-nine slayings in himself." Ms. Rogers said she just "can't accept" the fiber evidence linking her son to the other murders. In her words: "We know well that Williams didn't do it by himself!" The mothers suggested that others may have been involved and that there was a police "cover-up."

Despite Williams' conviction, many in the community, including mothers of the missing and murdered children, were unaware of all that had transpired during the trial and the extent of the evidence connecting Wayne to the young people who had been on the list. I assumed there had been follow-up by police agencies with the families of the victims. But at that time, there weren't any victim and witness assistance programs that are common in the criminal justice system today. I couldn't understand how anyone familiar with the evidence at trial could have doubts about the identity of the serial killer who had terrorized Atlanta. But many people in the community, including the families of many victims, were unfamiliar with the evidence. Instead, they focused on bizarre rumors of castration of victims, Klan involvement, and plots to harvest bodily fluids from victims. There had been little follow-up by law enforcement agencies, leaving the family members with a simmering suspicion of the police, and even suspicions regarding the city administration, now headed by longtime community leader Andrew Young.

Over the spring and summer, as court reporter Susan Northington completed each additional portion of the transcript, I outlined the testimony, with references to the page numbers I would need to refer to in future legal proceedings. By August, Northington had finished the entire transcript. Binder, who was experiencing health problems and was working on the case from five hundred miles away, asked to withdraw from the case. Judge Cooper now appointed the public defender of Fulton County to work with Lynn Whatley on the case. Tommy Chason, a veteran public defender, joined the defense. Despite having the resources of the Fulton County Public Defender at his disposal, Whatley invited two private lawyers to assist him, Bernard Freamon and Robert Klepak. Freamon was a New Jersey lawyer and associate law professor at Seton Hall University Law School, and Klepak was a Georgia lawyer.

Whatley filed a motion asking to reinvestigate the entire case. I objected. Pending before the court was a motion for new trial, a review of the rulings and evidence presented in the nine-week trial concluded on February 27, 1982. This was not a "redo" of the case. Judge Cooper entered an order allowing Freamon and Klepak to sit at the table with Lynn Whatley, but denying Whatley's other requests. Cooper scheduled argument on the motion for new trial for December 15, 1982.

A motion for new trial gives a judge a chance to correct mistakes made at a trial. Only rarely does a judge overturn his own rulings. The motion for new trial serves normally as a warm-up for an appeal to a higher court. A lawyer can try out various arguments before the trial judge and use the best arguments later before an appellate court.

Whatley still wanted to turn the motion for new trial into a retrial of the case. He was persistent. Before the hearing, he filed more motions, along with affidavits from lawyers, an affidavit from a man known as "the Dog Man," and an affidavit from Charles Morton, the fiber expert the defense chose not to call as a witness. None of the affidavits appeared relevant to the case. The "Dog Man," who had engaged in searches during the murders, had not testified and could add nothing to a review of the record. The fiber expert's complaints about not having enough time at the lab mattered little, since the defense declined to call him as their expert.

I was surprised by the amount of public interest and media attention at the hearing. I had assumed that interest in the case had subsided. I was wrong.

At the hearing, Cooper reminded Whatley to confine his arguments to matters appearing in the record of the case. Each time the defense lawyers went too far afield, I objected.

Whatley attacked the admission of the ten similar cases and claimed circumstantial evidence was not proof, but speculation. He claimed there was no pattern at all and that we won the trial by innuendo, speculation, news releases, and character assassination. He claimed to have newly discovered evidence. He avoided the facts.

Having heard the arguments, Judge Cooper denied the motion for new trial. Judge Cooper's involvement in the case was now at an end. Once Williams' defense team filed a "Notice of Appeal" to the Georgia Supreme Court, jurisdiction over the case would move to the high court.

Chapter 19

THE GEORGIA SUPREME COURT REVIEWS THE CASE

𝕴 n 1982, the Georgia Supreme Court consisted of seven justices, the term "justice" being generally reserved for the
highest court of a jurisdiction. While technically subject to
election by the people, most justices found their way onto the
court through appointment by the governor, usually filling a
vacancy resulting from the death or resignation of a justice in the
middle of a term.

Lynn Whatley filed a notice of appeal in the Georgia Supreme
Court in early January 1983 in the case of the *State v. Wayne
Bertram Williams*. That notice alerted the clerk to gather all tran-
scripts of evidence presented at trial and all motions, responses,
and orders filed in the case since Wayne Williams was indicted.
These documents were then delivered to the Georgia Supreme
Court, which logged in, or "docketed," the case, now titled *Wayne
Bertram Williams v. State of Georgia*.

Because of the length of the trial and the complexity of the issues, the Supreme Court relaxed customary rules in regard to the
length of briefs and time allotted to file them. The brief on behalf
of Wayne Williams, with thirty-three enumerations of error, was

filed in early April of 1983. Enumerations of error are allegations of mistakes made by the judge in the trial that might justify granting a new trial. The party appealing must then show, from the record and transcripts, the existence of the mistakes and why the mistakes were so significant that they prevented a fair trial.

I had argued my first case in an appellate court in Ottawa, Illinois, thirteen years earlier. Since then, I had moved to Georgia, rotated among various divisions in the district attorney's office in Fulton County, and been promoted to head the Appellate Section. Appeals were my specialty, and I prided myself on keeping up with the never-ending flow of decisions from appellate courts in Georgia and the United States Supreme Court. By reading and taking notes on each new decision from Georgia's appellate courts, I was able to provide a resource for the trial lawyers within the office. After years of adding to the three-inch black binder I used at trial, I had a case to cite in response to almost every situation.

In their appeal, Lynn Whatley and assistant public defender Tommy Chason touched on every key ruling made by Judge Cooper. They alleged that fiber evidence was unreliable and had been admitted without legal basis. They complained that their experts were not afforded sufficient time to inspect the fibers and that laboratory reports were not submitted to the defense in a timely fashion.

The Williams team took aim at the ten similar cases and complained about everything from jury selection to closing arguments. They argued that there was not enough evidence to convict Williams and that Judge Cooper should have suppressed much of the evidence. They claimed Williams' own lawyers were ineffective and that Cooper had tainted the jury with prejudicial comments. They insisted he should have declared a mistrial, without even being asked, when a drawing with the word "guilty" underneath was discovered in an area where jurors ate meals.

Writing my brief involved a month of tedium, connecting transcript pages to events in the trial, adding arguments and citations from Georgia Supreme Court and Court of Appeals cases. In 1983, computer word processing was only a dream, and I wrote my brief in longhand, section by section, on yellow legal pads. As I wrote, a secretary who provided administrative assistance to me and five other lawyers, worked dutifully on a typewriter. The final product was wrapped with a light-blue backing as required by Supreme Court rules. On May 6, 1983, I carried my 127-page brief the one-block walk to the Supreme Court Clerk's Office in the State Judicial Building. Ten days later, we would argue the case before the seven justices of the Georgia Supreme Court.

As head of the Appellate Section in the district attorney's office, I made frequent visits to the Georgia Supreme Court. I felt comfortable in the sixth-floor courtroom that was then home to the court. The Judicial Building, circa 1954, featured courtrooms for both the Supreme Court and the Court of Appeals of Georgia. The courtrooms were bland mid-1950s modern. Other than the presence of a wall of white marble rising behind the long bench shared by the seven justices, there was little of note in the high-ceilinged courtroom. Etched in the white marble behind the justices was the Latin phrase *Fiat Justicia Ruat Caelum*, or "Let justice be done though the heavens fall." Around the walls of the windowless courtroom, a dozen large portraits of stern-looking former justices peered down.

I was no stranger to the seven men who sat on the Supreme Court. Fifty-nine-year-old Harold Hill, a stocky reformer with wavy gray hair, had been on the court for eight years and, as the most senior justice in years of service, was serving as the Chief Justice. Next in years of service was Thomas O. Marshall, a tall, stately, gray-haired gentleman who carried himself with such dignity that he seemed to have been plucked from central casting to play the role of a judge. Justice Marshall, sixty-two, had served for over seventeen years as a judge in the south Georgia town of Americus before being appointed to the Supreme Court by Governor George Busbee in 1977. He had been on the court for six years.

Harold Clark, a balding fifty-five-year-old, had been on the court for four years and had served previously in the Georgia General Assembly and as president of the State Bar of Georgia, the organization that licenses and regulates the practice of law in Georgia. In past years, I had tangled over legislation with Clark in his role as president of the State Bar. We were, at best, on cordial terms.

Hardy Gregory Jr., in his forties, was one of the younger justices, coming from a law practice in Cordele, Georgia. His youth was evident from his full head of dark hair. Gregory had been on the court for two years and had an easygoing and affable manner.

Another justice with whom I had a history was fifty-six-year-old George T. Smith. George T., as he was known, was a hell-raiser of the first order. Unlike the many other members of the court, George T. had not been appointed by the governor. He ran for the office and was elected. He had served on the Court of Appeals for four years and remained consistently controversial, unpredictable, and argumentative. He often described himself as the defense lawyers' representative on the court. I had appealed one of George T.'s Court of Appeals decisions to the Georgia Supreme Court, where I referred to his reasoning in his Court of Appeals decision as "trampling common sense." The Supreme Court of Georgia agreed and reversed his decision. George T. was proudly one of the few people in Georgia history to serve in all three branches of government, having served in the legislative branch as Speaker of the Georgia House of Representatives, in the executive branch as lieutenant governor, and then in the judicial branch in both the Court of Appeals and Supreme Court.

Charles Weltner, at fifty-five, was best known for his stand against segregation in 1963. As a congressman from Georgia, he was one of only seven southerners to vote for the Civil Rights Act of 1964. In 1966, he gave up his congressional seat rather than sign the Democratic Party loyalty pledge to support the Democratic candidate for governor, segregationist Lester Maddox. Weltner had lost to Maynard Jackson in the 1973 race for mayor of Atlanta but was later appointed by Governor George Busbee to the Superior Court of Fulton County and later to the Supreme Court. Justice Weltner was both a scholar and a reformer, and I admired the logic often expressed in his decisions.

The seventh and newest member of the court was sixty-three-year-old Richard Bell, a short, stocky veteran of twenty years as DeKalb County's district attorney and six years as a Superior Court judge. Bell was gruff and unpolished and, like George T. Smith, had won his seat on the Supreme Court by way of election, rather than appointment.

The lawyers representing Wayne Williams attempted in every way to undermine his conviction. They criticized every decision we had made as prosecutors and accused Judge Clarence Cooper of repeatedly ruling inappropriately during the trial. As the lawyer representing the state of Georgia, my job was to defend every phase of the prosecution and every decision made by Judge Cooper. In a way, I was defending much of my own work on the case, as I had personally argued for many of the decisions made in our favor by Judge Cooper.

In the scores of appeals I had previously authored, my work usually began when the work of others finished (i.e., someone else had tried the case). This was different—I had been a major contributor in shaping the legal issues I would now defend before the court.

I followed my usual ritual for preparing. Time would be limited, and arguments would have to be succinct. I could expect the justices to ask questions that would interrupt the flow of my argument. I would have to have the most important evidence and the relevant law at my fingertips. As was my custom, I started with a legal-size accordion-type file folder, into which I would place a series of thin manila folders, each covering a single issue and containing a summary of keywords, facts, phrases, and quotes from cases supporting my position. In large letters on the cover of each file, I would write keywords that I could see from a distance, allowing me to quickly pick up the right folder. During my argument, I would spread the folders like playing cards on the counsel table, where I could glance down and grab the right folder. My file overflowed with dozens of the thin manila folders labeled with words like Similars, Fiber, Bridge, Statements, Closing, Polygraph, Pretrial Publicity, and Access to Crime Lab.

Before any presentation, I am always anxious. Have I missed something? Do I have everything? Is my pen going to run out of ink? Is my hair combed? Will I lose my voice? I had lost my voice once during an argument in 1976 before the Georgia Supreme Court, and it was embarrassing. It led me to quit smoking and had perhaps saved my life.

Sleep was always difficult the night before an argument. On this day I woke early, arrived at the office early, and reached the Supreme Court early. On the sixth floor of the Judicial Building, I checked in with the clerk of the Supreme Court, seated in the courtroom at a small desk to the left of the long judges' bench. It was not yet 9:30 a.m., and the courtroom was already full for our 10:00 a.m. argument, the only one scheduled for the day. News photographers packed the small space behind the clerk, jockeying for the best position to get good shots of the podium from which we would argue.

I tried to shut out all distractions and retreated to the lawyers' lounge, located off a hallway near the main doors to the courtroom. The murmur of people seeking entrance penetrated the quiet of the small lounge, furnished with a leather couch and a few round tables where a lawyer could nervously make final preparations before entering the courtroom. Most important, the lounge contained small restrooms, so essential to a lawyer under these circumstances. That was my last stop before taking a deep breath and entering the rear door of the courtroom.

I clutched my bulging accordion folder under my arm and made my way to the front of the courtroom, where an associate held a seat for me on the front row of the public seating area. The area directly in front of the long bench, soon to be occupied by the seven justices, featured a large, stained-wood podium and two massive counsel tables. A four-foot-tall railing separated that inner area of the courtroom from the rows of benches that made up the public seating area. In order to gain entry to the counsel tables, a lawyer had to negotiate one of the swinging brass gates positioned on each side of the court. I had seen the confidence of many lawyers shaken when they approached the gate and didn't know how to open it.

When the justices entered the courtroom, the clerk would formally announce their arrival, which required everyone to rise. Directly behind the long bench was a marble-covered double door that slid open with a whirring noise and reminded me of something out of a 1950s *Flash Gordon* movie. These doors would open, and the seven robed justices, somber and unsmiling, would file in to take their assigned seats on the bench, with the newest justices on the far ends and the chief justice in the center.

Chief Justice Harold Hill then addressed the clerk: "Madam Clerk, please call the next case."

"Case Number 39641, Wayne Bertram Williams versus the State of Georgia. Mr. Lynn Whatley and Mr. Bernard Freamon for the Appellant; Mr. Joseph Drolet for the Appellee."

This was our cue to stand and make our way to the brass gate providing entrance directly in front of the justices. I successfully negotiated the gate, took possession of the table on the left, and quietly spread my files in front of me. I pulled out a legal pad to take notes on points argued by opposing counsel. A pitcher of water and small paper cups helped with the dryness I would experience in the coming minutes.

Lynn Whatley argued first, dividing his time with Bernard Freamon, who had assisted at the hearing before Judge Cooper. As counsel for the appellant, they had the burden of showing that significant errors had been made during the trial of Wayne Williams. I would respond and refute their claims, and they would then have a brief final opportunity to speak.

Whatley called the prosecution a "witch hunt" and claimed that Williams was a convenient scapegoat in a rush to blame someone for the rash of murders that had terrified Atlanta. The justices listened patiently as Whatley went through many of the high points of his brief, as did Freamon, who took particular aim at the fiber evidence, arguing that it was voodoo science, unreliable, and inaccurate.

When my turn came, I ticked off responses to each claim. Justice

George T. Smith tore into my arguments, calling the introduction of similar cases "bootstrapping," pulling one case along by another. I sparred with Smith and used the opportunity to point out how significant and damning the fiber evidence was, as well as how obvious the connections were between the cases. Time flew as I covered each subject until it was suddenly over. The chief justice thanked us for our presentations and declared the court adjourned. The seven justices stood, turned, and filed back through the double doors and out of the courtroom. I gathered my files and notes and waded through the crowd of onlookers lingering at the rear of the courtroom. I avoided an encounter with Homer and Faye Williams, who had been seated prominently in the front row of the spectators' area.

Now my mind raced. Had I covered everything? Had I said anything that was inaccurate? After every big presentation, I tended to question my own competence. It was always difficult to remember exactly what I had said in the heat of an argument. I returned to my office and placed my large accordion file in one of the half-dozen boxes of files from the trial. I wondered whether I would be needing that file again.

The next morning, newspaper photos showed me waving my hands and gesturing, a habit I have been unable to break after years of arguing cases. The *New York Times* snapped a shot as I held up a crime lab report for the justices. The *Atlanta Constitution* published a photo of me seated at the counsel table, looking ever so serious as I'm studying my notes. This case was now over until the Georgia Supreme Court rendered its opinion, which would be months into the future. I resumed my more mundane life as an assistant district attorney.

Months passed. There would be an occasional news story mentioning the case, but things were generally quiet. On December 5, 1983, a deputy clerk in the Supreme Court called to say they were releasing the opinion. A copy was available if I wanted to walk up to the clerk's office. Normally decisions were physically mailed and you would learn what happened when you received that mail.

I walked as fast as I could the one block up the hill to the State Judicial Building and into the clerk's office. A thick mailing envelope with my name on it was waiting. I ripped it open and searched for the keywords: judgment affirmed. The court, in an eighty-page opinion, had upheld the verdict. Justice George T. Smith had dissented and written his own opinion explaining why he would have granted a new trial. He didn't like the similar transactions or the questioning of Williams near the bridge, and he was unimpressed with fiber evidence. Six justices ruled otherwise, and Justice Richard Bell was listed as the author of the opinion.

I rushed back to the Fulton County Courthouse to let Lewis Slaton know we had won the appeal. Slaton, like the rest of our team, was pleased but showed less emotion than I had expected. Personally, I was excited—the opinion of the court was a validation of all our work.

Whatley and the team representing Williams filed a routine motion for rehearing a few days after the order came down, to which I filed a written response. Not surprisingly, the Georgia Supreme Court, which had spent over six months considering the case, was not about to suddenly change its mind. The motion was denied.

At the time, I felt certain that my job was finally done.

Chapter 20

IT ISN'T OVER

wo months after the Georgia Supreme Court ruling, a new book, serialized in some newspapers, attacked the initial investigation. *The List* was written by one of the investigators for the defense, Chet Dettlinger, along with *Los Angeles Times* reporter Jeff Prugh. In the book, which was replete with factual errors, Dettlinger claimed to be the only one who knew the real pattern of killings but no one would listen to him.

With some validity, the book suggested that the list of cases investigated by the Task Force was somewhat arbitrary, since there were many murders taking place in Atlanta between 1979 and 1981. What the book didn't acknowledge was that when the Task Force was organized and a group of cases were assigned, no clear pattern had yet developed. Many of the early cases on the list, like the cases of the two girls, turned out to be unrelated to the bulk of cases that followed. Only in hindsight did a pattern emerge.

More than anything, the book was an attack on the handling of the case by Atlanta police. Wayne Williams' mother, Faye, was later quoted in the *Atlanta Journal* and *Constitution,* saying, "I think he [Dettlinger] has a vendetta to settle against the police." On this matter, Mrs. Williams appeared to have it right.

Dettlinger trashed Judge Cooper and the Georgia Supreme Court.

He trashed me in the book as well, saying I didn't understand the pattern. "It is so poorly conceived as to be ludicrous," said Dettlinger. He also said that Lynn Whatley's brief "put the prosecution's brief to shame." Having prevailed in the appeal, I tended to disagree. While the book was less than complimentary of my work, I enjoyed its inclusion of a pronunciation guide for my oft-mispronounced last name: "Drolet (pronounced 'Dro-LAY')." Not long after it came out, I found a copy in a markdown pile at a small bookstore on Ponce de Leon Avenue in Atlanta, on sale for $6.98.

Later that year a man named William Northrop wrote an article bluntly titled "Wayne Williams Is Innocent," published in *Penthouse* magazine. Northrop identified himself as the chief investigator for the Wayne Williams defense team, but he was not one of the team members I had become familiar with during the nine-week trial. Northrop's command of the facts was suspect, but to the casual reader, that may not have been obvious.

Then in June of 1984, an article in the *Atlanta Constitution* reported that Camille Bell, the organizer of the mothers during the killings, was consulting with movie producer Abby Mann, who had gained fame for the movie *Judgment at Nuremberg*. The *New York Times* would go on to report that a movie was in development and that the author of *The List*, Chet Dettlinger, was an advisor on Mann's production. It was beginning to look like the case was not yet over.

Then came Geraldo.

In October of 1984, Lewis Slaton called me to his office to tell me that Geraldo Rivera, with the ABC News show *20/20*, would be coming by for an interview. Being well-versed on the case, when anything about it came up, Slaton liked to have me sitting on the couch, to the left of his desk, while he spoke with reporters sitting directly in front of him.

Geraldo arrived on schedule, and his film crew began setting up cameras and lights. Geraldo was friendly and deferential as we prepared for the interview; he was also much shorter than I expected. As the lights came on and the camera rolled, Geraldo asked Slaton if the killings had really stopped after Wayne

Williams was spotted on the James Jackson Parkway Bridge. Slaton said that they had and that Nathaniel Cater was the last victim to be dumped in the river.

With great drama, Geraldo now stood and slapped an official-looking report on Slaton's desk, directly under his nose. In an inquisitor-like fashion, he asked Slaton to explain what the document revealed.

Slaton calmly looked down at the report, then turned to hand it to me as I leaned forward from the couch. He said, "Joe, call the medical examiner and see which case this is." In my hand was an autopsy report, dated June of 1981, with no name attached, only a Fulton County medical examiner case number. It described a young Black male wearing only undershorts, dead of asphyxia, and retrieved from the Chattahoochee River. If a body had been pulled from the river in June of 1981, after Wayne Williams' last known victim, then it would appear that the murders had not truly ended.

I soon had the medical examiner on the phone and received an answer. The report was the autopsy on Jimmy Ray Payne, one of the two victims we had convicted Wayne Williams of murdering. This was not a new, post–Wayne Williams victim. Dr. Zaki, the assistant medical examiner, had performed the autopsy in April, when Payne's body was found in the river; however, the report had not been transcribed and filed until June 16, 1981, several weeks after Williams became a suspect.

I stepped back into Slaton's office and handed him the report. I enjoyed calmly saying, "That's Jimmy Ray Payne's autopsy. It's not a new case." Slaton then shared my findings with Geraldo and his crew, who had been eagerly anticipating a panicked on-air response. The steam quickly went out of the interview, which appeared on the November 8, 1984, airing of *20/20*, hosted by Barbara Walters.

MORE EVIDENCE

During the trial, Homer Williams had provided rental car agreements to show that his son had *not* been driving the family's red Ford LTD from August through mid-October of 1980. After the trial, fiber expert Larry Peterson had stopped by my office. We were both interested in what fibers might be found in the rental cars, so I shared copies of those rental agreements with him. Fibers from a Ford trunk liner had been found on victim Charles Stephens in October, and we had assumed that they came from the red LTD. Homer Williams' evidence was intended to prove otherwise.

When these documents were offered in evidence, we were amazed to see that Homer Williams had rented similar Ford automobiles that would've contained the same fiber types found in the trunk of the red Ford LTD. But the agreements ultimately revealed much more. Homer Williams had rented three 1980 Ford Fairmonts—one brown, one yellow, and one white. We had been unaware of these three vehicles, all of which had been used by Wayne Williams during an eight-week period in the late summer of 1980.

During that period, Earl Lee Terrell, Clifford Jones, and Charles Stephens had either disappeared or been found dead. Clifford Jones' case had always been particularly perplexing. His strangled body was found laid out on his back, missing undergarments. On his clothing were four of the rare green trilobal Wellman carpet fibers, eight of the violet acetate fibers from Wayne Williams' bedspread, and four dog hairs similar to those recovered from Sheba, the Williamses' dog. Also present were fibers commonly used in the trunks of Ford products of that period.

What was perplexing was an abundance of over two dozen beige carpet fibers loosely clinging to Jones' hair, body, and clothing. They appeared to have come from wherever his body had been immediately before he was left next to the dumpster. I had wondered if perhaps his body had been wrapped in a piece of beige carpet before being placed where he was found. As far as we knew, the red Ford LTD was the car Williams was driving at that time. The source of those fibers had remained a mystery.

In late fall of 1984, Larry Peterson left a message saying that he had found the three rental cars. The next day he reported that the brown Ford fibers matched fibers found on Earl Terrell. Homer Williams had rented that brown Ford the day before Earl disappeared.

In August of 1980, he had rented the yellow Ford. During that time, Clifford Jones had been murdered. Fibers from the beige carpeting inside that yellow Ford matched the twenty-seven mystery fibers that had been so prominent on Clifford's body and clothing. The trunk fibers from that same Ford also matched fibers found on his body.

The white Ford had been rented in September and early October of 1980. The fibers from that trunk matched the fibers found on the body of Charles Stephens, who, like Clifford Jones, had been found on his back, his arm out to the side, bent at the elbow. Additionally, both boys were missing clothing, their bodies had been prominently posed where they were found, and they had died of asphyxia.

Counting the initial three, we could now point to six different vehicles driven by Wayne Williams as sources for fibers found on victims. Most significantly, the different fibers found on the bodies corresponded precisely with the different cars driven by Williams. When he stopped driving a certain car, the corresponding fibers would no longer appear; when he began using a different car, different fibers would be found on the victims. The fibers reflected the pattern of the murders as he changed cars.

THE KLAN?

Late in 1984, Lewis Slaton called me to his office for a meeting with Phil Peters, director of the Georgia Bureau of Investigation. Peters, whose name now adorns the GBI Headquarters Building, wanted to share some information about the missing and murdered children's case. I took my usual place on the couch near Slaton's desk.

During the time of the murders, the GBI had conducted an investigation of the Ku Klux Klan, though not many saw the Klan as a serious threat. To the extent that it existed, it was a shadow of the organization that had once wielded considerable power in Georgia as it terrorized rural minority communities. The investigation had started in March of 1981. For nearly two months, the GBI watched Klan members, searched their properties, interviewed various witnesses, and tried to find any evidence that the Klan was involved in the murders. The investigation yielded nothing connected to the missing and murdered children. No matching carpet fibers, no matching dog hairs, and nothing associated with any of the victims. The GBI closed the investigation on April 24, 1981, nearly a month before Wayne Williams was stopped near the James Jackson Parkway Bridge.

This information had not been shared with the Task Force or with the district attorney's office. Since the investigation had failed to reveal anything related to the murders, Peters had kept it separate and confidential. However, word had recently leaked to the press, and Peters wanted us to be aware of it. I could already see the headlines.

THE CBS MOVIE

We continued to hear rumors about an upcoming CBS movie. A lawyer close to the defense team had shared part of the script with our office. It was difficult to tell where the production was going, but it was novel to see our names as characters in a movie.

In January of 1985, the CBS public relations apparatus geared up. The movie was being distributed to CBS affiliates all over North America, as part of an effort to win the top TV ratings for the Spring Sweeps period of 1985. As part of the promotion, these nationwide affiliates would call and tell me that actors such as Morgan Freeman, James Earl Jones, Martin Sheen, or Jason Robards were in their studio and suggesting that Wayne Williams was innocent. They would want my comments. With each call, I offered to debate the evidence with whichever actor was there. Not once was that offer taken.

The CBS affiliate in Atlanta was WAGA-TV, Channel 5. A reporter at the station had covered not only the entire Wayne

Williams trial, but also the murders leading up to it. He offered Lewis Slaton and me the opportunity to view the movie at an advanced showing. We traveled to the station's studios, where we watched the two-segment, five-hour production. It was dreadfully inaccurate, creating dramatic images that conflicted directly with known facts. Unfortunately, Abby Mann's success with his award-winning blockbuster documentary *Judgment at Nuremberg* lent credibility to what was now being billed as a "docudrama taken directly from the official trial transcripts of the trial of Wayne Williams." For anyone not intimately familiar with the trial evidence and the actual transcript, the film seemed to suggest that Williams had been framed and that the real killer was still at large. As a courtesy, WAGA-TV provided us a copy of the movie.

Articles about the movie, and the controversy surrounding its accuracy, ran almost daily in Atlanta and throughout the country. From the *Christian Science Monitor* to the *New York Times*, our work on the case was again in the news.

Meanwhile, neither the Atlanta Chamber of Commerce nor the new mayor of Atlanta, former United Nations Ambassador Andrew Young, was happy with the upcoming movie and its negative portrayal of Atlanta. They asked if I could be available to assist them in challenging the accuracy of the movie. Soon I was joining former governor George Busbee and BellSouth president John Clendenin for chili dogs at the Varsity restaurant near Georgia Tech's campus. They were arranging a highly publicized visit to CBS headquarters in New York to take on the network. And I was to be their ammunition.

We would be meeting with six CBS officials at the network's offices on Fifth Avenue. It would be my job to point out discrepancies between the movie and actual events. My weekend prior to the trip was consumed with preparation. Alone in a conference room in the district attorney's office, I watched each scene of the movie, taking notes on how the scenes diverged from the truth. As I had done for my Georgia Supreme Court argument, I created a manila folder for each scene; in each folder, one sheet of paper contained a description of the movie version of the case, and on a second piece of paper I set forth the facts and evidence that had been presented at the trial. In some cases, I copied pages from the trial transcript to offer as evidence to our audience at CBS.

On the morning of February 4, 1985, we gathered at Peachtree-DeKalb Airport. Our contingent consisted of former governor George Busbee, now a high-powered lawyer with a prestigious Atlanta law firm; Mayor Andrew Young; Atlanta Police Commissioner George Napper; business executive and power broker, Jesse Hill; and our host, Chamber of Commerce president John Clendenin. And me. We boarded the BellSouth jet, and each of us took a place in one of the well-appointed cubicles, made comfortable for business travel. With a small desk in my own private area, I had plenty of room to go over the material I would present to CBS.

Absorbed as I had been in my preparations, I had forgotten that a community group in which I was conspicuously active had planned to publish a full-page ad in the *Atlanta Constitution* urging former president Jimmy Carter "not to destroy historic Atlanta neighborhoods with a 'parkway' built on lies, deceit, and corruption." In his race for mayor, Andrew Young, my former congressman, had garnered my support and that of other neighborhood leaders based on his consistent defense of Atlanta's reviving in-town neighborhoods, threatened by the construction of what many deemed unnecessary expressways. After winning a close election, Young agreed to help his old friend Jimmy Carter, who wanted to build his Carter Presidential Library on highway land through seven in-town neighborhoods, including my own. The Department of Transportation had agreed to let Carter have his library between the eastbound and westbound lanes of the defunct Stone Mountain Freeway, which Jimmy Carter himself had stopped in 1972. To get the Presidential Library, Andy Young had to agree to the construction of a highway through our neighborhoods, something we in the community had been fighting for years.

As our aircraft cruised somewhere over the state of Virginia, Commissioner George Napper, whom I had known for years from our involvement in neighborhood politics, broke the silence. Napper shouted to Andy Young, who was in his own cubicle forward in the plane. "Andy, did you see that full-page ad Drolet put in the paper about you this morning?"

I looked up. Andy Young responded, "I saw it."

Napper went on, "What are you gonna do about it?"

Young said, "Don't bother him now; he has to make the presentation. We'll talk about it on the way back."

I chuckled to myself as the interlude had at least partially distracted me from the task in which I was engrossed.

As we were deposited in front of a Fifth Avenue skyscraper with the enormous letters, "CBS," at the top, I began to feel a bit nervous. The success of our mission was on me. We were escorted to a conference room, where a large table had been set up with six seats for CBS vice-presidents and lawyers on one side and six seats for us on the other side. I sat with Governor Busbee to my right and John Clendenin to my left. Clendenin gave brief opening remarks about why we were there and suggested that there were gross inaccuracies in the CBS movie. He then said, "Mr. Drolet here is going to tell you about some problems with your movie." I was on.

I had already begun laying out my file folders, and I explained how I compared each major scene in the movie to the known facts. I started with relatively minor scenes and built to the major ones. One scene depicted Morgan Freeman, in the role of a disenchanted Atlanta police detective, imploring a group of fellow detectives that Wayne Williams could not have thrown a body off the bridge; it would be impossible. In the movie, the bridge was a steel-girder bridge with high steel railings, cross beams limiting access, and a wide sidewalk, making it impossible for a car to get close to the railing to drop a body. I showed the CBS executives a photograph of the actual James Jackson Parkway Bridge, with its narrow sidewalk and low, easily accessible concrete railing.

Scene after scene, I pointed out distortions and misrepresentations of what had actually been presented at trial. Then, well into my presentation, I got to a scene that I knew would cause CBS concern.

At trial, Assistant Fulton County Medical Examiner Saleh Zaki had testified that Jimmy Ray Payne had died of asphyxia. The defense claimed he might have drowned. Based on the surrounding circumstances, including the time of year, the area of the river where the body was found, and a lack of water in the lungs, Zaki had concluded that the death was a homicide.

In the movie, Dr. Zaki tells a detective that there is no evidence of strangulation; if it weren't for all this other information, he says, it might have looked like an accidental drowning. Later in the movie, the actor playing Zaki is on the witness stand. He is asked by actor Rip Torn, playing District Attorney Lewis Slaton, "Dr. Zaki, and what was the cause of death?"

Actor Zaki responds, "Asphyxia, *due to strangulation!*"

People watching the movie would conclude that Dr. Zaki had just committed perjury, swearing there was evidence of strangulation when there was none.

I passed a page from the trial transcript to the folks across the table from me. "As you will see from the transcript, Dr. Zaki never said those words. Those three added words make him guilty of a felony. He is a public official in Atlanta and a licensed medical professional. And you have made him out to be a felon."

At that point, former Governor Busbee, to my right, interrupted and said, "Mr. Drolet, may I say something?"

"Certainly," I responded.

Busbee then firmly lectured the CBS row across from us. "I do not now represent Dr. Zaki, but when we return to Atlanta, I will be calling Dr. Zaki to let him know that should CBS air this movie on February 10, with this scene in the movie, I will happily represent him. And CBS is now on notice that this scene, should it air, could subject CBS to considerable liability. Thank you, Joe, you can continue."

I finished up the presentation. We took a break, and both groups caucused. We decided to demand the removal of the three offending words they had put in Zaki's mouth. We also wanted warnings after each commercial break, before the resumption of the movie, clarifying that it was not a documentary but rather a largely fictionalized drama and not based on the trial transcripts.

CBS agreed to continue negotiations the next day. We read an agreed-upon statement to a large pressroom filled with reporters, including representatives from many of CBS's rivals.

We had not won anything yet, but we certainly had their attention. On the BellSouth jet back to Atlanta, the mood was jubilant. Andy Young never said a word about the full-page ad. George Busbee rewarded my performance with bear hugs. A crowd of reporters met our plane at Peachtree-DeKalb Airport. We would meet at Busbee's law office the next morning to continue our discussions with CBS over the telephone.

Ultimately, these negotiations proved productive. The *Washington Post* reported that "after a prosecutor ticked off a list of dramatic liberties taken with the facts, sources said, CBS promised to delete three words of trial testimony never spoken by a county medical examiner." CBS took out the offending dialogue attributed to Dr. Zaki. On February 6, 1985, the *New York Times* published an article with the headline "Atlanta Murder Film to Get CBS Advisory." The advisory, to be spoken in addition to appearing on-screen, warned that "this is not a documentary, but a drama based on certain facts surrounding the murder and disappearance of children in Atlanta between 1979 and 1981. Some of the events and characters are fictionalized for dramatic purposes."

On February 10, 1985, the movie premiered its first half. "Trial by TV" was how the *New York Times* described it. The article blasted the docudrama genre: "A docudrama is elastic; using the form, one can prove Brutus did *not* stab Caesar." They labeled the movie an "irresponsible piece of work."

After the whole movie was broadcast, six of the twelve jurors from the case weighed in with interviews with the *Atlanta Constitution*. They found the movie distorted and inaccurate. Claryce Jones said, "You had to be there and see and hear all [that] we did." These jurors were dismayed that the movie had condensed and changed so much, in particular leaving out so much of the evidence of Wayne Williams' guilt.

WAGA-TV, the Atlanta CBS affiliate, added a special program to air following the conclusion of the movie on the evening of February 12, 1985. The station made the program available to CBS affiliates nationwide. I appeared live from the courtroom where the trial had been held, along with former police commissioner Lee Brown. I clarified what had really happened at the trial and the real evidence against Wayne Williams.

Later that year, CBS changed their rules for the production of docudramas. Material distortions of historical events were no longer acceptable.

After the movie was broadcast, I was once again preoccupied with defending the case. Former Mayor Maynard Jackson asked me to accompany him to a gathering of citizens concerned about what they had seen in the movie. I addressed concerns and explained the inaccuracies in the movie.

ANOTHER APPEAL

Against the backdrop of the CBS movie and the revelation of an investigation of the Klan, a new appeal to the courts was inevitable. It came on November 11, 1985.

Wayne Williams now had an expanded defense team with some big-name lawyers. Lynn Whatley was still a part of the team, and he was joined by Alan Dershowitz, William Kunstler, and Bobby Lee Cook.

Bobby Lee Cook was a colorful criminal defense lawyer from Summerville, Georgia, reputed to be the basis for the titular TV character Matlock. Cook was probably the highest-profile criminal defense attorney in Georgia. He was thin, sporting a goatee that made him look a bit like Colonel Sanders. He spoke with a deep, southern drawl, and often dressed the part of a flamboyant lawyer.

William Kunstler, a New York civil rights lawyer, had made his name by representing the "Chicago Seven," alleged organizers of violent protests that disrupted the 1968 Democratic Convention in Chicago. Kunstler had frequently sparred with federal judge

Julius Hoffman during that trial and established his reputation as a disruptive nonconformist, irreverent toward the establishment and the law. Kunstler's trademarks were his bushy, wild haircut, booming voice, and a pair of ever-present reading glasses perched on top of his head.

Alan Dershowitz, a Harvard law professor, seemed to pop up in high-profile cases in which he could make professorial pronouncements. The thrust of the new appeal was based on a practice endorsed by Dershowitz in his book, *The Best Defense*. As Dershowitz proclaimed in the preface to the book: "In representing criminal defendants—especially guilty ones—it is often necessary to take the offensive against the government: to put the government on trial for *its* misconduct. In law, as in sports, the best defense is often a good offense." The new filing, a writ of habeas corpus, avoided talking about the guilt of Wayne Williams. As noted in Dershowitz's book, "It is the job of the defense attorney—especially when representing the guilty—to prevent, by all lawful means, the 'whole truth' from coming out."

The writ of habeas corpus was filed on November 11, 1985, in the Superior Court of Butts County, Georgia, where Wayne Williams resided at the Georgia Diagnostic and Classification Prison. The appeal to the Georgia Supreme Court had been a direct appeal, a review of each legal decision made at the trial. A writ of habeas corpus was referred to as a "collateral" attack, based on any newly discovered or peripheral error in procedure not previously known or part of the original direct appeal. Such a writ would challenge whether Wayne Williams was being lawfully detained.

The writ was filed with great fanfare and news coverage. It claimed that we, as prosecutors, had hidden a host of important material evidence, including the so-called Klan investigation. The claim was based on *Brady v. Maryland*, a 1965 United States Supreme Court case which held that material evidence "favorable to the accused" could not be hidden from the defense.

For five years after filing the 1985 claim, their case languished as Lynn Whatley and his expanded stable of lawyers amended the petition and continued to ask the Superior Court of Butts County for extensions of time.

OPEN RECORDS

Meanwhile, other controversies had erupted. In 1986, Brooklyn-born Jack Jersawitz, a rotund, balding, self-proclaimed Communist, began demanding the release of certain Task Force files under Georgia's Open Records Act. Jersawitz, with wild white hair flowing from his sideburns and around to the back of his neck, hosted a TV show on one of the rarely watched public access channels in Atlanta. He called his program *Brainstorm*. Over the years, clad in his open work shirt and wide suspenders, he attacked a variety of public institutions, frequently filing, and occasionally winning, lawsuits demanding agency records.

Jersawitz, alone in a makeshift TV studio, would have chairs lined up for his invited guests. For his programs about the Wayne Williams case, there was a row of empty chairs, one chair with the name "Joseph Drolet" handwritten on a piece of paper taped to the seatback. Similar empty chairs would be set out for Maynard Jackson, Andrew Young, Lewis Slaton, Lee Brown, Judge Clarence Cooper, and others associated with the Wayne Williams trial. Most people didn't take Jack too seriously.

Jersawitz took aim at the files maintained by the Atlanta Police Department relating to the missing and murdered children's cases four years earlier. During his open records litigation, which was defended by the Atlanta city attorney, the case caught the attention of the local newspapers and local TV station WSB-TV, an ABC affiliate. Soon, Jersawitz was a secondary player as the *Atlanta Constitution*, the *Atlanta Journal*, WSB-TV, and ABC entered the fray.

I was a witness in the litigation. I explained in a deposition that we still had open files on all the cases as long as there was any possibility of retrial. Records in open criminal cases were generally not subject to public scrutiny; the records became public when the cases were closed. Nonetheless, the court ordered most of the files released to the public. The city of Atlanta, on behalf of its police commissioner, appealed the ruling to the Georgia Supreme Court, where the name of the case became *Napper, Commissioner of Public Safety versus WSB-TV*. On May 6, 1987, the Georgia Supreme Court sided with the TV station and allowed the records to become public.

SORTING THROUGH EVIDENCE WITH HOMER WILLIAMS

Every year or two, Homer Williams, Wayne's father, would come by my office and ask for the return of items seized from the Williams home. Mr. Williams also wanted to retrieve the floor panel from the tailgate area of the 1970 Chevrolet station wagon his son had been driving when he was stopped near the James Jackson Parkway Bridge. Before I retired from the Fulton County District Attorney's Office at the end of 1991, I agreed to go through all the evidence with Mr. Williams and release whatever items had no apparent evidentiary value.

Larry Peterson, the GBI fiber expert, helped arrange a meeting at the Georgia State Crime Laboratory, part of the Georgia Bureau of Investigation complex on Panthersville Road in DeKalb County. Homer Williams, along with attorney Lynn Whatley, met with Larry and me around a conference table in the GBI complex. Large black plastic trash bags were brought into the room, and one by one, I removed items from the bags, compared them to an inventory of items made during the 1981 searches, and checked to see if they were of any significance in the case.

There were lots of Wayne Williams' shirts and other clothing, as well as miscellaneous items, picked up during the execution of search warrants. The rear floor panel from the Chevrolet station wagon was there too. Larry Peterson noted that bloodstains may have been on that panel. Homer Williams said that he wasn't surprised and had expected some bloodstains would be found on it. The floor panel was not released.

As I pulled out clothing items, I came to one item labeled on the inventory as a "blue jacket." As I looked at the jacket, I could see that it was not just a blue jacket, it was a blue *police* jacket, the same type worn by Atlanta police officers. I sighed, agonizing over the fact that this would have been a prime exhibit at the trial, had we known it existed. It had remained unnoticed in a pile of otherwise irrelevant clothing. I told Mr. Williams we were not releasing the blue jacket.

Next, there were boxes of Kodak color slides, the kind you show with a slide projector on a white screen. I opened a box of the slides and held one up to the light. I said, "It's a picture of a young man posing—" Before I could finish, Homer Williams erupted, "Those are Wayne's, those aren't mine. I don't know anything about those." Shocked at Homer Williams' reaction, I looked over at Larry Peterson, who seemed as surprised as I was. I then looked at the name on the box of slides, the name that had been hand-written on the sales order when the film was turned in for developing. I said, "Mr. Williams, this has your name on it. It says 'Homer Williams' on the box of slides."

"That has to be a mistake! Those are Wayne's!" he said emphatically.

The color slides were not incriminating, but Homer Williams sure acted as if they were.

CALLED AS A WITNESS FOR WAYNE WILLIAMS

In 1991, the celebrity team of lawyers handling Wayne Williams' habeas corpus case in Butts County, Georgia, was finally ready to call witnesses. Alan Dershowitz, William Kunstler, and Bobby Lee Cook, along with Lynn Whatley, had filed the case in 1985 with great fanfare, and it had rested in a near-dormant state for nearly six years. They seemed to be in no hurry, and I suspected it was because they had nothing of any substance to present.

At the close of 1991, I ended my tenure at the district attorney's office and opened my solo law practice in the Candler Building, an Atlanta landmark built in 1906 by Asa Candler of Coca-Cola fame. In my first month in the building, a process server dropped by, handing me a subpoena to appear as a witness for the "Petitioner" in the case of *Wayne Bertrand Williams v. Walter Zant, Warden*. In other words, I would be a witness for Wayne Williams. I was amused that Wayne's middle name of "Bertram" had been misspelled on the subpoena from attorney Bobby Lee Cook, the Colonel Sanders lookalike. I was to appear at the Butts County Courthouse in Jackson, Georgia, at 9:30 in the morning on February 17, 1992.

For anyone, being summoned for questioning under subpoena is an intimidating experience. It is no less intimidating when you are a lawyer accustomed to asking questions, not answering them. I knew that I would be accused of not turning over documents that would now be characterized as vital for Wayne Williams to get a fair trial. By definition, I would be on the defensive.

Many of Williams' claims were based on the 1966 United States Supreme Court decision in *Brady v. Maryland*. In recent years I had read a host of cases based on the ruling in *Brady*. It had been years since I had actually read the original case. So, I read it again. I was shocked to find that the case was a far cry from what had evolved over twenty-five years. The original decision was very limited as to what evidence needed to be disclosed to a defendant in a criminal trial.

On the morning of February 17, 1992, I drove the fifty miles to the small town of Jackson, Georgia, and parked in one of the diagonal parking spaces provided free for folks visiting the sleepy town square. I made my way to the classic Victorian-era red-brick courthouse, complete with a bell tower and surrounded by the usual flags and monuments to Confederate dead found in a typical town square in Georgia. I climbed the well-worn wooden stairs to the second floor, occupied almost entirely by a large ornate courtroom that had witnessed nearly a century of justice.

There was already a witness on the witness stand. I would not be called to testify until later in the day, so I took a seat and listened. Bobby Lee Cook was grilling a witness from the GBI about the Klan investigation. TV, radio, and print reporters took notes.

I watched as Cook would ask a question and then turn slowly toward the audience and the media, as if to seek approval. Cook was very effective in establishing his presence, strutting back and forth as if he were in a play. When I appeared with Bobby Lee months later, at a forum for criminal defense lawyers, I regaled the audience with what I had learned that day: how to turn away from the court and smile for the cameras.

After lunch, my turn as a witness arrived. I stepped onto the platform that held the aged wooden witness chair and took my seat. I rose to be sworn in by a deputy sheriff, and as William Kunstler approached, I felt nervous. Kunstler had been a larger-than-life legal figure back when I was in law school. Now Kunstler went through basic questions about my education and my period of employment with the district attorney's office. Kunstler then asked if I was familiar with *Brady v. Maryland*. "What does it say, in essence?" he asked.

I was certain that he, like me, had probably not read the original decision in a long time. Having just read the decision, however, I was able to clearly explain the case. Prosecutors never told Mr. Brady that someone else had admitted to being the triggerman. Despite this, the Supreme Court ruled there was no legal problem with the conviction because someone else's confession would not have been admissible in Brady's trial. The Supreme Court actually upheld the conviction itself, while granting Brady only a new sentencing hearing.

Kunstler was frustrated; this was not the answer he wanted. After some questions about more recent cases following the *Brady* decision, I acknowledged that prosecutors were required to turn over clearly exculpatory evidence in their files, particularly evidence so material that it would have changed the result of the trial if it had been known to the defense. But I had reached a level of comfort and was no longer intimidated by this imposing character with a booming voice and glasses perched on his head.

We talked about the Klan investigation, about Dr. Zaki's altered death certificate for Jimmy Ray Payne, about statements made by various witnesses, and the criminal records of state's witnesses.

Kunstler seemed disappointed by many of my responses. "You're taking the position in answering all of my questions that nothing we are putting up here amounts to *Brady* in your opinion, is that correct?" For several more hours of my testimony, Kunstler and I continued to spar. Court recessed for the day. I would have to return the next day, which I did, and after more than five hours on the witness stand, I was done.

Or at least I thought I was done. The case continued to linger for four and a half years until I was called again as a witness in 1996, this time by the Georgia Attorney General's Office. The attorney general represents state agencies and had been defending the case since Wayne Williams was transferred to a state prison. This time Deputy Attorney General Mary Beth Westmoreland asked questions to help clarify any misconceptions that might have arisen from my examination by Mr. Kunstler. After two hours of relatively friendly questions, I endured two additional hours of hostile examination, this time by Lynn Whatley. Whatley, along with Lee Sexton, a Clayton County lawyer, represented Wayne Williams at my deposition. Kunstler had died in 1995 and I don't know what happened to Alan Dershowitz and Bobby Lee Cook.

One year later, Mary Beth Westmoreland asked if I would help in the final stages of Wayne Williams' habeas corpus case. I was again part of the team defending the work we had done fifteen years earlier; as such, I was designated a "Special Assistant Attorney General." I helped Mary Beth draft a proposed final order to be submitted to Judge Hal Craig, who had presided over the habeas corpus case for the previous twelve years. Judge Craig had invited each side in the proceeding to propose what he should say in ruling on the long-simmering litigation. In early 1998, we submitted our proposed order; on July 19, 1998, he issued his own sixty-page order. In regard to the Klan investigation, the judge noted that "although there might have been suggestions or suspicions, none of those suspicions proved to be supported by fact or evidence, and Petitioner has failed to show any basis upon which he could have obtained any admissible evidence had he had access to the entire [Klan] investigation." In essence, there was no evidence against the Klan, and there never had been.

Williams' team of lawyers appealed Judge Craig's decision, and the case returned to the Georgia Supreme Court. The court reviewed the entire record of documents, testimony, and depositions collected over twelve years. After a year of review, the Supreme Court sent the case back to Judge Craig to supplement his findings. Williams' defense team had failed to press Judge Craig to rule on two of their original claims—that Wayne Williams was denied "the effective assistance of counsel" and that part of our prosecution closing argument was improper. The judge had simply noted that Wayne Williams had abandoned these claims.

Judge Craig again allowed both sides to offer proposed orders, based on all the evidence that had been amassed. On June 9, 2000, he entered a supplemental 121-page order outlining the lack of merit in Williams' claims. Now the two orders combined went before the Georgia Supreme Court as an "Application for a Certificate of Probable Cause" to appeal the final denial of the long-pending habeas corpus case. The Supreme Court again reviewed the entire matter, including the material in the additional 121-page order. The Supreme Court found no error and denied the application on December 14, 2001. It appeared, yet again, that the case was over.

THE CASE KEEPS COMING BACK

To my surprise, interest in the case continued to flourish. A flurry of books and television productions, many spouting conspiracy theories and cover-ups, continued to pop up. In 1995, FBI profiler John Douglas wrote *Mindhunter*, which has since been turned into a TV series. There is a section in the book on the Atlanta case and Douglas, at one point, confuses my role with that of my fellow prosecutor Gordon Miller. In 1998, Bernard Headley authored *The Atlanta Youth Murders and the Politics of Race. Those Bones Are Not My Child*, by Toni Cade Bambara, came out in 1999.

A Showtime TV movie called *Who Killed Atlanta's Children?* was released in 2000. In that version, it looks like the Klan may have committed the murders. The History Channel produced a short semi-documentary with no conclusions. CourtTV (now TruTV) produced a program in late 2000—in that version, the Klan seemed to be involved, and I was apparently part of one of those conspiracies. It was the only such program that generated telephoned death threats to my home. In 2001, A&E produced a fairly balanced program as part of their "American Justice" series, hosted by Bill Curtis.

Having lost the most recent case in the Georgia Supreme Court in 2000, Williams' defense team now sought refuge in federal court. With Lynn Whatley and a new group of lawyers, a habeas corpus petition was filed in 2002 in the United States District Court for the Northern District of Georgia. Gone from the legal team were Alan Dershowitz and Bobby Lee Cook. After four years of digging into this latest case, Judge Beverly Martin dismissed the petition, which was, in many respects, based on issues that had been raised in the state habeas corpus case years earlier. The United States Court of Appeals for the Eleventh Circuit declined an appeal on December 21, 2006.

REOPENING CASES

In 2005, Lewis Graham, a former Atlanta police detective, was named chief of police in DeKalb County, Georgia. Shortly after being appointed, Graham announced with great fanfare that he was reopening the Task Force murder cases that had taken place in DeKalb County. He vowed to find "the real killer." Five of the bodies of young Black males had been found in DeKalb, and we had used three of them as similar transactions in the trial: JoJo Bell, William Barrett, and Patrick Baltazar. The reopening of the cases once again created a national news event, and with that came the usual wave of interviews and requests for comment.

Lewis Graham's actions reopened not only the case, but also the hopes of some of the grieving mothers. Like the greater public, these women had probably never heard the full weight of evidence against Wayne Williams. Those who did not trust the outcome of the trial were now given hope that a new killer would be unmasked. Meanwhile, a local radio personality visited Williams in prison and gave him a forum for live interviews from the state prison.

In June of 2006, Lewis Graham left the DeKalb Police Department. No new suspects had emerged. No new killer had been found. The new acting chief, Nick Maranelli, quietly closed the investigation.

THE TWENTY-FIFTH ANNIVERSARY

In June of 2006, the *Fulton Daily Report*, the local legal publication for the Atlanta area, did a special report on the twenty-fifth anniversary of Wayne Williams' arrest. "Why Do They Still Haunt Us?" was the headline for their June 29 article, followed by "Fiber Links Still Powerful" on June 30. In their issue on the fiber evidence, experts from the National Center for Forensic Science, the American Academy of Forensic Sciences, and the John Jay College of Criminal Justice at the City University of New York reviewed the fiber evidence. They concluded that the evidence showed conclusive connections between Wayne Williams and the victims presented at the trial. They also validated the methods used by the experts we had relied on at the trial.

DNA

The *Fulton County Daily Report* went one step further—the newspaper began calling for DNA testing of hairs found inside the shirt of Patrick Baltazar and dog hairs found on various victims. DNA testing had been available to the Williams defense team for years, and they had been talking about DNA since 1999—but they had never asked for it. I personally suspected that they were afraid of the results.

The *Daily Report* articles stirred up the issue. On November 28, 2006, the defense team filed an "extraordinary motion for new trial," asking the Fulton Superior Court to permit testing. Lynn Whatley was quoted as saying, "I'm really more excited about this than some of the appeals. We're dealing with science now." Jack Martin, an experienced and well-respected criminal defense lawyer who had joined the defense, acknowledged that Williams was taking a risk: "If it comes back that the hair is from his dog, then the mystery is solved. If it doesn't, then that is pretty powerful evidence for a new trial."

Tests were done on three animal hairs recovered from the head of victim Larry Rogers, three animal hairs found on Charles Stephens' pants, five animal hairs from Jimmy Ray Payne's shorts, five animal hairs from the hair on Nathaniel Cater's head, and three animal hairs found on Patrick Baltazar's shirt. In June of 2007, mitochondrial DNA testing revealed that all the hairs shared the same DNA characteristics. Sheba could not be excluded as the source of the hair. In addition, the same dog hairs had been found on a total of eighteen victims.

Weeks later, results on the human hairs found inside Patrick Baltazar's shirt were revealed: the hairs shared the same DNA characteristics as Wayne Williams' hair. The report based on mitochondrial DNA testing showed that "due to the closely related sequences obtained from specimens, Williams cannot be excluded as the source of the hair." The extraordinary motion for a new trial was denied.

The case, it seemed, was finally over. What else could happen? It had now been more than twenty-five years since the trial.

In 2010, my fellow prosecutor Jack Mallard published a book on the case, covering the basic trial events. Jack sent me a copy.

In 2011, CNN finished production of a documentary about the case. I was invited to watch a preview on June 3, 2011. Viewers of the program would be able to call in to vote on Wayne Williams' guilt or innocence; viewers were given a third alternative as well: not proven. In the CNN interview, Wayne Williams, for the first time, claimed he was a trained CIA operative, part of a special program for high school students.

After viewing the film, I could not resist asking a producer: "How can you ask people to vote on guilt or innocence without presenting most of the prosecution evidence?" Apparently, the program would not be interesting enough for the audience if Williams' guilt was clearly established. Despite not hearing much of the evidence, fifty-five thousand people registered opinions, with 68.6 percent of viewers voting Williams guilty, 27.1 percent voting "not proven," and 4.3 percent voting innocent.

Years passed, and again I assumed the case was finally forgotten.

PODCAST

Early in 2018 came a new version of the story, a podcast. *Atlanta Monster* claimed to be taking a fresh look at the murders and the question of Wayne Williams' guilt. The ten segments aired over consecutive weeks and meandered through conspiracy theories, misinformation, and often irrelevant interviews. Most interesting were the interviews with Williams himself. He seemed to love the attention, and with his typical bravado, he yet again gave entirely new versions of his stop on the James Jackson Parkway Bridge. He also gave new accounts of his supposed CIA training and his family's involvement in the Manhattan Project (the development of the atomic bomb during World War II).

MORE TELEVISION PRODUCTIONS

In 2019, Investigation Discovery did a three-part program about the case. This was followed in 2020 by HBO and CNN productions, and a piece by the *Daily Mail*.

The publicity brought out something unexpected: two more would-be victims who had escaped from Wayne Williams. One of these now-middle-aged men wanted to make sure Wayne Williams was not being "recast as a victim."

A MEMORIAL

In 2019, Atlanta Mayor Keisha Lance Bottoms asked the police and district attorney to take one more look at the cases and review the evidence. She also created the "Atlanta Children's Memorial Task Force." I was appointed a member of this Task Force, as were some of the mothers, Maynard Jackson's widow, and the radio personality who visited Williams in prison.

On January 16, 2020, in the atrium of Atlanta's City Hall, I sat alongside them, as well as family members of the missing and murdered children. We were all there for a reception honoring the artist chosen to create portraits of the many victims.

Behind me sat Lois Evans, mother of Alfred Evans. Clifford Jones' mother, now frail, sat in the front row. Directly in front of me sat the mother of Curtis Walker and the stepmother of Patrick Baltazar. At the end of the program, I hugged one of the mothers.

After nearly four decades, here I was, still personally involved in the case. The controversy was still there, as were years of pain and grief.

For me, and all those touched by this case, perhaps it will never be over.

ACKNOWLEDGMENTS

Thank you to all who patiently read my work and shared their thoughts and suggestions. You know who you are.

Particular thanks to my daughter, Amy Drolet, for her counsel and support, and to Rebecca Keel, my significant other, for her patience and encouragement.

Additional thanks to Katherine Diamandis for her unending help and to Larry Peterson for his wisdom and technical assistance.

Special thanks to Alexa Selph for showing me the value of a good editor and to Mary Sage for turning my ideas into visual art.

ABOUT THE AUTHOR

Joseph Drolet is a lawyer and activist. He received degrees in both economics and law from the University of Illinois and began his legal career in Illinois as an assistant state's attorney. After moving to Atlanta, Georgia, he joined the Fulton County District Attorney's Office. It was during his twenty years with that office that he became a participant in the prosecution of serial killer Wayne Williams.

Today, Joseph Drolet is one of the foremost authorities on the Williams case and trial. He has been featured recently in documentaries on CNN, Investigation Discovery, and HBO. He and his partner, Rebecca, live in Atlanta with their dog, Zuzu.